Divorce Strategies & How To

MW00388154

For info/ contact:

Second Life Press
Dallas, Texas

SECOND·
LIFE

E-mail: ALooking1@yahoo.com

Dedication

This book is dedicated to: 1) the 640,000 alimony payers and; 2) the 2.5 million people divorced each year, with their struggles.

I was one of the permanent alimony payers, _causing me to research and write this book!_ I needed to move on and did it, so you now need to read about the pathway to your future.

A _special_ Thank You to the tenacious editing by Dr. D!, another payer dedicated to the cause.

Divorce Strategies & How To Be Alimony Free

If your rope needs to be broken

INTRODUCTION

If you see a divorce in your near future, I recommend you quickly learn about pre-divorce strategies and what can happen to you. This needs to be done before you file for divorce or have been served with the papers, as the impact upon your monetary assets and future quality of life can be enormous. Unfortunately the advice you get from friends is well-intended but pretty poor, and some of it is incorrect. Surprisingly you will learn you can't depend upon either the lawyers or the mediators to be pro-active and steer you on a straight course, as many do a poor job advising you. If this change in life is coming at you, you need to study Chapters 1 and 2 before you get run thru the divorce wringer. Be particularly wary of lawyers; they are generally hourly, and most will have no hesitation to "churn" your account to create as many billable hours for themselves as possible, with little regard to your outcome.

This is the worst that can happen to you … *"**Permanent Alimony until Death**"* …

So where do you start? … Will this become your outcome for 10+ years of marriage? … Beware you may already be another or soon-to-be alimony slave. Remember marriage is not supposed to be a life sentence, but the <u>consequences of divorce can be a life sentence.</u>

Post-divorce I had to ask myself – Did I even see this alimony life sentence or *Alimony Re-Marriage* coming? My answer was **NO**!

Didn't know beforehand about: 1) the 10 – 20 year marriage rule granting <u>Permanent Lifetime Alimony depending on the state in which you get divorced</u>, 2) required documentation for non-comingled pre-marital assets, or they will be considered marital property losing the premarital status, and 3) I had also figured during my brief pre-divorce analysis that an equitable distribution state was better than a community property state in which to have the divorce conducted. Wrong on <u>all</u> counts with $40,000 in legal bills, another lesson not to be repeated.

A word of explanation: "Plan A" is live your life normally; "Plan B" is what you do when you cannot do "Plan A." So if circumstances force your hand – for example, permanent alimony – you may opt as I did, for "Plan B," which means circumventing the unforgiving unfair law and seeking a new life.

What really bothers me to this day, was all thru the divorce proceedings, <u>never</u> at any time were there any court questions, negotiation or discussion about my future life sentence of permanent alimony. Believe it or not, I never was asked, nor did anyone talk to me about this subject. Instead I was told that from legal precedence with no state published laws or guidelines, <u>this was my life sentence</u>. The rationale is often "justified" by the legal profession as "this is the legal precedent" (not state law) with reference to legal cases of the distant past. I was flashed one page from another person's settlement with the same life sentence as further proof that this is "right." Is this proper justification? – Absolutely not! So I agreed to it and settled with my Plan B already being prepped, but it was coercion. It is kind of like this - If someone comes up to you in an alleyway with a gun and says, "Give up your wallet," would agree to give up your wallet? That's how the divorce courts treat a person with 10+ years of marriage exposed to lifetime alimony. <u>So this is how I began my journey</u> …

Most of us at the beginning or after this divorce life changing event, do not have the benefit of a coach/mentor who has done it before to advise and instruct us. How do you discuss the topic of "*How to Avoid or Escape From Alimony*" with anyone? So typically one begins discretely asking friends or with internet searches starting with "*Alimony Escape, Escape from Alimony*" ... Over time after not finding any relevant material, the search will drift off and evolve into the 2nd deeper phase with: "*Avoid the Alimony Dilemma, Offshore Banking, How to Hide, Disappear, Hiding Assets, and New & False Identity*" only to name a few. Surprisingly this topic's info at any level is difficult to find and research, but if one spends time and studies, the ropes can be learned. My 5-year journey led thru this maze to here with this manuscript for you to use, which is a record of my self-directed tutorial. I did not want to be a post-divorce participant in "*Permanent Maintenance Until Death*" or equivalent to "*Alimony Slavery.*" So with my large financial exposure and desire for total post-divorce freedom, this written collage became my plan ...

Your study trail may quickly lead to the 3 – 4 divorce alimony internet blogs including "*Alimony Expatriates* and *Alliance for Freedom From Alimony*", that have valuable info coming from frustrated alimony payers fighting both the state(s) legal system and their Bar Association, but both are extremely stoic and slow-to-change. Then lawyer websites providing abbreviated advice to seek clients, but none of it comprehensive on where to go. In fact, every lawyer website I've seen purporting to give advice was really only to get clients to that particular firm.

As there was no roadmap of any kind, I continued to dig deeper for better guidance, but had the alimony $5000/month clock ticking. Does that sound like a fortune? It does. It was not only my sentence, but the sentence of the editor of this book, so don't think it can't happen to you. The editor's ex-spouse sat on their every-growing behind and ate bon-bons, did nothing more, living on the alimony and child support.

A handful of books surfaced, but nothing focused on the issue "*How to Beat My Alimony Wrap.*" I went quickly thru skip tracer web sites like "*Escape-Artist & Privacy-World*", the Canary Press book publisher message board, and many pseudo privacy advocate books, but the "*How to Be Invisible*" book proved to be the best initial resource. This planted the privacy seed for me on how to proceed. Then the monumental step of finding "*Alimony Expatriates*" – a Yahoo Groups website focused on permanent alimony payers with a platform of state alimony reform, provided the best backdrop and nationwide perspective of other individuals in the same shape or worse. My study trail continued gaining momentum, and this book became my real plan on "*How to Do It*" and not dream about it. I moved on to blaze my own trail.

During my discovery, I was also awakened to the wide breadth of quiet alimony sufferers out there (640,000 nationwide, see page 2 for details), and how many of these people's lives are consequently severely ruined post-divorce. In the research about the alimony and child support monetary collection mechanisms outlined in Chapters 11-12, I became aware of the really sad plight child support payers are living. I also observed the state-by-state alimony reform efforts stonewalled by politics, lobbyists, and the lawyer bar associations. Only one state, Massachusetts, has had partial meaningful alimony reform. One can easily conclude any significant nationwide or state alimony reform likely will not occur in our lifetimes.

ALIMONY AND CHILD SUPPORT

The focus of this book is on alimony, not child support (CS). In the research process, I came across "*Fathers and Families*" an incredible group trying to solve the separate child custody injustice. I found universally an extreme high percentage of fathers take no issue with child support, and I also support this CS life responsibility obligation.

The resultant sole issue that occurs with combined CS and permanent alimony, it generally forces the payer to live on less than 33% of their gross income, which is impossible to do unless you make over $125,000/yr. For most this is impossible, frequently resulting in arrears, expenditures of large amounts of money in courtroom dramas, bench warrants, imprisonment, bankruptcy, and further depletion of their post-divorce financial resources.

Combining CS and alimony also puts the alimony in a "different category" in terms of arrears collections since there are strict federal laws regarding collection of child support, but not for alimony. When the two are combined, it is all considered CS, and all subject to the harsh federal regulations and enforcement.

MY PERSONAL JOURNEY

My initial assessment revealed that for many prior alimony escapees there were two typical escape routes: 1) liquidate all your assets, put them into a shoe box or safe deposit box, and then attempt to lead invisible lives as a fugitive, constantly moving while living in an RV, or 2) leave the country, the USA.

I decided neither option was the suitable route for me and made a conscious decision to find an alternative to allow me to continue leading my normal productive life in the US, not as a fugitive. I wanted to continue working, as I was not ready mentally, physically or financially for retirement. To do this, I had to learn how to become invisible as an individual, and make my employment and financial assets become equally invisible.

I had the necessary conviction to learn how it could be done so that my trail would become a cold case. I also decided in the future I have no intention of: 1) ever returning back to my divorce decree state court to argue my retirement Change in Circumstances (CIC) to stop or reduce the alimony, or 2) after 3 – 10 years post-divorce face a surprise request from my ex-spouse for more money, which incidentally can be done for a 2-year court review interval. So I began the process of reorganizing my life. The alimony nightmare or re-marriage was going to end.

And then unexpectedly it happened to me! Two or three months before my scheduled Plan B great escape to stop the alimony payments ... I lost my job and had to fully finish implementing my Plan B escape in short order. It became time to get a new job, move, and finish moving all financial assets ... to leave no discovery trail behind. I saw firsthand: 1) what happens when you are suddenly thrust into a scenario with no wage income, but have to continue paying substantial alimony from your life savings; 2) the perils of not being able to afford health insurance; and 3) finding a new job which, if you are 50+ or in a rural area, is tough or nearly impossible. That is why further depletion of your savings and bankruptcy can be the ultimate tragic outcome for many payers after a job loss.

Fortunately I was rehired 3 months later with my implemented Plan B in effect. In retrospect I was lucky with my life circumstances and confidence to have pre-planned an escape, with this self-taught methodology becoming my Plan B. But always remember, the ex and the asset searchers will come looking for you and for your money. As of the publishing of this book, my Plan B has been in effect for over 3-1/2 years. But I still continue always looking behind my back, keeping my invisibility while standing (always looking) in the shadows. Still, my life has moved forward.

FOR THOSE OF YOU THAT WANT TO JUMP AHEAD WITHOUT READING THE BOOK

It is suggested that you jump to:
- Chapter 7 - page 81 - Planning Your Escape
- Chapter 11 – page 169 – How an Arrears Judgment is Enforced
- Chapter 13 – page 195 – Your Planning Steps

SO WHY, HOW & DID I WRITE THIS BOOK?

I hope that with your study of this book, it will help you plan your divorce strategies beforehand and then if needed implement your Plan B, rather than be post-divorce reactive like most of us. If I had had this book's knowledge 2 – 3 years before my divorce finalization, the outcome would have been entirely different. Unfortunately I never found any book on alimony avoidance or this Plan B topic, and I looked really hard. So I researched and produced my own playbook.

One may ask where did the material come from that generated the factual material for the book? The sources came from many governmental and legal websites, as well as public message boards. I spent 24 months analyzing, rewriting, and reassembling the information into a cohesive outlined document. I was personally fortunate that 4 months before my divorce finalization with the initial beginnings of this book, that I knew my destiny, as my Plan B outline had been pre-planned. I just had to finalize the divorce and then make the post alimony invisibility details happen. My surprise was that the implementation of the roadmap details took longer than I initially thought.

Of real significance to those who read and need this book, the info and techniques presented are current and state-of-the-art as of the publishing of the book. I have tried to instruct you on how-to-do it, rather than tell you this or that could be done, and incorporate the decision making process background you will go through. After reading it, you will concur, "This book is the most comprehensive you will find on the subject."

There is more information presented than may be necessary, but to be successful one has to have a full understanding of the searcher's abilities, their tools, and the legal mechanisms that can come after you.

So to make your Plan B work, be sure to read and study this book taking the careful stance that the slightest error can result in your being caught. The ex-spouse will come after you to some degree. The long arm of the law will cross state lines and come after you if you owe CS. It does not come easy, but instead takes a lot of effort with the end result … your **Freedom** is back!

Good luck in your endeavor, as "*You Will Be Next*" and can then say, ***"Been There, Planned it, and Did it!"***

CHAPTER 1

ALIMONY - EQUIVALENT TO SLAVERY

What is wrong with our alimony state laws, and why are many forced to leave our present trapped and unfair lives? Permanent alimony or "*Lifetime Alimony Until Death*" ruins a person's life. Do the courts and law-makers really wonder why people go on the run, break the law with a contempt charge, and maybe get jailed for non-payment? Of course not, but maybe they should realize their laws are creating the problems.

First, there should be the sense of fairness. You may be going broke with no job and still be in court trying to get your alimony reduced. The court will say the alimony must continue, and your lawyer will be only concerned about collecting their fee. One lawyer recently told their client, make the support payments even if they had to sell their kidney.

The decision at hand for you – will you defy the courts, the alimony marital settlement agreement (MSA) and the divorce decree, as **Indirect civil contempt** may be the option for you? From here, it will take your willpower, conviction and confidence.

POST DIVORCE OUTCOME

After the divorce, you start thinking - do you fight in court and continue to live and work in the US with only half your net earnings as your own, or do you now disappear by becoming invisible? Court time with outdated laws and judgmental prejudices stacked against you can be really expensive, and with $300+/hr. lawyer fees, you may count on $20,000+ legal fees. You will learn quickly "*Perpetual or Lifetime Alimony Until Death*" can be the serious outcome from your prior marriage.

The Court – via the lawyers – will require a detailed financial statement from each party in the divorce. I am convinced that they use this information to determine how much they can charge you in fees. One of this book's editors spent over a half million dollars in legal fees while earning approximately $250,000/year.

If alimony is in the marital settlement agreement's (MSA) property settlement, and the agreement is incorporated into the final decree, the court doesn't have the power to change a dime of it, except by a separate expensive filing for "Change in Circumstances." A change in circumstances is generally a catastrophic event such as full age retirement or a disability severe enough for the Social Security

Administration to begin payments for disability. But if the court sets the alimony $$ amount, it maintains complete control as to whether it can be raised, lowered, or halted.

So ultimately, what is the long term toll on your life as a payer to be? Pay until death, no retirement, and forget about having fun or any money. The alternative is to plan your alimony escape. Even with the assistance of this book, this implementation effort will take 6 - 24 months minimum. So read, study and do it, as it now time to move on with your life …

DIVORCE STATISTICS - MOST ARE WORSE OFF

- 2.5 million people divorce each year nationwide; 50,000 avg. per state.
- **640,000** ex-spouses pay alimony (IRS 2013**); 96% are men, 4% women estimated.
  - 20,000 alimony payers have $0 annual income (IRS 2011).
  - 375,000 alimony payers have annual incomes $1 - $100,000 (IRS 2011).
  - 225,000 alimony payers have annual incomes over $100,000 (IRS 2011).
  - $11.3 billion annual alimony payments   (IRS 2013), calculates to $17,600 avg. alimony payer/year.
  - A majority of alimony payers live on 1/3rd or less of their gross income in a subsistence life style.
  - Big picture, there are so few alimony payers in the US with 12,800 avg. per state, no meaningful alimony reform is likely in the foreseeable future.
- 300,000 couples over age 50 divorce annually, and in 2030 will balloon to more than 400,000 busted marriages.
- 16% of divorce cases request alimony; given in 6-15% approx. or 150,000 cases per year.
- 85% of the time wives begin the divorce proceedings as they want out, and some do it for the security of the money while getting rid of you. The result after divorce, most parties get screwed.
  - Post-divorce 100% of alimony payers experience a drop in their lifestyle standards. Those with incomes less than $100,000/year really suffer as they cannot afford to live on 1/3 of their gross salary.
  - The recipient ex-spouse who was fortunate enough to divorce a payer spouse with an income over $100,000/year, generally may have an increased lifestyle (as 25%+/- cohabitate) often with another mate on $100K plus, with a nicer house, more expensive food, and nicer vacations after the divorce.
- Child Support:
  - 85% of custodial parents are mothers, and 45% of children living with a divorced mother live at or near the poverty line.
  - Only 50% of custodial parents are awarded child support, and only 45% receive the full amount.
  - $32 billion annual child support collected for 17 million children (2013 OSCE report), or $18,000/ child in IV-D program.
  - $7 billion (27%) of the money collected annually for child support is spent by federal and state Child Support Enforcement agencies for enforcement. (2009 OCSE report).
  - There is $89 billion in uncollected or past due child support.
  - 11,000 approximate child support-related suicides annually.
- Divorce is a $50 billion/year nationwide business spent on CS/alimony payments and legal expenses, with the courts spending $21 billion/year of the total. This is why the avg. divorce costs $50,000.
- ** The 2013 IRS archive records show 640,000 alimony payers who listed alimony as a tax deduction on their 1040 tax form filings, but this count includes both permanent and limited term alimony payers. To clarify, the 640,000 payers we are considering are alimony only, and do not include child support, as CS is not tax-deductible. So let's say of the reported total paying alimony, the best estimate is that 50% of the 640,000 are permanent payers or 320,000 individuals nationwide.

Post retirement when your wage income goes close to $0, and you are living on your Social Security with declining savings while still paying alimony, you will only be filing tax returns if your income is above $11,000 year. So your alimony deduction will not be taken and you are not included in the 640,000 count. As such, I believe there are approximately **500,000** permanent alimony payers nationwide.

OPINION – THE FAIRNESS?

You made a marriage commitment and a contract. If you opted out with a divorce, you have to settle up your side of the contract, but it should not be for life. All income from both parties belongs to both people, but was the contract you made for life? For the privilege of breaking the contract you have to offer a settlement or be ordered to keep your partner on equal footing with you financially speaking, until you die or until your ex-spouse remarries. That money would have been theirs if you had stayed in the marriage. Seems fair?

That's why there are prenups, and next time why you should think carefully before getting married. In the end, it's all about antiquated financial, contractual state law.

- Example - Married at 22, divorced at 37. 29 years till retirement.
  - You were married 12-15 years... Now you are responsible for lifetime alimony.... Paying alimony for 40 more years.
  - Paying 35% of your gross income... so you cannot retire until 67.
  - After 62-67 and if you go into arrears, your retirement social security money can also be garnished 50 – 65% to fund your ex-spouse's retirement. This is on top of the Social Security your ex-spouse can collect merely because that spouse was married to you for ten years, which is 50% of the social security you receive.
- It does not matter if your ex-spouse:
  - Was/is capable of working and makes a good living wage, you pay forever.
  - Was unfaithful, you pay forever.
  - Abused drugs or alcohol, you pay forever.
  - Abused you, you pay forever.
  - Now cohabitates and shares expenses with the new live-in lover, you pay forever.
- It does not matter if you re-marry, you will pay the first spouse forever.
- Even if you are married longer the 2nd time than the first, you pay the 1st ex-spouse forever.
- If you don't pay your alimony due to lack of money, you can be scrutinized once again by the courts, and get to wear an ankle bracelet or be put in jail.
- Reality Check, Unbelievable but True: A 40 year old guy married for 20 years who murders their ex-spouse and is sentenced to 20 years in prison, will be better off financially at age 65, than an ex-spouse who divorces and is hit with lifetime alimony.
- Another Amazing Alimony Fact: At the time of divorce, the retirement assets are split. But when the alimony payer retires, they still must continue paying alimony using only the payer's portion of the retirement money! It is utterly insane, the ex-spouse recipient gets to double dip at the payer's expense!

ANOTHER PERSPECTIVE

Why is only one ex-spouse ordered to continue providing maintenance to the other? This is a mystery to logical thinkers, as in most marriages the participants make different contributions. In a traditional marriage the husband earns the money to support the family, while the wife bears children and stays home to rear them while performing domestic duties. When such a marriage dissolves it is not uncommon for the husband to be ordered to continue his former contribution to the ex-wife in the form of monetary support, aka alimony. But what of the ex-wife? Should she not then be ordered to continue part of her former contribution to her ex-husband? Cooking, cleaning, laundry, shopping, something? Anything? A foolish suggestion? Why is it any more foolish to suggest the ex-husband should continue supporting his ex-wife with alimony and receive <u>nothing</u> in return? An ex-spouse to whom they are no longer related? Should the equal protection clause come into play here?

It is time to plan your escape, as this is the time and opportunity for you to move on with your life.

GENDER BIAS PERSISTS IN THE COURTS

Gender bias does persist in the Courts; not against women, but against men. The courts almost always order a man to pay child support when the woman has the children, but usually delay in ordering a woman to pay child support if the man has custody, and may pressure the man to waive child support regardless of how much money the woman earns.

The courts are quick to throw a man out of the marital house, even if it is clear the woman is causing all the problems. If a woman says a man hit her, he is arrested and ordered to stay away from his home and children, even if he can prove he was not home at the time or there are witnesses who affirm the woman hit the man. When a man is caught lying he pays the price, but when a women is caught lying no one cares. Women nearly never get jailed for violating a court order, but men often do.

Women who earn money off the books are not held accountable, but men have income imputed to them. Imputed income means the amount of money the Court believes the person "should" be earning. Men are usually ordered to pay more support than they can afford, and a woman is usually given more than needed when coupled with income she does or should earn. Advocates patrol the social welfare networks seeking women to help, and no one is there for the men. Courts give mothers custody even when the forensic expert recommends the father, but never give the father custody when the forensic recommends for the mother. Why waste time and money on forensics when judges often ignore the recommendation?

Bottom-line, the courts are very biased against men and the majority wage earners, and in favor of women.

TEMPORARY SUPPORT GUIDELINES

So why did my attorney tell me that I would have to pay a certain dollar amount of pre-divorce spousal support before we even went to court? How did they figure out this amount?

If an attorney gives you an exact dollar figure for your upcoming temporary spousal support, in all likelihood they are using a formula or computer program to determine the exact amount of spousal support payable. Even though using these programs is valid for determining child support, these programs can only be used to determine <u>Temporary</u> Support, not post-divorce spousal alimony/maintenance or <u>Permanent</u> Support. Generally these are not binding, as the judge is given "judicial discretion" for making such determinations.

Temporary support has one party paying the other until the divorce proceedings are finalized, which is until the final judgment of divorce. Temporary Support is usually only determined by <u>your current gross income alone</u>. Courts cannot rely upon computer formulas to determine the amount of Permanent Support, as they must weigh the factors listed in the respective state's Family Code. Therefore, an attorney who tells you the exact amount of your post-divorce spousal support payment is likely guessing or discussing temporary support only. The final amount of permanent spousal support determined by a court or the marital settlement agreement (MSA), <u>might be quite different</u> from the temporary spousal support amount. For alimony, one can expect up to 33% +/- of your <u>gross</u> income to be the spousal support level granted.

<u>Recommendation</u>: Get a low paying job (50% or less of present income) three years before divorce filing. They generally look back three years, but not longer. Make this a <u>high</u> priority.

ALIMONY

Alimony is the money the ex-spouse pays to the other by court order for support/ maintenance.

In recent years, <u>alimony</u> due to negative connotations has been relabeled to <u>maintenance</u> or spousal support. Generally, alimony was awarded traditionally to the wife and paid by the husband. However, during the 1970 - 80's judges occasionally began to award alimony to the husband. Alimony is now awarded to either spouse in an effort to maintain the standard of living that both parties were accustomed to during the marriage.

Alimony or <u>temporary support</u> awarded prior to the divorce is called <u>pendente lite</u> alimony. If ordered by the court, it is tax deductible to the payer, and becomes taxable income to the recipient.

At the time of the divorce if alimony is awarded, it can be one or a combination of the following:

- **Permanent:** This alimony type is to be paid until either the "*death*" of the payer or the remarriage of the recipient. This is the <u>worst</u> scenario that can happen to you for a 10+ years marriage scenario. Smarter marital settlement agreements (MSA) should include: 1) a "cohabitation" clause that states alimony ends when the recipient cohabits with another person in the avoidance of marriage and 2) <u>automatic</u> curtailment when the payer reaches full retirement age (so you don't have to go back to court for a Change in Circumstances and maybe get denied). But the attorneys do neither of these proactive defenses for you. So you continue to pay …

- **Lump Sum**: This alimony type has one payment instead of periodic (usually weekly or monthly) payments. This alimony is taxable, so consult with a CPA experienced in divorce to determine the lump sum payment tax consequences prior to agreeing to it. Beware of the IRS's 3-year tax recapture rule (see page 41.)

- **Temporary**: Lasts for a specific period of time such as one to two years, and may be awarded when the persons are on almost equal ground but due to certain circumstances, one person may need temporary financial assistance to "get on their feet," or for any other reason the Judge wants to give.

- **Rehabilitative**: This is the most common awarded alimony for situations where the recipient is younger, or able to eventually enter or return to the work force and become financially self-supporting. May include payments for the education necessary to enable the recipient to become self-supporting.

Every state has its own criteria for determining the need and extent of alimony, however the following general factors may be considered:
- Marriage duration.
- Age, as well as physical, mental, and emotional state of each party.
- Earning capacity of both parties, and difference in income.
- Other income, including but not limited to interest and dividends.
- Education of the two parties.
- The contribution by one spouse to education and furtherance of career of the other.
- The contribution of one spouse as a homemaker.

- How much earning power will be affected by the parenting requirements of the custodial parent.
- The children.
- Your premarital or inherited property.
- Any pre-nup agreement.

The judge may consider any economic circumstances of either party that they deem to be just or proper. The amount of alimony payments are generally ordered based on the above considerations. As with any other aspect of your divorce, you should try to negotiate your alimony within the marital settlement agreement (MSA), rather than have a judge arbitrarily determine if your situation will include alimony and how much will be awarded.

ALIMONY GUIDELINES

Surprisingly after an extensive search, I found there are <u>no specific legal documented alimony guidelines</u> (only child support) for <u>any of the 50 states</u>, and certainly <u>no consistency from state-to-state</u>. As there is no basis a Court can apply, what has resulted is that judges use their own particular parameters to help them decide about the amount of alimony.

Courts have not settled on a method to calculate any resulting payments, so it's left to the Court's judgment that plays into the MSA development.

Alimony guidelines have been in existence for some time, but there is nothing in most state statutes that quantifies the alimony percentage, dollar amount, or duration. In 2007, the Chicago-based American Academy of Matrimonial Lawyers (AAML) tried to provide a starting point when it recommended alimony guidelines. The stated goal was more predictable and equitable results. The group studied approaches in different parts of the country to produce a formula that could work across jurisdictions, but this has no legal basis. Attorneys have seized on this lack of direction to give them an opportunity to bring their clients to court again and again to fight about alimony, creating an ongoing "cash cow" for the attorneys. As far as Judges' rulings, well remember they are first and foremost attorneys themselves.

The income discrepancy between you and your spouse is generally the most important aspect for the judges to consider when determining alimony. When it comes to facing divorce, many men believe winning in court is how you win your divorce, and unfortunately 90% of those men learn that nothing could be further from the truth.

If the court does reward your ex-spouse post-divorce spousal support or alimony, you can appeal years later the MSA or the court's decision with an expensive <u>Change in Circumstances</u> filing. So it is better to be proactive now to enhance your chances of having lower or nonexistent alimony payments. Hence, it's critical you build a very solid case before divorce, and here's why:

- Men in the same situation can pay drastically different amounts when it comes to alimony. So why do some ex-spouses get excellent alimony agreements and others don't?
- Your strategy and approach may strongly influence how much if any alimony you will owe.
- At its simplest, your case should be built around providing evidence that your ex-spouse can get by on the amount you feel is fair based on their ability to work, not on your spouse's defined financial need. Be aware that the Judge may not even consider the spouse's earning capacity, or it may be a tiny factor in consideration.

- You can do this by providing documentation of your ex-spouse's income or job posting they would be qualified for, and the level of income those jobs would provide to the ex-spouse. You can also hire a forensic expert, but don't count on that expert's findings to be respected by the court, even if unrefuted.
- All of this helps the court understand how much money the ex-spouse really can get by on and maintain a reasonable standard that doesn't bankrupt you. Never forget the Court's decision may simply be a whim of the judge.
- <u>Action Plan</u>: If married for more than 10-15 years, permanent alimony will be your only outcome in most states if you are the larger wage earner. In California and New Jersey for example, you can be married from age 20 to 30, then pay permanent alimony for the rest of your life. Incredible but true.
- To cover your bets, get a lower paying job three years before the divorce if possible. This is the most important factor, your ace card. Of course, that means you know divorce is in your future, and you can put up with living with your spouse for those three years.

No matter what your strategy is or how well you play your cards, if there is an income discrepancy, alimony is likely to be part of your future. The amount is all up to the Judge.

HOW MUCH ALIMONY WILL YOU HAVE TO PAY?

That is one of the hardest questions for a divorce lawyer to answer. The real answer is "<u>They don't know</u>," and no lawyer wants to say that to a client.

The reason they don't know is that alimony is <u>left up to the judge's discretion</u> based on several <u>factors</u> (age, health, income, length of the marriage, etc.) set forth by the state legislature. The Court doesn't and cannot use a statistical approach to determine alimony based upon the state laws.

The results vary widely from case-to-case and bewilder anyone who has tried to plot alimony against incomes and marriage duration, as there seems to be little rhyme or reason. As an example, recently several attorneys were given the same hypothetical facts and asked to write out an alimony award, and they all provided different alimony awards.

While no state has yet enacted strict quantitative formulas akin to federal sentencing guidelines for post-divorce alimony, bar associations and legislators are nevertheless providing their own quantitative guidelines suggesting they be used rather than relying on independent judicial discretion. Codified guidelines for temporary support or alimony while a divorce is pending, known as alimony pendente lite, are becoming more common; however, they only offer judges a framework for determining permanent awards.

The American Academy of Matrimonial Lawyers (AAML) report suggests the following framework: Take 30% of the payer's gross income minus 20% of the payee's gross income. That amount when added to the gross income of the payee, should not exceed <u>40%</u> of the combined <u>gross</u> incomes of the parties. The duration of the award should be calculated by multiplying the length of the marriage by a certain numerical factor between 0 and 1.

It would be nice to have a starting point that this is more or less what you're going to get expect. Again, judicial discretion will trump such calculations, and thus they are of limited value. Too bad.

MORE STATES ARE LOOKING AT ALIMONY SPOUSAL SUPPORT FORMULAS

Many agree that divorcing spouses deserve more predictable outcomes. As a result some states are starting to examine the uncertainty of alimony awards, as some policymakers take aim at a spousal support system that's been attacked as antiquated, unbalanced and unfair. Alimony – it is argued - should last for a "reasonable period of time" until the recipient becomes self-supporting, usually about 2 - 5 years, but this is not the case. Remember the legislators are lawyers, and Bar Associations are rich matrimonial lawyers who want the divorced individuals to have as much "in court conflict" as possible in order to increase their income.

Judicial Discretion

Many lawyers say that allowing a judge's discretion to weigh these factors offers flexibility that formulas don't. States usually provide judges with factors to consider in reaching an alimony decision, including the length of the marriage, the age and health of the parties, standard of living during the marriage, and the ability of each party to acquire assets in the future. The previously given list (page 5) is reasonably accurate in terms of what the judges are "supposed to" consider.

Others say the answer may be avoiding the issue altogether. One solution may be an upfront lump-sum payment in lieu of alimony, if there are enough marital assets for this option. An ex-spouse can be awarded alimony, but that doesn't guarantee they're going to receive payment. If they get a lump sum, then it's over and done with it. However the real downside is the payer is financially destroyed first by the award of at least half the marital estate, and then followed by a monetary lump sum to provide a future lifestyle for the recipient ex-spouse. This clearly is not fair and doesn't work either. And to make matters worse, the recipient ex-spouse can later go back to court and receive a court order for the paying spouse to pay again!

ALIMONY/ CHILD SUPPORT GUIDELINE SOFTWARE CALCULATORS

There are at least 3 well-known calculator programs that provide estimates, but are not binding for alimony:

MarginSoft Support Program: A calculator for the family law attorney provides an easier way to quantify support based on some state guidelines. The software program was developed by a Michigan family law attorney who reviewed a myriad of child support and alimony cases over the last 30 years, and incorporated alimony/maintenance theories into the program. It is available for the 6 states of Florida, Kentucky, Maryland, Michigan, Washington and Maryland, but not for the other 44 states.

The DissoMaster (California) and another program by Traxler Software are similar, but these three programs are about it. Child support has formula guidelines in most states, but for alimony spousal support there are no guidelines. It is important to note that these software guidelines are not binding on the court and if a court relied on them alone, it would be reversible error. Some judges use the guidelines as a starting point for analyzing cases, and certainly they will be used by attorneys in settlement negotiations. Most importantly, lawyers may be able to give at least a preliminary answer to the "how much" alimony question.

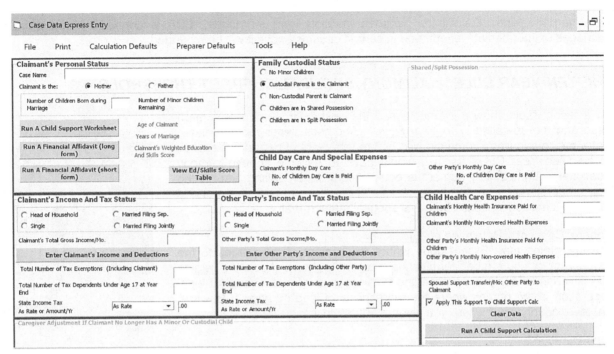

MarginSoft Alimony/ Child Support Calculator

LIMITED DURATION VS. PERMANENT ALIMONY

In divorce cases where alimony is an issue, it is not merely a dollar amount issue, but the length of time must also be decided. Before 1990 there were only two types of alimony - permanent and rehabilitative. Then many state laws were amended circa 2000 to add limited duration and reimbursement alimony.

By statutorily allowing limited duration alimony (LDA) for a term of years, the legislature gave the courts the authority to do what attorneys had been doing for their clients all along through negotiated agreements. This flexibility has been helpful to divorce litigants, since not all cases warrant permanent or rehabilitative alimony.

However, what is the line of demarcation between an award of limited duration alimony and permanent alimony? Unfortunately there is no clear line, and the ultimate resolution depends on the facts of each case, as well as the judge's perspective. In attempting to resolve this issue, case law is instructive in distinguishing between the two types of alimony.

Limited duration alimony is available to a dependent spouse who made contributions to the marriage, if the marriage is of short duration. Permanent alimony is awarded after a lengthy marriage, in recognition of prolonged economic dependence and sustained contribution to a marital enterprise.

While all the statutory factors in determining alimony must be considered (such as need of the party, ability to pay, health of the parties, standard of living during the marriage, etc.), the duration of the marriage is the defining distinction between whether permanent or limited duration alimony is awarded. Yet the question remains, what is considered a short term marriage, and what is a long term marriage? And what is known about intermediate length marriages? There is state-to-state variation.

Generally it can be gleaned from case law that marriages between 10 - 12 years are of intermediate length, and marriages of over 20 years are considered long term marriages. Although it is not known whether long-term starts at 13 years or some other number, it is known that permanent alimony will be awarded in a long term marriage, and LDA will be awarded in short term marriages. LDA is considered appropriate for marriages of intermediate length, and in certain circumstances it will be extended.

THE TEN-YEAR RULE - ALIMONY SPOUSAL SUPPORT THRESHOLD

On a recent radio show a listener raised the post-divorce spousal support issue and the so-called "*Ten Year Rule*." Another listener recommended that a previous caller divorce his wife before ten years of marriage because of the "Ten Year Rule," as they would have to pay the spouse alimony indefinitely. Immediately numerous other callers began calling and stating their understanding of this rule. This response showed the general audience's misconceptions about this spousal support matter.

General Concept – Retainage of Jurisdiction
The law states that "Except upon written agreement of the parties to the contrary or a court order terminating spousal support, the court retains jurisdiction indefinitely in a proceeding for dissolution of marriage or for legal separation of the parties where the marriage is of long duration." Beware, whatever county court where you divorce will retain jurisdiction forever.

Long Duration
Any marriage that is longer than ten-years can be presumed "lengthy." However, in some states under limited circumstances, even shorter marriages may be deemed "lengthy."

Setting the Duration and Support Amount - How Long Does Alimony Last?

When a court determines the amount and duration of permanent spousal support, they are supposed to weigh eleven factors.
- The extent to which the earning capacity of each party is sufficient to maintain the standard of living established during the marriage;
- The extent to which the supported party contributed to the attainment of an education, training, a career position, or a license by the supporting party;
- The ability to pay of the supporting party, taking into account the supporting party's earning capacity, earned and unearned income, assets, and standard of living;
- The needs of each party based on the standard of living established during the marriage;
- The obligations and assets including the separate property of each party;
- The duration of the marriage;
- The ability of the supported party to engage in gainful employment without unduly interfering with the interests of dependent children in the custody of the party;
- The age and health of the parties, including, but not limited to, consideration of emotional distress resulting from domestic violence perpetrated against the supported party by the supporting party where the court finds documented evidence of a history of domestic violence against the supported party by the supporting party;
- The immediate and specific tax consequences to each party;
- The property brought to the marriage by either spouse;
- The balance of the hardships to each party;
- The goal that the supported party shall be self-supporting within a reasonable period of time.

Except in the case of a marriage of long duration, a "reasonable period of time" generally shall be one-half the length of the marriage. However, nothing is intended to limit the court's discretion to order support for a greater or lesser length of time based on any of the other factors listed, the circumstances of the parties, and any other factors the court determines are just and equitable.

You may have noticed in the first example, that Jane received an award for support for half the length of her marriage. In circumstances where the marriage lasted less than ten years, it is "reasonable" (and quite common) for a court to set the duration of support at half the length of marriage, but that does not mean that the court must set the amount exactly at half the length of marriage. With marriages that last longer than ten years, the half the length of the marriage formula is generally not followed, and the court may weigh the factors listed above – including any other factors the court feels are pertinent to determine the duration of support.

Conclusion
The Ten Year Rule is not a magical number that states a court will automatically award spousal support with indefinite duration, as the duration of support will be determined on the judge's interpretation of the circumstances of each case. However the ten year threshold is important, since it may affect the court's ability to revisit the issue of spousal support again, and reissue or change the amount of support - absent any agreements between the parties regarding this matter.

Hindsight
How many of us would have handled things differently if we knew about the mystical 10-year rule for permanent alimony awards? California is 10 years, many other states are 12 - 15, but what would you have done differently in hindsight? How many of your lawyers told you about it during the divorce proceeding (most are not candid). Even though this is common knowledge among matrimonial attorneys, did you learn about it during the pre-trial final settle-up right before the divorce? How many of you would have taken a lower paying job for three years before the divorce, and moved to a different state advantageous to your future plight? Trust me, your recipient ex-spouse was coached by their lawyer on what their future benefit would be, if they proceeded with the divorce at your expense. How is that for incentive to be proactive before the divorce?

COMMUNITY VS. EQUITABLE PROPERTY DISTRIBUTION STATES

Nine (9) states have *Community* Property rules: Arizona, California, Idaho, Louisiana, Nevada, New Mexico, Texas, Washington, and Wisconsin.

In contrast, the other 41 states follow *Equitable Property* distribution. Why is this important?

Community Property – The Better Option
These states consider all property as being in two categories: separate property or community property. Separate property doesn't need to be split at the time of divorce, but community property does.

In a community property state all income and assets acquired during the marriage are considered community property and are assumed to be **equally** owned by both parties regardless of how much money each spouse makes. Even if one spouse does not work at all, the property is assumed to be owned 50/50. Similarly, any liabilities incurred during the marriage such as loans, mortgages, and credit card balances are equally shared at the time of the divorce.

Separate property includes all assets owned by one party before the marriage, inherited by one spouse during the marriage, or purchased after the date of separation. Those assets remain with the party who owned them after the divorce. If there is a way to trace payments before the marriage to one spouse, that payment towards an asset can be considered separate property. Separate debt works the same way. If debt is taken on by one spouse before the marriage, that debt is wholly owned by that person, but it has to be provable.

Equitable Property
The more common Equitable Property distribution rule allows for consideration of which spouse earned the property, but beware ... Beware the payer or higher wage earner spouse can receive between **1/3 – 2/3rds** (not 50/50% when the property split is determined) of the property. The method the judge uses for determining the split is subjective, as consideration of the following is made:

- Length of the marriage.
- Beware in long duration marriages the majority wage earner will receive less than 50%, and not 50/50% of the marital property.
- If one spouse stayed at home to raise children or chose not to work with no children.
- Each spouse's income level.
- The health of the spouses.
- Abuse and infidelity.
- Any actions to waste or destroy property.
- Whether the property is needed to maintain a household for the children.

<u>Conclusion</u>: A community property state is better with pre-defined 50/50% distribution, as equitable distribution will award larger percentages (greater than 50%) and be to your disadvantage if you are the only or larger wage earner and have more money.

THE CURRENT STATE OF ALIMONY - NATIONWIDE PERSPECTIVE

Alimony is alive and well, and people assume it's a thing of the past.   The 13th Amendment to the Constitution of the USA states otherwise …

> "*Neither slavery or involuntary servitude shall exist in the land except for punishment for crime.*"

So if marriage is concocted to be a crime, should we start alerting people to keep them from getting caught by a long term marriage?

<u>Where Did Alimony Come From</u>?
In a divorce proceeding, the court generally considers five major issues: grounds for divorce, property division, custody/visitation, child support, and alimony.

Four of these five issues make intuitive sense. The ordinary man or woman understands why a divorce court must verify that proper grounds for divorce exist; determine which property shall go to which spouse; determine custody of the children; and allocate funds for their support. Indeed these are tasks which unmarried couples often perform themselves, without any court assistance upon breakup of a relationship.

In today's world, there is no intuitive sense behind the fifth issue: <u>alimony</u>. Some time ago this was not true; the ordinary person did understand what it was and why it was required. Divorce was based on fault, women could not support themselves; thus when the marriage broke down because of the husband's fault, the wife needed lifelong support or she would face starvation. Perhaps this understanding of alimony support still exists in cases where divorce occurs after a traditional long term marriage in which the wife did not work. But many marriages today are not long-term, and very few women are entirely removed from the work force. By and large, the marriages of our grandfathers and grandmothers do not exist today.

<u>Historical Perspective</u>
As economic, social and cultural factors have changed the financial fabric of marriage, we have lost our understanding of the purpose of alimony. Around the country, some courts and commentators, and even a few legislatures, have reasoned that since women now work, alimony should be drastically curtailed or even abolished. Most states have not taken such a drastic step, so alimony stumbles along based upon habit and precedent as much as logic, as part of the modern divorce case. We have difficulty explaining its precise purpose; yet at some level society is reluctant to get rid of it. In short, commentators agree that the law of alimony is in the midst of an identity crisis.

As recently as forty years ago, divorce and alimony were fairly well understood. Society expected that people would marry in their youth, and remain married until death. The courts and indeed the law as a whole were determined to make this view of marriage a reality. They did so by imposing upon every marriage an implied term of permanency. When a marriage really and truly broke down, that permanency provision was breached. It was therefore the law's duty to seek out and punish the guilty party.

Pursuant to this view, the first task of the court hearing a divorce case is to determine who is "guilty." If no one was guilty, then there was no legitimate reason to end the marriage at all. The parties were told to leave the courtroom, still married, and live together as husband and wife. If both spouses were guilty, then they deserved each other, and the same result obtained.

Most commonly, the courts found one party alone to be guilty. If that party was the wife, she was cast out from the marriage and left to survive on her own, with no legally-required support at all. That was a harsh result, for women generally had little or no earning capacity. But in this instance if the wife brought the problem on herself by her own misconduct, the law had little sympathy for her position.

When the guilty party was the husband, punishment required something more forceful than mere inaction. That is where alimony entered the picture. Since women usually did not or often could not find employment, the innocent wife had a much higher standard of living while married to the husband than she could ever obtain on her own. The marriage had to end because of the husband's misconduct, but the marriage equitably should continue, as the law believed all marriages were by nature intended to be permanent. Thus where other factors were equal, the wife was entitled to the benefit of her bargain - the standard of living she enjoyed during the marriage. Since she could not reach that standard on her own, she needed a financial supplement, a weekly or monthly payment sufficient to permit her standard of living to remain unchanged by the divorce. That supplement was what the common law meant when it spoke of alimony.

In the middle part of the twentieth century, two social changes wrought havoc upon the policy basis behind the traditional rules of alimony. First, separation and divorce lost much of their unfavorable stigma. The reasons for this change are best examined by stating the proposition conversely: society became less attracted to the notion of universal and permanent marriage. Second and equally importantly, women began moving into the workplace in increasing numbers. These rents in the social and financial fabric of marriage could not be ignored.

The first reform attempt was the <u>Uniform Marriage and Divorce Act</u> of 1970 that was promulgated by the National Conference of Commissioners on Uniform State Laws. The alimony provision of the UMDA provided that alimony could be awarded only if party seeking support "lacks sufficient property to provide for their reasonable needs," and "is unable to support themselves through appropriate employment." By stressing that property division is the primary method of support, this language suggests that support is not necessary where a reasonable amount of property is awarded to each spouse. To stress the complete break with older notions of alimony, the UMDA renamed alimony, "<u>maintenance</u>." This reform freed the law of alimony from the outdated notion that alimony is punishment for marital misconduct. This reform, however, did not provide a clear rationale for alimony, and it suggested that "reasonable need" was never present if employment was available. By so doing, it changed the law applicable to that set of spouses most in need of alimony: dependent spouses in <u>long</u> marriages.

To make a bad situation even worse, state court decisions in the 1970 – 80's tended to overestimate the employability of women. Judges appeared to reason that because women could in theory qualify for any job in the nation, any individual woman could therefore find employment at a reasonable salary within a short period of time. They held to the UMDA maintenance provision, that there was no need for alimony if a spouse seeking support was able to obtain employment appropriate to their skills, regardless of the level of earnings available through that employment.

Because of these flaws, many states resisted the UMDA reform. Alimony legislation since the early 1990s has been mainly a response to widespread criticism of support awards during the previous two decades, especially after longer marriages. This legislation constitutes the new wave of alimony reform. By expanding the list of factors which the court must consider in awarding support, and by requiring the court to make findings explaining the reasoning behind its award, the new legislation encourages courts to base their support awards more upon the facts of the case and less upon broad assumptions. To emphasize the new nature of alimony, these statutes generally eschew the term <u>alimony</u>, and substitute "<u>spousal support</u>." Of course, "a rose by any other name…"

Nowhere is this change more evident than in the increasing use of vocational experts to measure earning capacity. This change more than any other, lies at the heart of new wave reform. Traditional alimony law was wrong to assume that women were close to unemployable; but the first "reform" in the law was equally wrong to assume that the theoretically unlimited employability of women translated into timely and sufficient employment of any specific former wife. The employability of any spouse is a question of fact and not law, and a question upon which experts can speak with much more authority than legislators or judges. By basing assessments of employability upon evidentiary facts and expert testimony, the courts can avoid the broad justified assumptions in both directions present in former case law. The vocational expert plays the same role in the law of spousal support as the valuation expert plays in the law of property division. Note that using these "experts" increases the cost of litigation.

<u>Who can get alimony</u>?
First for the court to award alimony, the court must find one spouse is "<u>dependent</u>." The divorce court state statute will typically state:

- The court shall award alimony to the dependent spouse upon a finding that one spouse is a dependent spouse, that the other spouse is a supporting spouse and that an award of alimony is equitable after considering all relevant factors.
- To be "actually substantially dependent" and thus entitled to alimony, a spouse must have an actual dependence on the other in order to maintain the standard of living to which he or she became accustomed during the last several years prior to the spouses' separation. To be "substantially in need of support" means that the dependent spouse would be unable to maintain their accustomed standard of living established prior to separation without financial contribution from the other.

The list of factors contained in the statute is not meant to be exhaustive, since the overriding principle in cases determining the correctness of alimony is fairness to all parties. And though the statute does not state that any one factor is more important than any other, the recent case law stresses property, earnings, earning capacity, and the accustomed standard of living of parties. One recent case also stressed the role of caretaker to the marital children. At the least, the court must at least make findings sufficiently specific to indicate that the judge properly considered each of the factors for a determination of an alimony award.

<u>Parties to a divorce must remember that the determination of alimony is a matter left to the wide discretion of the judge based on their notion of "fairness."</u> One recent case said that in determining amount of alimony, consideration must be given to the needs of the dependent spouse, but the estates and earnings of both spouses must be considered. "It is a question of fairness and justice to all parties." Such vague terminology gives lawyers the chance to drool at the number billable hours for the arguments they can make.

<u>How are earnings and earning capacity figured</u>?
The court must consider a party's total income, undiminished by savings contributions including investment income, severance pay, gifts, and any source of funds available for support. The court must also consider a party's earning capacity. This means the amount a person can earn using their best efforts to earn income commensurate with their skills and education. The purpose is to prevent payers from quitting their job and claiming an inability to pay.

<u>How do taxes figure into this</u>?
Under federal and state income tax law, alimony is deductible by the payer ex-spouse and reportable as income to the dependent ex-spouse, provided that the following criteria are met: (1) the payments are in cash and not in kind; (2) the payments are made incident to divorce or to a separation agreement; (3) the parties have not designated the payments as non-alimony; (4) the parties are not living in the same household; and (5) the payer has no liability for payment after the death of the payee spouse. While the parties may privately agree that the tax deduction and the taxable income aspects of federal alimony law shall not apply, the parties may not by private stipulation create "alimony payments" that do not meet the five federal criteria and yet attempt to obtain the tax deduction for the payer.

How is alimony paid?
An award of alimony may include, in addition to a sum of money in lump sum and/or periodic payments, transfer of title or possession of personal property and an interest in property, a security interest in or possession of real property. Both periodic and lump sum payments may be for a limited, specified term. In fixing the amount of alimony, the court must consider all the factors enumerated. Alimony shall be in such amount as the circumstances render necessary, having due regard to the estates, earnings, earning capacity, condition, accustomed standard of living of the parties, and other facts of the particular case.

When does alimony terminate?
The court can order alimony for a definite period, thereby providing a definite termination date. Certain events will also cause alimony to terminate. Chief among these are the <u>remarriage</u> of the dependent spouse or the continued <u>cohabitation</u> of the dependent spouse with a person to such a degree that the supported spouse's expenses are lessened, and the <u>death</u> of either party.

An important exception exists to the rule that alimony terminates on the remarriage of the dependent spouse. Sometimes parties enter into a global settlement agreement, fixing their property rights and spousal support rights. When the provisions of the property division and the alimony are "integrated," that is dependent on each other, then the alimony provision cannot be terminated on remarriage. For example, a spouse might give up a valuable property right in exchange for the stream of income that alimony provides. That stream of income cannot then be terminated on remarriage, because it was a bargained for right.

Can alimony be modified?
Alimony that is not lump-sum but for a definite period, may be modified upon a showing of a "<u>substantial change in circumstances (CIC)</u>." This means a change in circumstances from those that existed at the time of the original order to the time of the petition for a modification. This would include a change in income or assets of either party, a change in earning capacity (e.g., a job loss or a new graduate degree), or an unanticipated change in expenses. A dependent spouse cannot, however, deliberately increase expenses and run up bills in an effort to increase alimony. Alimony that is part of an integrated property settlement agreement cannot be modified, because it is a bargained for right.

More often, this "change in circumstances" is invoked when the payer loses a job, or has a decrease in income through no act of their own, and due to circumstances beyond their control. This brings both parties back to court (with their hourly-billing lawyers, no surprise there...) where the payer will claim the "change in circumstances" was voluntary, and the payor will claim the change is not voluntary.

But this court procedure is not automatic. Here are some examples:

Just before the "real estate bubble" burst, mortgage brokers were doing quite well with some earning close to a million dollars a year. After the bubble broke, in many cases the payer's income may have fallen by 80% or more, due to circumstances truly out of his control. Judges would usually favor the position of the alimony recipient despite the clear evidence to the contrary.

There are also documented cases of individuals with terminal illness where the Court in its "infinite wisdom," would force the dying payer to continue paying, despite the fact that this decision forced penniless payers into the cheapest hospice facilities available, rather than permit the dying individual to spend his final months at home with family. Documented stories like these are abundant and horrific, and many can be seen on the website of the New Jersey Alimony Reform (NJAR).

As a perspective of the court's fairness, one of the editors of this book suffered a brain injury and could no longer practice emergency medicine. Two separate disability insurance companies and the Social Security Administration all agreed he was truly disabled through no fault of his own. Despite this, with his income dropping by approximately 70%, the Judge lowered the alimony from $5,000/month to $3,500/month, and lowered CS by about a $1000/month.

Clearly this is not equitable Change in Circumstances administration by the courts. So beware!

<u>Can the parties agree on alimony instead of having the court decide it</u>?
The law encourages parties to come to a marital settlement agreement (MSA) regarding their rights and obligations instead of leaving that to the court. Thus the parties can agree to all the possible terms of alimony: the right to receive it, for how long, for how much, when it can be modified, and when it terminates.

When parties decide to fix the alimony obligation by agreement, the agreement must be untainted by fraud, must be in all respects fair, reasonable, just, and should have been entered into without coercion or the exercise of undue influence, and with full knowledge of all the circumstances, conditions, and rights of the contracting parties. The Court does not consider the very real threat of, "You had better sign this agreement otherwise you may have tens to hundreds of thousands of dollars in lawyer fees and even higher, life-long alimony payments" as coercion.

<u>How are alimony orders enforced</u>?
Alimony can be paid by wage income withholding or garnishment, lump sum payment, periodic payments, or by transfer of title or possession of personal property or any interest therein, or a security interest in or possession of real property, as the court may order in its discretion. In most instances, garnishment of wages is the rule.

The court may require the supporting ex-spouse to secure the payment of alimony or post-separation support so ordered by means of a bond, mortgage, or deed of trust, or any other means ordinarily used to secure an obligation to pay money or transfer property, or by requiring the supporting spouse to execute an assignment of wages, salary, or other income due or to become due.

The same remedies of arrest and bail, attachment and garnishment, injunction, receivership, criminal contempt, civil contempt, execution, income withholding, and remedies also available to creditors are available in actions for alimony. However, alimony payers can be jailed for non-payment. While this country is not supposed to have any "debtor's prison," this imprisonment is considered justified, because the alimony is re-named as a "duty" rather than a debt. Semantics only, but enough to permit the Court to jail an alimony payer who has run out of money and run out of options.

<u>Conclusion</u>
The 1995 statute revision was a step towards the UMDA's idea of non-support for those who can support themselves. The statute however retains traditional notions of fault and providing for dependent spouses after long marriages. With these principles in mind, it is far better for parties to negotiate property and alimony awards, than leave it to the wide discretion of the judge.

THE PREDETERMINED PATHWAY TO YOUR PERMANENT ALIMONY

Above all, remember mediation is mandated by the courts and parties are urged to settle before trial, typically with a Marital Settlement Agreement (MSA).

When a person files for divorce, there are a series of procedural steps dictated by the court that must be followed including, but not limited to: serving papers to the respondent, preparing financial affidavits, and in some states attending a court ordered mediation. The purpose of the mediation is for the soon-to-be-ex-spouses to try to settle the case before taking the court's time and resources to settle the divorce through the judicial process.

So the parties are subject to a court ordered mediation to try to settle the case before they ever get to see a judge. Should the case be settled during one or more mediations, a Marital Settlement Agreement (MSA) is signed by both parties and afterwards, presented to the judge to accept the MSA and issue the Final Judgment.

Either agree to pay permanent alimony, or spend tens or hundreds of thousands of dollars on a trial, and then be ordered to pay permanent alimony. Here is why ...

Currently in many states, a long term marriage is defined as lasting 10-15 years or longer, and permanent alimony is the default judgment for long term marriages, unless there are very unusual circumstances in a particular case. Even if a couple is married fewer than 12 years (but more than 8-10 years), permanent alimony can be the judgment in some states.

What is heard over and over again is that during mediation, those married 15 or more years are advised to agree to pay <u>permanent</u> alimony if they are the higher earning spouse. These folks are told that they can agree to it in mediation, or go to trial and spend substantially more on legal fees, and then be ordered by a judge to pay permanent alimony.

Further, what exacerbates the situation is the lawyer for soon-to-be ex-spouse is also advising their client they are entitled to <u>permanent alimony</u>.

<u>Does Anyone Really Agree to Pay Permanent Alimony</u>?
Those who try to buck the system and fight, usually learn the expensive way that they were fighting a losing battle all along. If a couple is married less than 12 years, the fight may pay, but it may not. A person who has worked a lifetime to build up a nest egg now gets to understand that it will be split between the spouses, less of course the legal fees. Beware judges may order the paying spouse to pay the legal fees for the dependent spouse.

When you are told by your attorney that you will likely be ordered to pay permanent alimony, your soon-to-be ex-spouse's attorney is also telling them to expect awarded permanent alimony. So is it worth the further gamble of your nest egg to go to court and fight what would most likely be a losing battle?

The answer depends on you. Some people fight to the bitter end, while others take the more cautious and often prudent approach, and sign a MSA agreeing to pay permanent alimony. In most states, about 1% of matrimonial disputes end up in Court. These trials are always adjudicated by the presiding judge; jury trials are not permitted. This can bring in particular problems by itself. Suppose there is prejudicial information that would not be permitted in Court that is brought up before the Judge. Even if the Judge is asked to rule, and rules the information or legal exhibits cannot be brought into evidence, the Judge has already seen the "evidence." Do you then go to the extreme measure of asking the Judge to recuse himself/herself, a decision left totally up to the Judge? The answer is not an absolute <u>yes</u>.

Let's recap:
- Judges order the parties into mediation. Refusing mediation is not an option, as it is a judicial order. Remember, mediation results in billable hours not only from each party's lawyer, but also from the mediator, who is always an attorney.
- Attorneys advise their clients to settle, and as a last resort to use the court to settle a case.
- Although the law indicates that permanent alimony should only be used when there is no other form of alimony that would be acceptable, permanent alimony is still ordered more than not for marriages over 10 years.
- After the emotional toil is taken and retainer fees are used up, the paying party is often told that permanent alimony will probably – or definitely - be ordered by the judge anyway.
- Many times the lower earning spouse is told by their attorney to <u>expect</u> to receive permanent alimony before they even go to trial.
- Most potential permanent alimony payers conclude on the advice of their attorney, that it is beneficial to agree to pay permanent alimony and sign a MSA rather than go to trial with further depletion of their nest egg on legal fees, and then be ordered to pay permanent alimony anyway.
- Bottom line, payers who agree to pay permanent alimony in a MSA are essentially coerced into doing so, even though they understand that permanent alimony is payment until death or a successful retirement change in circumstances court fight, or face jail if they don't.

<u>Will a Substantial Change in Circumstances Modify a Marital Settlement Agreement</u>?
Almost all MSAs have a provision that alimony is modifiable if there is a substantial change in circumstance, unless the agreement specifically states it is non-modifiable. While new alimony laws could be considered a

substantial change in circumstances under which a person could seek to modify their agreement, ambiguity and inconsistency in the courts will inevitably result in one judge allowing it, and another judge not allowing a modification.

THE STATE'S $$ RATIONALE BEHIND CHILD SUPPORT ENFORCEMENT - Not *Deadbeat Dads, More like Dads Beaten Dead!*

A recent 7-year Arizona State University study found that less than 5% of those that are in child support arrears are true deadbeat dads – the ones with the younger trophy wives and sports cars, who don't want to pay anything. The truth of the matter is that according to the Federal government, over 66% of those owing child support can't pay because they are unemployed, underemployed, disabled, dead, or in some cases the mothers don't want support.

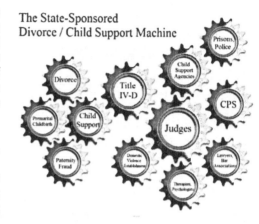

The State-Sponsored Divorce / Child Support Machine

Judges order such onerous child support amounts in some cases, along with alimony, daycare, medical expenses, life insurance, and other expenses, that the father can't survive. He ends up becoming despondent, leaves (or is fired from) his job, drops out of sight, and loses all contact with the children because he cannot afford the court-ordered child support.

They always have a motive behind what they do and the laws they make. It's all about money, power and control. Judges refuse to reduce child support and alimony when a man loses his job due to the current economic climate. They tell the guy that it's too soon to reduce support because "you might get another job" in a short time, and that the change of circumstances is "temporary." Most often the guy never gets the same-salaried position and winds up making substantially less. All the while, he falls farther and farther behind in his CS and alimony "obligations" with no hope of ever making up the arrearages plus interest. The point to remember, fathers will generally make it a priority to pay their child support.

But do the courts reduce child support? Rarely. No, they keep it there until the arrears are so high, that the payer's credit is ruined (which happens after 90 days), and then they start putting warrants out for their arrest, even though they did everything they were able to do to comply with the law.

Judges then use a court order to hold the non-payer in jail, somewhat like bail. But it isn't bail, because child support is an "obligation, thus avoiding having a "debtor's prison." Keeping men in jail until they pay? Stupid is as stupid does, as it's not about the children! Keeping a man in jail to pay support is an oxymoron. And many of the family court judges are morons! How does one pay child support if in jail? Do they work in the jail making $10, $15, or $20/hour and have their wages garnished? Does this person invoke the Insolvent Debtors Statutes when they get out of jail, since they have no assets or income, and the jailing served as the remedy for the debt owed? Under the Bankruptcy Code for insolvent debtors, the debt has been paid once the person has been jailed for it and released. But the state will try and keep the arrears on the books.

The reason why judges grant high dollar orders and enforce them stringently is because the <u>Federal government pays the states</u> a <u>federal reimbursement incentive funding</u> (42 USC Section 658a) for child support amounts awarded, collected and enforced. This money goes into the state coffers, no strings attached (42 USC Section 658f). As a conflict of interest, state treasuries pay the judicial/state employee pensions and salaries.

Family Court judges continue to thumb their noses at the US Supreme Court mandates. They are obliged to disqualify themselves from these cases where they have a financial interest in the outcome. See the Machine dependence chart to the right.

Every other Circuit court has followed suit and hold that child support is a common commercial, civil debt. The child support enforcement industry is a total machine, and a $30 billion/ year collection industry.

FAIRNESS OPINION

The state(s) family court system and the judges are very concerned with the alimony recipient maintaining the lifestyle they had when married.

So why is the alimony payer not entitled to the same?
When a spouse is a homemaker, isn't it part of their homemaker job to maintain the home? So why do I now pay the ex-spouse permanent alimony and get nothing at all in return? Why is the ex-spouse not required to do a job maintaining the payer's home, as now the payer is paying the ex-spouse a salary? When is it my turn to maintain my lifestyle, while the ex is using my alimony money? As my retirement years approach, I am increasingly nervous. I've already given my ex-spouse half of everything – including half of my retirement funds. However I have now learned, the Courts generally will not end alimony at my retirement age even after going to court again, but instead will tell me to continue to pay. But I've already paid by virtue of splitting my retirement funds at the time of the "equitable distribution"? Is it unfair? The answer is, yes! Permanent alimony is unfair; it needs to end!

THE PUBLIC IS UNAWARE OF THE PERMANENT ALIMONY PLIGHT – WHY?

The public believes for several reasons:
- That alimony only affects the rich.
- They falsely assume that all those men paying alimony cheated on their devoted, selfless wives and deserve what they get.
- They may have read some articles or heard an interview, but philosophically believe the cases are exaggerated, and that the government and courts would not order such a thing.
- The public when hearing about alimony, only think of the recipient and how the lack of alimony payments will affect that person. No one thinks about the effect on the payer!
- It's interesting how many people are against a woman paying permanent alimony, but still feel it's ok as a man's obligation.
- The vast majority of people do not know anyone personally who is enslaved to permanent alimony until death. Therefore they believe it has no effect on them, so they are indifferent.
- They have total disbelief when hearing about the scenario that a working 2nd marriage spouse would have to contribute some of their 2nd marriage independent income to the 1st marriage ex-spouse's alimony.
- In reality, most people simply are not aware of the problem affecting 640,000 individuals paying alimony. Many people give "fairness" only lip service, and most simply do not care.

PLAN B – THE STRONG ARGUMENT FOR INDIRECT CIVIL CONTEMPT

This option is for alimony-only payers (not child support - CS), as this can be a complex issue with the authority of state CS enforcement agencies and one's morals). Indirect civil contempt of court is the violation of a court order outside the immediate presence of the court.

As the now-divorced majority wage earner, you have been ordered by the Court to continue to pay "until death" huge sums of money to an ex-spouse for alimony. Your financial burdens may be so absurdly overwhelming that many will feel they need to move to another country – away from the clutches of the Family Court and ex-spouse – in order to live and later to retire in any manner other than completely impoverished. So why is it necessary for the now divorced, majority wage earner after giving up a large % of what you put into the marriage, to be faced with the scenario that to have any future quality of life, it may be necessary to leave this country? I don't believe this is the right approach. Yes, you can stay in the US and continuing to work, as it is ***feasible and attainable***.

With 6-24 months of preparation, you can become invisible. You can continue to work and re-establish your life in the few years before you have left to retire. You probably will also have the misfortune to get laid off in the interim, but this happens to many in the current work environment.

The easy way is to bail and leave the US. Bottom-line, even if you leave the country, after 65 you will probably want to come back to the US for Medicare and Social Security, so why bail overseas now? You can stay, fight the legal system's stupidity, and get on with your life in the US. One day after 10 years of paying alimony have quickly gone by, you will realize no one told you to run. So don't wait, take off now, or do your Plan B in the US.

At no time did I agree to this lifetime obligation either in my wedding vows, or at any subsequent time up to the divorce proceeding's final court verbal summary. The surprising and infuriating thing is, many of us were told without negotiation by the lawyer and the court that permanent alimony is your life sentence, and for many without even speaking a word or being asked what you would consider to be fair in court. Life sentence! Even bank robbers get out in a dozen years!

I still say - Implement Plan B and forget your alimony life sentence, which may well exceed the length of your marriage. I am a proponent that it is not necessary to leave the country to escape. Just plan it and move on, staying in the US, moving out of your divorce decree state, and continuing working for a paycheck as you have done, but without the horrific alimony.

Alimony reform will just take too much time of the time I have left on this planet and too much of my hard-earned money. I have too little time and too little potential income to plan for any type of reasonable retirement.

Plan B... Move on with your life, with a priority of moving out of your divorce decree state. Do it and become an alimony expatriate <u>without</u> fear.

CHAPTER 2

PRE-DIVORCE STRATEGIES

Marriage is a partnership, but legislators are confusing it with being permanent and lifelong, which it isn't. You are not held to pay for your business partner, so you should not be held to pay in perpetuity for your former domestic partner. Your pre-divorce strategies are extremely important to your future, and you will need to implement them beforehand if you have any thought of an impending divorce.

There is <u>no</u> law that assumes every divorced ex-spouse has the right to a life of idleness after divorce, except your ex-spouse with a permanent alimony award. Anything beyond temporary or rehabilitative ex-spousal support is demoralizing and punishment, so here is how to move on.

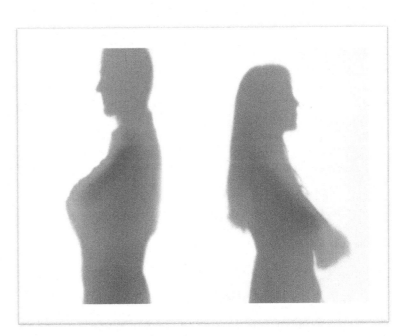

BLUEPRINT TO FACILITATE YOUR LIFE BEFORE DIVORCE

There are five essential periods when you absolutely need to concern yourself with the planning for your divorce strategy and asset protection: Before marriage, during marriage, before a divorce, after a divorce, and when you are facing a contempt of court hearing. Throughout, you must carefully avoid letting the lawyers take all of your money. While they are "supposed" to work for you (or actually as Officers of the Court, work towards "justice"), they all bill hourly, and all want more and more billable hours (preferably paid in advance).

Good asset protection planning should start very early, even before you are contemplating marriage or divorce. With the substantial possibility of divorce, planning for this eventuality should be done in the early stages when you think you might want to tie the knot. When the parties are in "heat" to get married, little thought is given to their financial future and everything seems rosy. As one of the parties to a future divorce proceeding, you need to protect what assets you have now ... not later.

You need to be concerned about your privacy, as protecting your assets is primarily concerned with finding legal, privacy methods to implement that are readily available and cost effective. Surprisingly enough, you don't have to resort to exotic and complicated remedies like going offshore to do so. You should be familiar with basic laws that regulate what you are trying to do, and develop an understanding how the courts view them.

Your goal needs to be to make your assets "bulletproof and invisible" from anybody and the courts to keep them safe from outside attacks or attachment. There are legitimate, commonly overlooked ways to protect your assets and future wage earning capacity, precautions to use, and considerations of which you weren't aware. The first thing to do before divorce is to protect what assets you have now, as after a divorce proceeding starts or... later, it will be too late.

By-The-Books Divorce
- Over a year of divorce struggles with the lawyers in control and vast sums of money expended.
- Afterward comes years and years of ongoing legal wrangling. Legal costs are usually @ $300+/hour. Then the ex-spouse's lawyer will attempt to assign to you their fees, as there is no motivation for them to be reasonable, and every motivation for them to sue you frequently. $25,000+ legal bill likely each time.
- Frozen assets.
- Loss of house.
- Loss of kids.
- Loss of >50% of your assets.
- Paying alimony for the rest of your life ... until death?
- Child support till 21-24 with college costs after the legal age (18) end of child support? (Commonly tacked into divorce settlements).
- Life insurance policy if you die or become disabled.

Do It The Alternate Way – *The PLAN B ESCAPE – PLAN BEFOREHAND*
- 3 years or so of pre-divorce prep work with your simple lower paying job close to your home. Be prepared for a lower standard of living for a while.
- Assets liquidated, gifted and divided where possible.
- Sell the house if possible.
- Now a quicker divorce, as little to fight over.
- Move to another state if you can.
- Then 3 years or so of post-divorce wind-down in new job.
- It is more likely your ex will be paying their own legal fees.
- You pay for your kid's college and support as you are able to and want to.
- Hide your identity and income and then move on.

PLAN B - PRE-DIVORCE STRATEGIES BEFORE YOUR ESCAPE FROM ALIMONY

So here is a quick more detailed summary of your prospective **Plan B**, protecting your future livelihood from a legal system that thinks that all working spouses should be reduced to slavery. Here are the steps:

Pre-Divorce
- The first step is to avoid jumping into the divorce, as once the divorce machine gears are moving, it is really too late.
- Do not let anyone talk you into filing for divorce too early. Keep your future plans to yourself in total secrecy. If you feel like you need to speak with someone, get over the urge!
- Assuming you have been married for a few years, you must rig your marriage to last for a couple more years while you get ready. Utilize tokens of love, romantic vacations, and gifts. Stall before your filing.
- Assets:
  - You have to understand that everything that you have - your money, investments, and home are really going to be divided and destroyed by the divorce. Your lawyer, your spouse's lawyer, and your ex are going to get much of what you have, and anything you have left may be attached to

provide the alimony and child support you will be paying. Your quality of life is going to go down, so plan a strong offense, spend it, or hide it now.

- o <u>Financial Statements and Passwords</u>: Shortly before the divorce filing, remove all of your bank and financial paper statements from the household. Then change the passwords for all these accounts. Don't allow this info hoard to be used against you during the asset discovery period by your ex-spouse.
- o <u>Premarital Assets</u>: Document what you brought into the marriage, as If years later you cannot produce the document trail, you will lose the status and the money will be split. Safeguard and document all records of your premarital assets, as you will need them later.
- o <u>Money Off The Table</u>: In the last 2 years, consider converting some of your financial assets into a zero interest tax reporting status (0% interest accounts or cashier checks) and holding onto them, getting them off the books, tax returns, and the grid. Make it a priority to take some money off the table, as you will need it later.
- o <u>Kids Future</u>: Set up trusts or 529 accounts for your kids' educations, but set them up so neither you nor your current spouse can withdraw them - only the kids should be able to get at them.
- o <u>Most Important of All</u>: Get all your current financial records, birth certificate and passport out of the household, <u>everything</u>!
- <u>Passport, Birth Certificate, Diplomas, Professional Certificates and Licenses</u>: Remove from the household and put in a safe place.
- <u>Mailbox</u>: Get a secret PMB (private mail box, also known as a CMRA box that is not a Post Office box), and use it to communicate with lawyers or divorce resources.
- <u>Email</u>: Next get a secret email account. Change your passwords on all existing accounts.
- <u>Public Message Boards</u>: Delete your Facebook, Twitter, LinkedIn or similar accounts. **Stay off with no** public identity, and no public message board posting.
- <u>Affairs</u>: Be good. No public affairs, until the divorce is complete to avoid any marital misconduct allegation. Sorry it's inhumane, but so is divorce.
- <u>Employment</u>: Now, <u>lose your present high paying job</u>. Find something that pays <u>less</u> than your spouse is making or 50% of your present income, and <u>keep</u> that job. Something close to home. You should be at that lower paying job for 3 years before seeking a divorce. Make it work.
- <u>Best State To File the Divorce</u>:
  - o A high priority alternate, research the best state to divorce to file with the least alimony and best division of marital property (Kansas, **Mississippi**, or Texas), as there are substantial differences. A community property state vs. equitable property distribution is also recommended. This is a critical step before filing; so don't blow it off as unimportant.
  - o Then take the big step and separate before filing for divorce, and seriously consider strategically picking the best state to move to. Don't wait for the spouse to file first, putting you at a disadvantage with required travel if you separate to another state.
  - o If you elect to separate before filing for divorce, be aware of the different state residency requirements before filing for divorce. Then after separation, file first to establish your divorce decree state, and make the spouse have the difficulty of traveling to your foreign state court for each court proceeding and to see their lawyer.
- Line up personal support systems and child care for your upcoming divorce. Make sure you have a few people to help, places to escape to blow off steam or relax.
- Should you elect to stay, do not move out of the house, because this decision can be important in child support determination and community property states (see Watt's & Epstein credits on page 34). If you stay, beware domestic violence charges against you may ensue, and this issue will not be a factor. This is another reason to separate and move to another state of your choice.

Divorce Filing & Proceeding
- Then finally you file for divorce. If you have no money, file <u>pro-se</u> (representing yourself), as this makes it difficult for your ex to pile the legal fees on you.
- <u>Children Involvement</u>: If there are children involved, do not move out of your residence. Ask your spouse to move (but not the kids, they stay). Be very nice to them. Then shut your spouse out of the bedroom - put a new lock on the bedroom door and put your spouse's stuff outside the room - or move it into another

room. Do not get into arguments with them, or raise your voice. Do not raise your hand to your spouse, no matter what they do. Retreat to your lockable room with the kids if they get crazy. Beware false allegations of domestic violence may ensue.

- You may lose your house, lose custody and pay child support, but you will be giving yourself as much freedom as possible.
- Be generous dividing things. Give your spouse what they want if you can, but track costs. Make sure that your spouse is demonstrably somewhat ahead of you in the division.
- Hidden Assets: Contemplate hiding some of your assets or money, putting into a certified check or into an account with no interest and sitting on it 1 – 3 years before the divorce. Do not list them in your asset declaration at the initiation of the divorce.
- Tax Returns: Do not agree to filing joint tax returns during the divorce proceedings, as the alimony temporary support tax deduction will be lost if you file jointly. File separate returns, as getting the spouse's signature can be problematic, and they will then want the ½ of the refund.
- Privacy Mode: Shut down all unnecessary communication lines with your casual friends, initiating your privacy mode.
- Watts & Epstein Credits – Community Property States Only: This housing associated credit of the marital residence is a complicated issue, but you can request the soon-to-be-ex-spouse to pay for staying in the house during the divorce. See page 34 for an explanation.
- Mailbox: If you did not do it before, it is now imperative to get a secret private mail CMRA box (not a USPS Post Office box), and use it to communicate with lawyers or divorce resources.

Post Divorce

- If you did not do this before or during the divorce, consider now moving to another state or another country. Your need for a new job might be a good motivation.
- Sell and divide the return from the sale of the marital house. Time to move on.
- If you move, don't buy, instead rent from a private party.
- Do not fill a USPS change of address form, as this can be used to easily locate you.
- Obtain a copy of your employer's wage garnishment for your records, if you were not provided one at the divorce marital settlement agreement (MSA) finalization. Many never receive a copy of their 1st garnishment order.
- Keep your escape plans a secret. Discuss with no-one except trusted friends who can keep a confidence. Do not tell your lawyer, as the lawyer may feel "obliged" to share this with the Court as the Lawyer is supposed to be an Officer of the Court. Shut down all unnecessary communication lines with your casual friends, initiating your privacy mode.
- After the divorce for the next 3 years or so, continue to stick with your present easier, lower-paying job while paying alimony. You want the ex-spouse to have moved on with their life before you start to accumulate any assets or start earning any more money.
- Keep your earnings and assets from here on a secret and live modestly, developing your own privacy strategies. Women have taken men back to court many years after their divorce, and won new alimony and support arrangements that have kept men on the hook past retirement. You don't want this to be you.
- Employment Lay-off: Never planned, but this can happen to you and can really complicate your plan. But it provides an opportunity to stop the current wage garnishment.
- Tax Returns: Even if required by your MSA, do not send your ex-spouse copies of your tax returns, as they will be used to come after you for more money. Beware you may be held in "contempt of Court" and risk arrest by "bench warrant" by setting foot in your previously "home" state for your arrears and failure to provide the tax returns.
- Do not wait until you are in arrears, and served with papers subject to a contempt charge with big financial payments and threat of jail. It is too late then. Plan B needs to be started before the arrears charges start coming, while you have time for the unforeseen.
- Plan B: So plan your escape. Examine your situation for what are the punitive damages of your stopping the alimony? If they: 1) find your new place of employment, or 2) you are caught by a divorce decree

state bench warrant or 3) a judgement is issued to seize your financial assets, generally arrears plus 6-12% interest and a nominal penalty (20% +/-) governed by individual state law.

Is it worth it? If you look at the time, money, and effort that goes into a "*By the Books*" divorce, and weigh your potential for being enslaved for the rest of your life, *Plan B, the Escape* seems worth it. Your "*By-the-Books*" divorce will likely drag out more than a year, and eat up a significant chunk of your monetary assets. Following the alternate **_Plan B_**, you will maximize your undivided assets, and have no debt servitude to your ex. Then move on.

THE DIVORCE PROCESS

First - you are married and later on years later you start thinking about divorce, like it might be a good idea. A friend will tell you are wrong, but they don't know your situation. Anyway out looks better than in, and you decide to move on and get...

Separated: Separation is where you divide your stuff from your partner's more or less informally, and make some arrangements for the kids to not be traumatized too much. You think you have done a good thing, and perhaps you have, but the IRS and your state thinks you are still married. You wouldn't think that was so terrible, but it is. You may live for many years in relative peace, being separated, and seeing to your ex's basic needs, thinking that all is well. It is not. You just haven't hit the bottom yet. What happens eventually is that someone for some reason, decides that they need to formalize this separation with a divorce, either for re-marriage or some other reason. So you ...

Seek a Mediated Divorce: Guess what. Mediators are all family court lawyers and are all invested in the system, and think that it is right, and the system says that the wage-earner has to pay through the nose. So the mediator will likely give you a solution that is as bad as or worse than one you would get in court. Your soon-to-be-ex who is normally a wonderful person, starts thinking about the many, many years that they will have to support themselves without any help, and how nice it would be to have that extra money that the mediator is hinting at between their words. The mediator probably keeps mentioning your kids in the process, trying to make their skullduggery sound highbrow. So you stop going to the mediator, and sensing blood in the water, your soon-to-be-ex (stbx) files for ...

Divorce Filing and Motions: Besides the basic divorce initiation your ex will file for a motion to freeze your assets, and impose an interim agreement for their temporary support. They may ask to have this taken directly out of your pay by wage execution. Watch out, this interim agreement is certainly not going to be in your favor. You will be told that it will be fine because the divorce will move along quickly, and this is just an interim thing, and if the final divorce goes more your way, you can get any overpayments back.

Repeat these words to yourself, "I will never see any money back." That is fact one. Fact two, "This is going to take a long time." Be sure that this interim agreement is one that you will be delighted with (or as much as possible) a year or two from now. Cases can and do get delayed that long. Oh, here is where you first get to enjoy the fun of legal fees. Theoretically the spouse that earns more always pays the other's legal fees, or a good portion thereof. Unless the spouse that earns more is female (sorry, speaking from experience), some other excuse will be trumped up to assign the fees to the man. Next comes ...

Discovery: You have to basically strip your financial, psychological, and general persona and display it for your soon to be ex-spouse's lawyer to see, very possibly with a forensic accountant. You might be advised to also hire a forensic accountant, which may or may not be a good idea depending on what assets your soon to be ex-spouse might have. You may find out things about your soon to be ex-spouse's in this process that surprise you. For instance, you may discover that your spouse has been happily misusing your credit since the separation. This is very common. And if your soon to be ex-spouse has already done this once, they probably done it again. Next the court orders you to go to Court-Ordered Mediation. This is a total waste of time and money for your lawyer and for the mediator ... Following that, you get to enjoy ...

Certifications: This is where you say why you think you shouldn't be enslaved, and where your soon-to-be ex-spouse makes up a lot of really imaginative and horrible stuff about you. At the end of your certification is a statement that says you will be punished if you lie. Don't you dare lie, but be confident that your soon-to-be ex-spouse will never be punished if they do. Next comes ...

Pre-Settlement: Oh, the joy. The group of bloodthirsty divorce lawyers once again all bought into the system, and now gather to review your preliminary filing and your stbx's preliminary filing. The point of Pre-Settlement is for the panel to tell you what the very busy judge would likely decide in a full trial, so that you don't waste their time and your money. Just as most people would prefer to know what kind of cancer they have right away, so this is better than having to wait for trial, but not as good as living in a state that doesn't believe in alimony enslavement. At some point around here, your lawyers start putting together a final agreement, but before that there is ...

Bench Trial or An Attorney Meeting At The Bench: Turns out the judge now after all has lots of time and may have read your certifications, and that judges like to meet with the lawyers only before any agreement is set in stone and say what they think they would have ruled. This is usually a very scary moment, because if the judge says something more bloodthirsty than the pre-settlement panel did (and the judge is likely to, just think about how they got this job), your soon to be ex-spouse's may want to revisit any settlement that you thought you had reached. After this horror where the judge tells you that they would have recommended far worse, you are left to finish negotiation, and if you can agree without trial, you get to come back into court for the actual ...

Divorce: The judge will ask you at length if this wasn't the best thing you ever did in your life, and if you don't love this agreement. You have to say yes or go through a trial, and have the judge do the horrible things they already explained in the bench meeting, and pay more legal fees (yours and your soon-to-be-X). Needless to say, you nod violently in the affirmative, while expressing your agreement that the wax fruit is yummy, sorry that the "Voluntary Execution" clause is correct. You probably celebrate that evening that this thing is over. It isn't, because people often spend more than they did on their divorce on their ...

Post Divorce Motions: OK, I can't tell you what will happen here, but if you made money, have bonuses, or if you ever change jobs or get married or just live, you will likely run up against your ex. They have interests that are not yours, want to stop you from living freely, and take any new income that you are making, or force you to continue to paying the same alimony and child support that you were before if you happen to lose your job or have some other unfortunate circumstance occurs. And if you did remarry, you will discover that in some states, the courts believe that half or more of the assets that your new spouse has brought to the marriage, and half or more of their income is available to satisfy any judgments against you, and that their finances are now entirely exposed. Your lawyers will tell you that this cannot happen, but it does. In divorce law, you are assumed guilty until proven innocent, and it is always possible that you hid funds in your spouse's accounts, and once and if your funds are/were co-mingled, those funds are 'tainted' - considered marital property. Enjoy these post-divorce actions. You will likely have several of them and regardless of your relative incomes, if you are male, you will pay for most of the legal fees generated by them. This is where you get to pay a lot of dollars for the legal teams.

DIVORCE FINALIZATION - MARITAL SETTLEMENT AGREEMENT (MSA) APPROACH

<u>Settlement</u>: 95% percent of all divorce cases are settled and do not go to contested trial, but the statistics for settlement of child custody cases are not as good. The illustrated case below of Mary and John ends in a settlement, but the results of the settlement will be (because they usually are) almost the same as the results of a trial. The advice your lawyer gives regarding settlements is based on the lawyer's knowledge of the law and the knowledge of how the judge is going to rule. A settlement should not be considered by your lawyer until the lawyer knows and understands all of the financial and child custody facts. The settlement is usually negotiated directly between the lawyers. Sometimes the lawyers decide to hold a "four-way settlement conference," that is a negotiating session in which both the lawyers and clients participate face to face. Four-way conferences may be

helpful, but in most cases are counter-productive, because some lawyers "showboat" at these conferences.

<u>Court Conducted Pre-Trial Settlement Conference</u>: If the case is not sooner settled, the judge conducts a pre-trial settlement conference. At this conference each lawyer submits to the judge a memorandum telling the judge all the essential facts of the case, proposing a settlement and attempting a justification for the proposed settlement based on the facts of the case and the law applicable to the case. The parties and their lawyers are in court for the settlement conference, but usually only the lawyers go in the judge's chambers (office) for the settlement conference. The lawyers each present their position and arguments to the judge. After this the judge will generally have a fair assessment of the facts of the case and the applicable law, and the judge will usually tell the lawyers something to the effect of, "If this case goes to trial and the facts at the trial come out as I now understand the facts to be, then my ruling is likely to be ..." The judge's pre-trial conference recommendations for settlement should be the blueprint for a settlement agreement, unless your lawyer believes the judge misapprehended the facts or misunderstood the law, and that at trial the lawyer can convince the judge to a different position. Remember going to trial against a judge's recommendation is going to trial with <u>the odds against you</u>.

<u>Finalizing the Settlement</u>: Settlement is finalized by a written "*Marital Settlement Agreement*" (MSA). In this example assume that Mary's attorney makes the first draft of the settlement agreement which after Mary's approval, is presented to John's lawyer, but it could well have been that it was John's lawyer who wrote the first draft. It will probably take Mary's lawyer more than one draft of the proposed agreement for it to contain all of the terms that are satisfactory to Mary and her lawyer. That draft of the marital settlement agreement will then be delivered to John's lawyer, and John and his lawyer will review the agreement, and in most likelihood will ask for changes to be made so that the proposed agreement is acceptable to John. This is part of the negotiations and is a back and forth procedure that may take some time before both signatures are on the agreement.

<u>Finalizing – the Prove Up</u>: Once the marital settlement agreement (MSA) is signed, it is merely a matter of docketing the final hearing before your judge. The hearing can usually be scheduled within about a week of the time the lawyer calls the courthouse to schedule the hearing. Usually only the plaintiff (in this case Mary) is required to attend the hearing and testify. Before the divorce prove up Mary's lawyer should inform her of the questions that will be asked of her. The actual hearing (the time Mary will testify) will only last about five minutes, but since there will be other divorces being finalized in the same time frame, Mary should allow about an hour for the court appearance. The questions to be asked will first be in order to prove the matters stated in the petition for divorce, which includes names and identities of the parties, the grounds for the divorce etc. The questions will also deal with Mary's understanding of the terms of the marital settlement agreement. As soon as Mary finishes her testimony, her lawyer will present to the judge the proposed

judgment of divorce, which the judge will sign. Both parties are now <u>divorced</u>, and the marital settlement agreement is made part of the judgment.

COLLABORATIVE DIVORCE - SOMETIMES TOO GOOD TO BE TRUE!

Of course you want to get your Dissolution of Marriage Judgment - the goal of your divorce, but you don't want to go through the adversarial expensive legal system to get it. Bottom-line, you don't want to get all tangled up with lawyers and courts, because the system is designed to work against you.

Instead of going through the legal system without hiring a lawyer, you should go around it and work outside the legal system, by making arrangements and reach an <u>agreement</u> with your spouse. By doing things yourself, you have far more control and far better solutions. Working outside the legal system is the way you get a low-conflict, low-impact, higher quality divorce.

To stay outside the legal system, neither spouse should retain an attorney. The key word is "retain." I'm not saying you should never get help from an attorney if you want it, just that you shouldn't retain an attorney unless you have no other choice. This is known as "<u>collaborative divorce</u>."

Retaining an attorney means turning over both your responsibility for your case and control of it. The attorney represents you as you sign a retainer agreement, then you pay a nominal $5,000 retainer and your attorney has now taken over control of your case. This is what they mean when they say, "<u>I'll take your case</u>." And they do take your case, right into the high-conflict, low-solution expensive legal system. They have to, it's the law.

Because you don't want to go into a system that works so hard against you, only retain an attorney when you have no other choice, as when you are facing immediate threat of harm. You need an attorney if you:
- Can't get support from your spouse and have no way to live;
- Believe your spouse poses a danger to you, your children or your property;
- Think your spouse is transferring, selling or hiding assets.

In such cases, you should get a good attorney right away. Otherwise, you only want an attorney for information, advice and maybe some drafting and paperwork. The attorney retainer is the poison apple - don't bite it.

There are three different kinds of cases that respond to self-help techniques:
- <u>No agreement</u> between the spouses is needed, or a spouse is not involved. An agreement isn't necessary or not possible if there are no children, very little property, few debts to worry about, or no need for support - in short, nothing to agree to. There are also cases where the respondent simply will not participate and will not file a response, because he or she is either long gone or simply doesn't care. This case will be relatively easy to complete.
- <u>An agreement</u> will be <u>fairly easy</u> to work out. If you think it will be no problem for you and your spouse to work out an agreement, the MSA portion of this article is about the many advantages of a good agreement. But an agreement may not come easily. This describes the situation for most couples going through divorce. If you don't think you can deal with your spouse, don't worry - you can learn how to deal with disagreement and negotiate a settlement and where to get help.
- <u>An agreement is needed</u>, but may not be easy to work out. If you have children, you should work out a good parenting plan in a written agreement. If you have income or property worth protecting, or lots of debts to be paid, or if you need to work out spousal or child support arrangements, you should definitely have a written agreement.

MSA Agreement Advantages

The marital settlement agreement (MSA) is your key to avoiding judges, lawyers and the legal system, but that's not all - it has many other important advantages. Your MSA actually becomes your <u>Judgment</u>, which means <u>you get to decide all the terms ahead of time</u>. Without an agreement, you can't be sure exactly what some judge might do. The MSA has far more depth, detail, flexibility and protection than a plain judgment. Almost anything that's on your mind or in your lives can be included and resolved any way you like.

Most states have simplified procedures that allow you to get your divorce <u>without going to court</u> — if you have an agreement. Without an agreement, you almost certainly will have to go to a hearing to get your Judgment. But what's most important is that you get a better divorce outcome when you work out an agreement. With an agreement, people tend to heal faster, and it just plain feels better. The MSA agreement you negotiate is very valuable and worth working very hard to get. If you work it out with your spouse outside the system, you beat the system!

The bad news about collaborative divorce - if one cannot come to an agreement, your team must be dismissed, and you have to start all over with traditional lawyers following the more expensive court route.

ADVICE FOR DEAILING WITH YOUR LAWYER

One expects that for the amount of money for services paid, your lawyer will proactively inform you of the path you should be taking, give you some advice on how to structure and protect your income and financials, and have recommendations on your tax filings and pre-marital assets. Beware, unfortunately most lawyers will not be proactive on your behalf. My personal experience has required me to hire 4 lawyers – 1st quit before being fired; 2nd one was very good, 3rd was fired; and 4th was above avg.

Lawyers serve an important negotiating function in this area of law, as they act as buffers. They can negotiate with the other attorney based upon a trade-off of bargaining items. That is, they can make conditional concessions based upon getting something in return. This is something which the parties cannot do nearly as well themselves.

Many people will wait before seeing a lawyer. They may feel overwhelmed or deny the reality of the divorce. They may fear that seeing a lawyer will inflame an already deteriorating situation. They may not realize how an attorney can help. But an attorney can be an important ally in a divorce. An attorney's specialized knowledge, training, and experience allows the attorney to give timely advice that can prevent some serious problems from ever arising. Much of the work performed by lawyers occurs without a lawsuit being filed. Selecting the right lawyer is part of the pre-divorce process.

When you interview a divorce lawyer, keep in mind that you'll need to rely on this person to safeguard your interests during a time of great emotional distress for you and your spouse.

Also make sure that your divorce lawyer is well-qualified. The settlement structure you create will have a long-reaching financial and emotional impact on your life. Part of the divorce settlement or ruling at trial will involve technical issues, such as taxes and health insurance. Trying to tackle these issues without a qualified lawyer could be a serious mistake.

While you may or may not feel friendly with the lawyer you choose, you should expect to develop a rapport. If your lawyer doesn't listen to your questions during the initial interview or after you have retained him or her, consider consulting another person. Not understanding what the lawyer says or finding that the lawyer is disorganized, are signs that you may not be speaking with the right lawyer for you.

You should expect to be given a clear picture of your attorney's billing and collection policies. The lawyer should explain the hourly rates of everyone in the office who will work on your case. You should learn how the lawyer charges for expenses, such as photocopies, long distance telephone charges, court reporters, and postage. Learn whether or not you're supposed to pay these expenses in advance. Different lawyers have different definitions of the word "retainer."

Read your legal bills before you pay them. You should be able to understand what work was performed and the length of time it took to complete the tasks. Never settle for vague answers to your billing questions.

You can't expect your lawyer to predict exactly how much their total fees will be. But your lawyer should be able to give you a ballpark figure for each stage of your case.

Look for a firm that's flexible. Every divorce case is different. So is every law firm. Some parts of a case can be handled by a paralegal or junior lawyer under supervision by an experienced attorney.

Different people have different expectations. You may want to spend most of your time talking with your attorney directly. Or you may prefer to talk with a paralegal to keep the bills lower. Be sure to discuss your preference with your lawyer during the interview process. Listen to what the lawyer has to say. Determine if your goals are consistent with the attorney's practice. Be wary of the lawyer who tells you what you want without listening to you.

Make sure you hire an attorney who has enough time to handle your case. For important discussions, you'll most definitely want to spend time with your lawyer rather than with a paralegal. If your lawyer is too busy to return your phone calls or spend quality time engaged in extensive settlement discussions or strategic planning, you may need to consider hiring another attorney.

While your case may not require that you spend a great deal of time with the attorney, being unable to schedule an appointment with that attorney or to get that attorney on the telephone within 24 hours of your first call can be very, very frustrating.

Some attorneys handle as many as a hundred cases at a time, making it difficult for any single client to have quality time with the lawyer. Others will limit their practice to make sure they have enough time for each client. When you first talk to an attorney, find out how many clients he or she has.

Divorce is not a "one size fits all" proposition. Clearly communicating your goals and concerns to your attorney will help produce the best results for your special circumstances.

PRE-MARITAL ASSETS - DOCUMENTATION REQUIRED

What about the things that I owned before or inherited before/during my marriage? The general answer is that they are non-marital and are not subject to equitable distribution in the dissolution of marriage proceeding. The surprise during the divorce proceeding is you now will have to with no notice, provide clear documentation of your pre-marital asset ownership, or it becomes dividable marital property. Believe it or not, your inheritance can become marital property if you cannot prove it. This may be difficult for a 20 – 30-year asset, when some of the parties or companies and needed paperwork are no longer in existence and cannot be located within a 30-day clock for the production of documentation. Bottom-line the status of big dollar premarital financial assets can be lost, and tossed into the division of marital assets.

Under the statute all assets acquired and liabilities incurred by either party prior to the marriage (and assets acquired and liabilities incurred in exchange for such premarital assets and liabilities) are non-marital assets and liabilities and not subject to equitable distribution. There are exceptions to this general rule such as where a party co-mingled their non-marital assets and liabilities with marital assets and liabilities or made gifts of their non-marital wealth to their spouse, for example by putting the non-marital asset into a joint bank account.

<u>If I inherited an asset during my marriage, will my spouse be able to claim part of that in our divorce</u>? Normally not. Assets acquired separately by either party by bequest, devise, or descent (and assets acquired in exchange for such assets) are non-marital property and not subject to equitable distribution. But beware you will have to prove it. However they may become marital property if you made a <u>gift</u> to your spouse or <u>commingled</u> them with marital assets.

<u>Can I still have property that's my own</u>?
Yes, you can have individual property. Usually this is property you owned before marriage. A personal gift or inheritance, no matter when received, also is individual property. For an item to be individual property, however, you must have records that prove it belongs solely to you. Otherwise the law presumes that all property owned by spouses is marital property, belonging to both of you equally.

Simply having only your <u>name on the title</u> to an item does not make it individual property. The spouse named on the title does, however, have the right to manage and control that property. The law requires the titled spouse to treat the non-titled spouse fairly if the item is marital property.

<u>Can individual property unintentionally become marital property</u>?
Yes during a marriage, individual and marital property can easily get jumbled together. The law presumes this mixed property to be entirely marital property, <u>unless records prove</u> that some portion is individual property.

For instance, say you had a savings account before you were married. Over the years, you deposit portions of your paychecks, which are marital property, and the account continues to earn interest. You often withdraw money to pay family expenses. That account has become mixed property and at least partially marital property. It becomes extremely complicated to trace a portion of that account as individual property because multiple deposits, interest earnings, and withdrawals have moved in and out of that account during the marriage.

Another example: You've owned a summer cabin since before you were married. After marriage, your spouse builds an addition to the cabin, without receiving compensation for their labor. That extra room boosts the cabin's value. The amount of increased value is marital property, even though the cabin's original value could remain individual property, if documentation so proves.

On the other hand, suppose you owned 100 shares of stock <u>before</u> you were married. You buy no more shares during your marriage, and the stock grows in value due to market changes. That stock along with its increased value <u>remains your individual property, but you will have to prove with account statement documents</u>. Chances are high you cannot produce your documents of ownership after all these years, as you have changed brokerage accounts, mixed leftover income with investments, etc., despite them being in your sole name.

It bears repeating, "*If you wish to maintain an item as your individual property, you must have <u>complete</u> records to trace the ownership, and you will have to <u>prove</u> it.*" So safeguard the records.

MARITAL MISCONDUCT - DOES IT COUNT?

Although now that all states have initiated no-fault divorce, it doesn't mean that you or your spouse won't have to answer in some way for any misbehavior during the marriage. It's what divorce lawyers and courts refer to as marital misconduct, and in certain states can affect the outcome of the property division, an award of spousal support, or an award of attorney's fees for the victim-spouse.

The legal definition of marital misconduct is any conduct that undermines the marital relationship. It becomes a factor in a divorce when the offender-spouse's behavior forces the victim-spouse to assume extra burdens in the marriage. It isn't meant to punish the offender-spouse or award them an inadequate amount of property or income, but to fairly compensate the victim-spouse.

The rationale behind this theory is that the victim-spouse is compelled to contribute more to the marriage because of the offender-spouse's misconduct, therefore he or she is entitled to have the offender-spouse's behavior taken into consideration when property or income are divided. Marital misconduct can be disregarded if both spouses are guilty of marital misconduct. In some states, marital misconduct is specifically disregarded as a matter of law.

In those states where misconduct is a factor, there are several broad categories of behavior that might be classified as marital misconduct. They are:
- habitual drunkenness or addiction,
- adultery,
- domestic violence,
- cruel and abusive behavior, or
- economic fault.

Once the offender-spouse's behavior has reached the level of marital misconduct, it is the court's responsibility to determine just how much weight to give to it in each specific situation. Some of the considerations the court looks at are the:
- length of the marriage,
- character of the misconduct,
- time period during the marriage when the misconduct occurred, and
- frequency of the conduct and whether it was continual.

Certain types of marital misconduct may have more of an impact upon a court's decision-making than others. For example, cruelty or domestic violence might not be a relevant or appropriate consideration for making an equitable division of property because this type of misbehavior typically isn't relevant to the acquisition of marital property. The same cannot be said for economic fault, adultery or an addiction, all of which can directly influence a couple's property. There are several types of economic fault:
- dissipation of assets,
- hiding assets,
- diverting marital or community income to pay for an addiction,
- spending marital or community income on an extramarital relationship,
- excessive or abnormal spending,
- destruction of property,
- the fraudulent sale or conveyance of property, and
- any other unfair conduct that prevents the court from making an equitable division of property.

Some divorcing spouses believe that once they are separated and a divorce has been filed, that marital misconduct, especially adultery or economic fault has no effect on the outcome in a divorce. That isn't actually the case. Each divorce is very fact specific and the same logic about the impact of marital misconduct on the division of property applies whether it occurred prior to the separation or during the time up to the actual divorce. This is particularly true for economic misconduct.

There are some states that have statutes that specifically permit a court to award a disproportionate or lesser share of property to an offender-spouse, particularly if the misconduct can be classified as economic. The facts of each particular divorce play a heavy role in how the court applies the law.

In cases that involve the dissipation, hiding or destruction of assets, the excessive or abnormal spending of income, or the fraudulent conveyance of assets, the court can't increase the size of the marital or community estate that actually exists. However, it can order a disparate division of the existing and known property to reimburse the victim-spouse for their loss in the couple's estate.

In addition to having a possible effect on the division of property, marital misconduct may also have an effect on the amount of spousal support an ex-spouse may receive provided he or she qualifies for such support. This can work both ways. If the spouse who may be entitled to receive support is guilty of the misconduct, their receipt of support may be in jeopardy depending upon the nature and level of the misconduct. On the other hand, a paying spouse might have to pay more, especially if their behavior caused the victim-spouse to give up or reduce the ability to earn income.

PRE-DIVORCE TEMPORARY SUPPORT - AN ALIMONY INCOME TAX DEDUCTION CONSIDERATION

During pre-divorce MSA negotiations, do not give up your rightful income tax deduction for alimony paid prior to the divorce. Here's why - You will be probably be receiving the refund after the divorce.

As a rhetorical question, how many people when signing their marital settlement agreements (MSA's), gave approval to losing their tax deduction for their pre-divorce alimony only payments and agreed to file jointly up to the time of the divorce? For a nominal $50,000 alimony/year payer, this equates to a $12,500 yearly loss to you on top of the permanent alimony. Who with or without the advice of their attorneys would have agreed to such language, when the US government gives this tax deduction right to every tax-paying citizen for free? Most attorneys will be silent on this issue and not be representing the best interests of their client.

So do not give up your alimony tax deduction rights before the divorce and file married filing separately. Filing separately keeps your life simpler, as the soon-to-be-ex will probably have 2nd thoughts about signing a joint tax return with you. Then later after the joint signing of the refund check, they will want half of the refund.

QDRO DIVISION – CIRCUMVENTING EARLY WITHDRAWAL TAX PENALTY ON RETIREMENT BENEFITS FOR DIVORCE EXPENSES

Couples who find themselves in divorce proceedings may realize that in this economic climate, they are in need of more cash than is available to them. There is often an ongoing need for more cash flow following a divorce than one's salary or maintenance payments may provide. The financial shortfall may operate to suspend negotiations regarding settlement, and this may prove to substantially reduce available funds.

Some divorcing couples have retirement assets which may help alleviate cash flow issues. Sometimes couples may question about using or liquidating these assets for pre-retirement needs, since most are of the mind-set that these assets should be reserved solely for retirement purposes. This may be in large part due to concerns regarding distributions from retirement funds prior to age 59 and the resulting 10% penalty tax.

This penalty tax may be avoided as there are four methods for receiving distributions from retirement accounts prior to age 59 without the fear of incurring the 10% penalty tax for early withdrawal. These methods may be employed by divorcing couples in order to take advantage of settlement options which may otherwise remain unexplored.

In general, the laws addressing retirement assets provide that taking a distribution from retirement assets before age 59 will result in a 10% penalty tax. The methods discussed below, when properly implemented, assist in the avoidance of the 10% penalty tax levied for early withdrawal. It must be noted, however, that funds withdrawn from a retirement account will be taxed as income the year those funds are withdrawn.

The first method relates to tax code section 72(t) stating that the 10% penalty tax will not be applied to funds withdrawn from a retirement account if the money is in substantially equal periodic payments (SEPP). IRA assets are eligible for section 72(t) treatment, but 401(k) assets are eligible only if the plan participant is no longer employed with the sponsoring employer.

The 2nd method for avoiding the 10% penalty is to annuitize an IRA. Pursuant to this method, the owner remits a sum of money to an insurance carrier in exchange for a payment, which is guaranteed over a specified period of time. The duration requirement is met when the annuitant selects a pay-out period that will span a number of years or, in the alternative, for as long as he or she lives. With these immediate annuities, the payment amount is fixed, thus, the SEPP requirement is met. Given the current economic climate, this method makes sense because the risk of investment is transferred to the insurance company which is obligated to transfer the required payment to the annuitant.

As a general rule, money cannot be withdrawn from most employer sponsored retirement plans while the employee is still employed there. The <u>third</u> method known as a <u>Qualified Domestic Relations Order</u> (QDRO), is an exception to this general rule. A QDRO may be used in order to transfer funds from the 401(k) of the participant to the alternate payee's IRA. When the money is transferred to the IRA, it is subject to the tax-deferral benefits of a traditional IRA.

The tax code also provides that money being transferred pursuant to a QDRO may be received by the recipient spouse (i.e., alternate payee) without incurring the 10% penalty tax. By utilizing a QDRO, the recipient will receive a lump sum of money which can be used towards the payment of bills such as college tuition, legal fees, and a down payment for a house. Further by utilizing a QDRO, the available funds in a 401k may be split with some of the money being transferred to the spouse's IRA and the remainder being given to the spouse.

QDROs may be used only with employer-sponsored retirement plans and are not available for use with an IRA. Please bear in mind that not all employer-sponsored retirement plans will allow the use of a QDRO. For example, some plans will not permit lump sum payments while others are addressed by a different section of the tax code. A final method for use in avoidance of the <u>10% penalty</u> applies to employees who leave an employer after they are 55 years of age. The tax code allows these individuals to forego the age 59 rule and start receiving distributions from a 401(k) without the worry of the 10% early withdrawal penalty. To properly take advantage of this method, the employee must truly have separated from service. The employee may not continue to work for the sponsoring employer even without compensation and utilize this method.

WATTS AND EPSTEIN COMMUNITY PROPERTY CREDITS, DURING DIVORCE ONLY - Only in the 9 Community Property States (see page 45)

(see page 45)

<u>Epstein Credits</u>: It goes like this: If you pay a community debt with earnings after your date of separation, you may receive credit for making that payment when the assets and debts are divided. However, this rule is somewhat complicated. For example, if you pay debts for your spouse which are equal to or less than what you would have otherwise been ordered by the court to pay in support during the same period of time, you probably will not get credit. Keep track of all debts paid and let your attorney figure out what credit you may receive.

<u>Watts Charges</u>: Under this theory, if you use an asset which does not have a debt on it or has a very small debt, you could be charged with a "phantom" amount when you divide your assets. For example, if you have possession of the house and are paying $500 per month for the mortgage, taxes and insurance, yet the house would rent for $1,500 per month, you could be charged with $1,000 per month ($1,500 less $500) for every month you stay in the house from your date of separation until the assets are divided. This can add up to a substantial amount of money if your case takes a long time to resolve. This theory can also be applied to other assets, including <u>vehicles</u> and businesses. You should discuss this issue with your lawyer to determine if you should make some changes during your divorce process.

<u>Epstein/ Watts Combination</u>: This happens when one spouse is using a community property asset after separation (e.g., the house) and the other spouse is making the payments on it. The spouse using the asset can be charged the reasonable rental value for using it, (Watts Charge), plus the payer spouse may get credit for making the payments (Epstein Credit) - a double whammy. This can result in a major charge against your one-half of the assets in the ultimate resolution of your case.

After separation one spouse stays in the family home while the other spouse pays the mortgage. What are the consequences?

It's often the case that after separation one spouse moves out of the marital home ("the out-spouse") while the other spouse stays in the home with the children ("the in-spouse"). The out-spouse, usually the husband, may offer to maintain the status quo by continuing to pay the mortgage payments and other payments such as property taxes to maintain the property. In such a situation the in-spouse should be warned that there may be serious consequences of such an arrangement at the time of trial.

We've already seen one consequence. The out-spouse paying the mortgage payments may be entitled to Epstein credits, because they are paying separate property earnings towards a community property debt, unless there was an agreement to waive such reimbursements or such payments were a form of child or spousal support.

The other major consequence is that if the reasonable rental value of the family home is more than the mortgage payments, the in-spouse may be required to reimburse the community for the difference in these payments between the date of separation and the date of trial. These are called Watt's charges after the case that established the rule.

The general rule is that where one spouse has the exclusive use of marital community assets during the date of separation and trial, that spouse may be required to compensate the other spouse for the reasonable value of that use. Consider this example: Bob and Jackie separate. Jackie and the kids stay in the family home after separation. Bob agrees that he'll continue to support the family and pay the mortgage and other expenses. The mortgage payments are $1,500 per month. If Jackie had to pay the fair market rent for the property she'd pay $2,500 per month. Bob pays the mortgage for 10 months from the date of separation to the date of trial. Bob could argue that he should be reimbursed Watt's charges of $10,000 ($2,500 - $1,500 x 10). In a division of community property he'd be entitled to an extra $5,000. Bob could argue that he should also be entitled to Epstein credits of a further $15,000 ($1,500 x 10) which would increase his share of community property by $7,500.

The only solution to this mess is for the parties and their attorneys to agree early on in the proceedings whether a spouse's payment of community debts (such as the mortgage) and one spouse living in the family residence should be treated as spousal support which does not generate Epstein credits or Watt's charges. If it's treated as spousal support any agreement or Order should contain explicit language that mortgage and other payments by the out-spouse and exclusive residence by the in-spouse in the family home "shall be treated" as spousal and child support and the paying spouse shall not receive any reimbursements such as Watt's, Epstein, Jeffries credits and charges.

How do reimbursement claims work in a divorce?

Do you (or your spouse) have <u>exclusive</u> use and control of the family home while the divorce is pending? If so, you better read on!

What are we talking about here?

As owners of a house which is likely a <u>community asset</u>, you and your spouse both have the right to equal use of and access to the house. Upon separation and until the date of trial and a final division of all assets, the community is entitled to continued use and access to this asset. By one of you remaining in the house after separation, and thereby preventing the other's access to the home, he/she is <u>using this community asset for their separate purposes</u>. By preventing the community's use of the asset, they will be charged with reimbursing the community for the <u>value of the loss of the use of the asset</u>.

What does the law say about this dynamic?

Family law contemplates that when a couple separates thereby ending the community, each spouse is entitled to the benefit of the assets accumulated during the marriage. In the case of a house, such as the situation here, the "ideal situation" is one where both parties move out of the house and set up their own households using separate property funds they have accumulated post-separation. Once this has happened, the community asset is then rented out at fair market value, with each spouse receiving <u>one half</u> of the rental value. In turn, they would each then pay for <u>one-half</u> of the mortgage and <u>carrying costs</u> of the house from their portion of the rent, and would keep whatever amount remains.

<u>An example</u> ...
Assuming that the house rents for $6,000/ month with mortgage and carrying costs of $3,000/ month. Each party would receive $3,000 as their portion of the rent, would then pay $1,500 as their portion of the costs, and would retain $1,500/ month as their income from the community asset. In this way, the community is fully reimbursed.

<u>What happens if one spouse stays in the home during the period between separation and the conclusion of the divorce</u>?
In the event that one spouse retains use of the community asset post-separation, such as wife's continued use of the house, the community is still entitled to the value of the asset. In the situation where a spouse is the one who is "renting" the home from the community, that spouse is obligated to reimburse the community for their use of the community assets post-separation, which works much in the same way as the rental of the home to a stranger.

<u>What this mean</u>?
This concept of reimbursing the community for post-separation exclusive use of an asset is known as a "<u>Watts credit</u>" and is the amount of money owed to the community to make up for the loss of income that could have been recognized had the asset been rented to a third-party. Whichever is the one who has remained in the home, they will be the one responsible for reimbursing the <u>community for their personal exclusive use of the asset</u>. The actual amount that they will owe the community will depend on the fair rental value of the home and the monthly carrying costs. You should retain an appraiser to determine the fair rental value of the home to avoid any later arguments over this figure.

<u>There is a "reverse" to this concept as well</u> ...
In addition to the "Watts credits" that are owed to the community, both parties may also be entitled to "Epstein credits," which are reimbursements to the individual from the community. Whereas "Watts credits" are the rights of the community to reimbursement for a spouse's exclusive use and possession of a community asset, "Epstein credits" are the right of each spouse to receive reimbursement from the community for separate funds expended on behalf of the community, such as for payment of community debts. The courts have determined that it is possible for both credits to exist in a marriage, even if they work together to the detriment of a single spouse.

<u>How do Epstein credits work</u>?
In this case, while one spouse will owe the community money for their use of the home, the community may end up owing that spouse money for their payment of community debts with money earned post-separation. This would include his/her payment of the mortgage on the house, credit card debt accumulated during the marriage, and the pay down of car loans, etc. In turn, the community will owe the other spouse for post-separation payment of any community debts as well. You should keep track of all of these expenditures for the purposes of calculating these various credits when the case moves towards resolving these issues. Please understand that these credits continue to accumulate throughout the separation, and must be accounted for at the conclusion of the dissolution, either through the allocation and payment of the credits, or through a waiver.

FACTORS DETERMINING MAINTENANCE (ALIMONY)

There are factors set out in the law (eleven really, and a catch-all "any other factor that the court expressly finds to be just and equitable"). No one factor determines whether maintenance will be awarded, and the judge doesn't have to give each factor equal weight – the judge only has to "consider" each factor.

The factors a judge has to consider when making (or denying) an award of maintenance includes:

1. The income and property of each party: Under state law, the court must consider the income and property (including marital and non-marital property) assigned to the party seeking maintenance. The court must consider not only the size of the property awarded to each spouse, but also the property's future income-generating potential as well. Consider for example, a case where one spouse is awarded the marital residence and the other spouse receives a six flat apartment building of equal value. The apartment building will produce income whereas the house will produce only tax liability, insurance costs, and maintenance expenses.
   There are no particular rules or formulas spelled out in the law. Each judge is left to their own devices when it comes to making these "property-and-income from property-vs.-maintenance determinations." What is clear, however, is that a spouse has an obligation to generate income from or use assets if possible and practical.

2. The needs of each party: The law permits courts to look at the needs of each party – not just the spouse receiving maintenance, but also the needs of the spouse who is supposed to pay maintenance. Where a spouse cannot meet every day needs, maintenance may be appropriate even if the spouse is employed. Where the couple lived a very frugal existence during the marriage, such minimum needs will not necessarily be the benchmark by which a court will measure its maintenance award – a more liberal award of maintenance may be justified. In one often quoted case, the court commented, "The reward of frugality should not be impoverishment."

3. The present and future earning capacity of each party: This factor helps even things out in couples where one spouse receives property that produces income or is readily convertible to cash. Care must be taken to ascertain the future income earning capacity of any retirement benefits allocated to the spouse receiving maintenance. Too often lawyers and judges overlook the fact that upon retirement, both spouses will be living off retirement assets – equitably divided at the time of the divorce, and will have no effective income. An argument can be made, however, that retirement income derived from plan contributions or investments made with post-judgment earnings constitutes income not considered by the court at the time of the divorce and is therefore, a separate income stream from which maintenance may be paid.

4. The "Homemaker Contribution": State law requires courts to consider the extent to which one spouse has sacrificed his or her career in order to stay at home and maintain the household and rear the children while the other spouse establishes and builds a career. At the end of the marriage, the employed spouse will be able to start a new life with the income, assets, and perks afforded by the career. On the other hand, the homemaker will have few resources with which to build a new life. The law permits judges to look at the effort and sacrifice of the homemaker as just as much of a contribution to the marriage as the effort and sacrifice of the breadwinner.
   The "homemaker contribution" can be very significant. Several cases spell out how a court should look upon the years of sacrifice made by homemaker spouses. On the other hand, many maintenance claims relying on the "homemaker contribution" fail. In many cases a stay-at-home-spouse can be said to be merely lazy and unproductive, and this may be true. The argument can be made that to award maintenance to a stay-at-home loafer serves only to reward the lazy with an undeserved windfall and to punish the hard working breadwinner.

5. **The standard of living established during the marriage**: This is the factor that everyone remembers from the movies, "My client must continue to enjoy the lifestyle to which they have become accustomed, Your Honor." However, because two households are more costly than one, most parties cannot afford the same standard of living they enjoyed as a couple once they live apart. In such circumstances, the court should balance the parties' claims against the available income and assets.

6. <u>The duration of the marriage</u>: There is no rule that ties the duration of a marriage to an automatic award of maintenance. Nevertheless as a general rule, shorter marriages result in lesser, or no maintenance awards and longer marriages beget greater, or even permanent, maintenance awards. Numerous cases have awarded maintenance for periods longer than the marriage itself.
7. <u>Whether a party is caring for children</u>: This factor is not as significant as one might think. It usually only applies in cases where children are very young and not yet in full-time school and usually only last until the kids can get into full-time school/ day care.
8. <u>The age and physical and emotional condition of both parties</u>: This is the factor that usually carries the most weight. In most cases where maintenance is awarded, the receiving spouse is unable to hold a job outside the home in any meaningful way – due either to age or health complications. In fact, some lawyers argue that where one spouse is considerably older than the other, the older spouse should be entitled to maintenance – especially if they are too old to maintain a career and the younger spouse is still employed. Age, however, is not always the heaviest factor. In one noted case, a 32 year old wife was awarded permanent maintenance.
9. <u>The tax consequences of the property division and the economic circumstances of the parties</u>: Judges have the power to offset deleterious tax consequences with maintenance awards. For example, if one spouse receives property laden with capital gains taxes, that same spouse may receive an additional award of maintenance to help make ends meet and keep the IRS satisfied. Care needs to be taken in considering this factor, however, as the general rule is that maintenance is a tax deduction for the payer and is considered as taxable income to the recipient.
10. <u>Contributions and services by the party seeking maintenance to the education, training, career or career potential, or license of the other spouse</u>: There was a fairly famous 1986 case where a wife helped put her husband through nine years of medical school, only to be divorced shortly thereafter. Her years of frugality, student-budget living, and contribution to his medical license resulted in nothing and his years of sponging off her gave him a lavish, professional, lifestyle. Today the law is different. Law specifically permits courts to consider the contribution one spouse may make to the education or career of the other.
11. <u>Any valid agreement (a pre-nuptial agreement) between the parties</u>: The court must consider any valid agreement (a prenuptial or post-nuptial agreement), and usually courts will enforce such agreements. The fact is that most divorce cases settle, and a good divorce lawyer will include a maintenance clause in a settlement agreement when it is advisable.

EX-SPOUSE REQUIREMENT TO BECOME SELF-SUPPORTING - THE GAVRON WARNING (California Only)

When a husband and wife are married for 10 years or longer, the California Family Code provides a built-in presumption that this is a marriage of "long duration." This classification is important in divorce proceedings, as it commonly entitles one spouse to receive permanent spousal support, as opposed to support that will terminate on a specific date. In recognition of the potential for the recipient ex-spouse to abuse this privilege, the courts have adopted several rules intended to prevent the supported spouse from resting on their laurels in reliance on a lifetime of support from their ex-spouse. The most frequently invoked such rule is called the "Gavron Warning."

The Gavron warning is frequently issued to the supported spouse at the time the permanent spousal support order is made, typically at the time of the divorce decree finalization. The warning essentially compels the supported spouse to make all reasonable efforts to become self-supporting within a reasonable time. If in the future the supporting payer spouse feels as though the supported ex-spouse has failed to make such reasonable efforts, the payer spouse can request a Change in Circumstance support obligation modification downward, based on the failure to comply with the Gavron warning. The courts then assesses whether or not the supported ex-spouse had made reasonable efforts, which is where the application difficulty lies.

So wouldn't this legal warning be nice in other states?

LIFE INSURANCE GUARANTEE FOR PERMANENT ALIMONY PAYMENTS

Keep in mind that awarded alimony will cease upon death of you, the payer. So the ex-spouse may ask for a potentially expensive life and disability insurance policy in an amount sufficient to replace the alimony if something happens to you. Because the ex-spouse has an interest in you being insured in case of death or disability, you the alimony payer will get to buy the policy. Watch out for this one if you earn a lot of money.

Required life insurance is often an additional clause which seems to appear in the final MSA judgment. It is often inserted without regard to the insurability of the alimony payer. For example, requiring a person to purchase additional life insurance when an ex-spouse is in their 50's can be a tremendous financial obligation, since it is in this age bracket when life insurance costs accelerate, especially if there have been any medical issues. For example, during your divorce if you have been treated for heart disease, cancer, depression or are a smoker, the cost of life insurance will rise significantly. It can also be a reason why you can be cited for contempt if you don't continue to show proof at regular intervals that the policy is still in effect.

A $1 million dollar policy can cost you in the range of $3250/year, that you will have to pay each year until you die. If this does get thrown at you, get a decreasing term life insurance policy instead of a whole life policy, to make insurance more affordable.

Don't have enough money to pay the premium? If so, *Go Directly To Jail, and Do Not Pass Go.* So keep this one out of your MSA. Recommend that if when one stops paying for the policy at the time of Plan B implementation, the policy will then lapse.

AVOID AT ALL COSTS - ALIMONY SECURED WITH LIFE INSURANCE

Here are the potential terms and what to avoid at all costs. Rise to the occasion and walk away from the MSA negotiations if this shows up. Remember at this level it becomes near impossible for them to divorce an ex-spouse if you become an absent ex-spouse, so don't negotiate over this optional benefit entitlement. Here are the typical terms:

Alimony *in futuro* shall terminate upon payer ex-spouse's death, and the recipient ex-spouse shall receive all of the proceeds from the life insurance policy. Payer ex-spouse shall obtain a life insurance on themselves, naming recipient ex-spouse as owner and irrevocable sole and primary beneficiary of said policy in the amount of no less than __ million dollars to recipient ex-spouse. Payer ex-spouse shall immediately transfer ownership of said policy to recipient ex-spouse and shall furnish proof of compliance of this section within thirty (30) days from the date of the request. Should payer ex-spouse fail to make payments on said life insurance, recipient ex-spouse shall have an option to continue making payments and to assess the cost of said premium against payer ex-spouse. Payer ex-spouse shall not have the right to borrow against the life insurance without written permission of recipient ex-spouse.

Upon payer ex-spouse's death, the life insurance proceeds policy shall not be taxable to recipient ex-spouse, as the parties agree that these proceeds are to cover recipient ex-spouse's support and maintenance until the recipient ex-spouse's death.

Should there be any obligation, alimony, child support, life insurance or other outstanding debt upon the death of payer ex-spouse, which obligation is not satisfied by the life insurance policy or by will or trust, then it will be a claim against the estate of payer ex-spouse for monies or things due or to become due in the future under this Agreement by the persons entitled to receive those monies or things.

WHY YOUR ALIMONY AND CS PAYMENTS ARE SENT TO THE STATE DISBURSEMENT UNIT (SDU)?

Federal (Congress) and state laws require that all child support payments be processed at one central state location, and unfortunately alimony only payments are also sent to the same State Disbursement Unit (SDU) location. The typical location is the state Child Support Centralized Collections (CSCC) operation, fancy words for a SDU that simplifies the wage withholding process, allowing employers to send one check to one address for the respective state alimony and child support payments. CSCC handles payments from employers that are made by Electronic Funds Transfer/Electronic Data Interchange, which is an easy and efficient method of remitting child support payments, and provides a good documentation trail for you. For alimony only, don't agree to mail the checks directly to your ex-spouse so there is an independent verifiable record of payments. So don't be alarmed that your alimony only payment thru your employer's withholding goes to the state child support disbursement unit (SDU). Then the check sent by the SDU to the ex-spouse for alimony only may have a child support logo or banner on it. Here is an example of how the alimony only payment gets branded with child support.

Alimony Only Payment Coupon (Florida example - processed thru child support SDU)

Single checks or electronic withholding payments for both alimony and child support are believed to be applied proportionally. So remember, if a partial rather than full payment or a payment for arrears is made, it cannot be applied to just child support first.

Understanding the system is important as if later on you become unemployed and decide out of survival attempt to make child support (CS) payments only (which you can't, see page 165), this proportional payment policy doesn't help your arrears situation at all.

SOME STATES COMINGLE ALIMONY WITH CHILD SUPPORT REPORTING TO RECEIVE INCREASED FEDERAL CS TITLE IV INCENTIVE FUNDING

Federal law requires all states to have single site, state disbursement centers (SDU's) where payments are sent for: 1) all child support (CS); 2) combined alimony/CS, and 3) most alimony only settlements where agreed to in the MSA or by the divorce decree.

At this SDU location is where the CS and alimony money comingling takes place. Some state's SDU's comingle process the alimony payment with child support payments to receive additional federal incentive compensation, as it boosts their CS incentive collection total on average (9/20 x 100) or by about **45**%. This is big bucks as about $26 billion of child and spousal support are reported per year to the IRS, while concurrently about $10.6 billion/year of alimony (not related to child support) was reported to IRS.

POST DIVORCE - AVOID ALIMONY 3-YEAR INCOME TAX RECAPTURE IMPACT

Recapture of Frontloaded Alimony
One item to watch out for if you do not have to pay permanent alimony is the 3-year payback rule. To prevent a property settlement from being disguised as <u>alimony</u>, a provision in the IRS federal tax law requires that when large sums of alimony (<u>over $15,000</u>) are paid in the first or second year following the divorce, but significantly less is paid in the <u>third</u> year, a portion of the alimony deducted by the payer in the first two years is recaptured by being <u>added back</u> to the payer's taxable income in the third year. This has the effect of "<u>recapturing</u>" the lost tax for the IRS.

If this recapture rule applies, <u>the ex-spouse who received the alimony</u> (and had initially been required to include it in income) is entitled to a corresponding <u>deduction</u> in the third year.

The rule does not apply to alimony paid under temporary support orders (i.e., before the final decree is issued), nor does it apply when the reason for the drop-off in alimony in the third year was that the recipient died or remarried, or that less alimony was paid because the amount of alimony was based on a fixed portion of the payer's income from a business, property, or other compensation.

When to apply the recapture rule:
You are subject to the recapture rule in the <u>third year</u>, if the alimony you pay in the <u>third</u> year decreases by more than <u>$15,000</u> from the second year, or the alimony you pay in the <u>second</u> and <u>third</u> years decreases significantly from the alimony you pay in the first year. When you figure a decrease in alimony, do not include the following amounts:
- Payments made under a <u>temporary support</u> order.
- Payments required over a period of at least 3 calendar years that vary because they are a fixed part of your income from a business or property, or from compensation for employment or self-employment.
- Payments that decrease because of the death of either ex-spouse or the remarriage of the ex-spouse receiving the payments before the end of the third year.
- The rules are so complicated, not sure <u>how the IRS keeps track of your circumstances</u> and enforces these specialized provisions.

SHOULD ONE APPEAL YOUR DIVORCE DECREE AFTER THE FACT?

For the alimony payer, this makes no business sense. The court has already heard the facts once, made a ruling, you both signed the MSA agreement, and you got the short end of the straw. Going back for an appeal will cost $15 – 25K and you probably will lose, unless you can miraculously prove your insanity under extreme duress at the time of the divorce. Unfortunately your role in life is now to work and pay for a long time. Remember the end game with any appeal, you may get to pay the other spouse's legal bills as a reward for your initiative.

It is far easier for the recipient ex-spouse to haul you back into court and request a Change in Circumstances or hardship has occurred for them. They simply have to state they are incapable of maintaining the prior marital lifestyle on their own.

The insanity of believing in this appeal approach is like the perception that retroactive alimony reform is going to happen in our lifetimes. It will never happen. One more time a touch of reality – Plan B for alimony payers is a believable option with a known outcome, and far cheaper. Make the right business decision for yourself and move on.

EX-SPOUSE'S 50% MATCHING CLAIM ON YOUR SOCIAL SECURITY BENEFITS FOR 10+ YEARS OF MARRIAGE

When the ex-spouse (62+ or older) makes a 50% matching claim on your SS benefits for the 10+ years of marriage, none of your retirement benefits are changed, reduced or penalized. Here is why, the Social Security Administration rules in a nutshell:

The ex-spouse can receive benefits based on your SS work record if:
- The marriage lasted 10 years or longer;
- You, the payer ex-spouse, are <u>age 62</u> or older;
- The ex-spouse (62 and older) is still unmarried, and the divorce was at least two years ago.
- Your ex-spouse is entitled to Social Security retirement or disability benefits (<u>worked 40 quarters</u>) and,
- Based on their work record the SS benefit they are entitled to receive is less than the benefits they would receive on your work record; and
- Even if you, the payer ex-spouse, are age <u>62 or older</u> and have <u>not</u> applied for benefits but can qualify for them; then the recipient ex-spouse (62+) can receive **50% matching benefits** from your work record.

THE OUTCOME GAIN AFTER STOPPING ALIMONY WITH SOCIAL SECURITY (SS)

So you finally have reached retirement age at 65-67 and decide to stop working, but unfortunately your alimony continues. You can now attempt to try an expensive Change in Circumstances court filing ($10 – 25K expense) in the divorce decree state, but the outcome of these filings generally is poor and unsatisfactory. Meanwhile if your ex-spouse is on the ball, they have or can be collecting the 50% matching of your SS for being married 10+ years. They can also garnish your SS to 65% for the arrears once you stop paying, if they follow thru and get a garnishment order. You need to look at the options.

Isn't this fair! ***Equal to slavery***, and it never ends ...

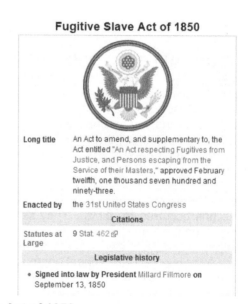

Fugitive Slave Act of 1850

Here is the fairness equation (or is it?), with a summary of how both sides fare:

Your Scenario 1	Their Scenario 2	Your Scenario 1A
You Retire And Continue Paying Alimony	**What They Can Get If You Stop Paying After Retirement**	**What You Get If You Stop Paying After Retirement Even with the SS Garnishment**
• $2600/mo. social security • **-$3500/mo. alimony** **-$900**/mo.	• $1300/mo. (For 10+ years of marriage, $2600 @ 50% matching of your social security) • $1690/mo. For arrears, $2600 @ 65% garnishment of your SS) **$2990**/mo.	• $3500/mo. - No alimony • $910 (from the remaining 35% of your garnished SS) **$4410**/mo. difference

This is a **$5310**/month ($900 + $4410) positive **CASH FLOW** swing for you after stopping the alimony. **WOW!**

This may be the time and circumstance for the recipient ex-spouse to gain wings and be on their own!

CHAPTER 3

BEST STATES FOR DIVORCE

DIVORCE STATES – THE BEST AND THE WORST – NO UNIFORMITY

With all the horror stories about <u>divorce</u> and then alimony, it can be an incredibly long and painful ordeal. A divorce lawyer sees their fair share of feuding couples, as people who are ordinarily rational and controlled become transformed during the divorce process into vengeful, abusive and money-crazed. The divorce lawyers may encourage such crazy behavior as it makes their clients want more motions against the other party and creates more billable hours. So in a typical contested divorce, that's when people start "divorcing ugly." When a divorce is uncontested, the understanding is that both partners are agreeable to the terms of divorce, and therefore have no need to prolong the process.

Overall, divorcing is not always treated fairly by family courts. An attorney once observed, "*A person who stands on their rights often stands on quicksand*." A well-prepared case may not ensure victory at trial, but an unprepared case almost always ensures disaster.

Not so long ago, a divorce could only be granted for a specific fault-based reason such as adultery or mental cruelty. Now all states allow "<u>no-fault</u>" divorce, where the spouse asking for a divorce does not need to prove that the other spouse committed some form of marital misconduct, making divorce a little less complicated.

Each state has different rules for awarding alimony, splitting up property, and deciding who takes care of the kids, and thus could be better or worse for you. The main issue isn't how quickly you exit, but how you carve up the pie. It pays to be picky as judges have a lot of <u>leeway with equitable-distribution rules, and you can end up with less than an equitable 50%</u>. Finally though fault isn't a factor in getting divorced these days, nearly half of all states still consider it when divvying up the goods.

Though many states will allow you to be single again in three months, business is booming in Nevada, the quickie divorce capital with the almost unparalleled six-week residency requirement. Most states demand that you live there at least six months and sometimes up to a year before you can file for divorce. One exception, Alaska where you can file the day you arrive, though it will take at least a month to get unhitched.

A wealthy spouse looking to keep all your money should steer clear of the 41 equitable distribution states, and head for one of the 9 states that divide property by the 50/50% community property method. The judge in an equitable distribution state may order a non-equitable distribution like 40%/60%, that will not be in your favor as the majority wage earner. Other significant factors you should want to consider before dissolving a marriage include provisions for permanent or lifetime alimony, child support and visitation rights, requirements for establishing residency, and waiting periods before a divorce can be finalized. These are all significant issues that will determine how the state marriage dissolution will progress.

There is no single best state to get divorced, as each has different rules for splitting up property, awarding alimony, and deciding who takes care of the kids. This could be better or worse for you depending on whether you're a breadwinning money-earning spouse or a 20-year homemaker with children nearly out of school. If you supported the ex-spouse through a professional degree and then got dumped, take heart! At least twelve states have ruled that professional degrees and licenses are marital property, whose value can be considered when dividing up property and determining support.

So seriously pick your state in which to file and get a divorce, because the decision can have tens to hundreds of thousands of dollars of impact. Stay away from any equitable distribution state, unless your wage income and your own non-marital assets are less than your soon-to-be-ex-spouse.

STATE ALIMONY SUMMARY - NO UNIFORMITY

One of the major pre-divorce items for consideration when getting married and particularly when filing for divorce, should be what state to establish residency and get divorced in, because alimony determination varies greatly from state to state. Most of us have no idea this will become a major factor in your divorce decree outcome. There are no state-by-state comparisons either, with only a few brief sound byte articles written by reporters. Similarly your friends and legal counsel have no nationwide perspective. Recommend that you try to pick your state before filing for the divorce. Remember you will have to establish residence. This summary is about as good as it gets, so here goes ...

Best States for the Alimony Payer: Arizona, Kansas, Mississippi, and Texas.

Worst States for the Alimony Payer – Permanent Alimony: Colorado, Florida, New Jersey, and New York.

Community-Property States, Nine (9): Arizona, California, Idaho, Louisiana, Nevada, New Mexico, Texas, Washington, and Wisconsin.

No-Fault States: All states are now no-fault, as NY was the last state in the country to switch in 2010.

<u>California</u>: Permanent alimony and community-property state. The statute indicates that any marriage of <u>10+</u> years (one case for 8 years) is considered a lengthy marriage with <u>permanent</u> alimony. Rule of thumb is that spousal support for marriages of less than ten years will last one-half the length of the marriage.

<u>Colorado</u>: Passed a 2013 alimony reform bill HB 13-1058. May now be one of the **worst** states, if you're the significant higher earner in a long-term marriage which can result in the highest alimony awards in the US. The formula asserts that the amount of maintenance is equal to <u>40%</u> of the higher income party's monthly adjusted gross income but less than fifty percent of the lower income party's monthly adjusted income. For example, if the higher wage earner makes $10,000 per month, and the other spouse earns $500 per month, the payer's payment will be $3750 ($4000 - $250) per month.

Now the courts have a table indicating appropriate alimony time frames. For example, in a marriage of 3 years, alimony would be paid for 11 months, or 31% of the length of the marriage. For a marriage of 13 years, maintenance would be paid for 80 months, or 50% of the length of the marriage. Retirement age attainment ending of alimony is now supposedly automatic, but you have to go back to court.

<u>Delaware</u>: Spousal support is usually <u>not</u> awarded in marriages of less than 10 years. Alimony payments last no longer than half the length of the marriage, unless the marriage exceeded 20 years, in which case payments may be ordered indefinitely.

<u>Dominican Republic</u>: Fly to the island and get divorced in 24 hours provided your spouse consents. Out of the US enforcement will be problematic, so this state could be a priority.

<u>Florida</u>: **Stay away**. Estimated to be 50,000 permanent alimony payers in the state. Based upon the new 2010 law, a short-term marriage is 7 years or less in duration. A moderate-term marriage is 7-17 years, and a long-term marriage is 17 years and more. Will send you to jail for alimony non-payment.

<u>Illinois</u>: New 2015 alimony law passed with family incomes below $250,000, the amount of maintenance shall be calculated by taking 30% of the payer's gross income minus 20% of the payee's gross income. The amount calculated as maintenance, however, when added to the gross income of the payee, may not result in the payee receiving an amount that is in excess of 40% of the combined gross income of the parties. Alimony is pro-rated and permanent for 15+ year marriages. No jury trial allowed.

Kansas: One of the **better** states, but an equitable distribution state. Alimony <u>cannot</u> exceed <u>10 years</u> or 121 months with the option of one extension of up to 121 months or 10 years. The spousal support timeline is two years for a five-year marriage plus 33% for each additional year married. Gives explicit guidelines to judges on the amount and/or duration of alimony. A few county bar associations have non-binding guidelines that provide spousal support should be <u>20%</u> of the difference between the parties' <u>gross</u> incomes when there are minor children and <u>25%</u> of the difference when there are no children.

<u>Maine</u>: Support may <u>not</u> be awarded if married for less than 10 years, and may be awarded for a term exceeding 1/2 the length of the marriage if married for at least 10 years, and not more than 20 years.

<u>Massachusetts</u>: The 2011 Alimony reform law limits the alimony longevity to include:
- In marriages lasting 0 – 5 years, no longer than 1/2 the marriage length.

- In marriages 6 - 10 years long, capped at 60% of the marriage length.
- If the marriage is 10 – 15 years, not longer than 70% of the marriage length.
- If the marriage is 15 – 20 years, not longer than 80% of the marriage length.
- The court may order alimony for an indefinite length of time for marriages longer than 20 years.
- General term alimony orders shall <u>automatically</u> terminate upon the payer attaining full retirement age, but only for <u>post</u> 2012 divorces and if you go back to court again for your CIC.
- The amount of alimony should generally not exceed the recipient's need or <u>30 -35</u>% of the <u>difference</u> between the parties <u>gross incomes</u> established at the time of the order.

<u>Mississippi</u>: The **best** state. Alimony is awarded only in marriage of <u>ten</u> years or longer, and limited to **three years** unless there are special, extenuating circumstances. Furthermore, the amount of spousal support is limited to the <u>lesser</u> of <u>$2,500 per month</u> or 40% of the payee's <u>gross</u> income.

<u>Nevada</u>: Lifetime alimony and community property state, so any assets are split 50-50. The best state to get a quickie divorce. It should be no surprise this state has the highest divorce rate. If you establish residency for <u>six weeks</u> almost unparalleled you may take advantage of the quick divorce laws, the shortest of any state after establishing residency then you can get an uncontested divorce in as little as 48 hours.

<u>New Jersey</u>: One of the **worst**. Had a worthless 2014 alimony reform bill approved with the only improvement – "permanent" alimony was changed to "open durational" alimony. Retirement curtailment is not automatic, so you get to go to court one more time. For 10+ years of marriage, permanent alimony will be awarded. Combine alimony and child-support together in the state disbursement payment centers, and many deadbeat dads for alimony only arrears get jail.

<u>New York</u>: When in 2010 the state law was revised to allow no-fault divorce, divorce filings spiked. Before the Empire State was one of the worst states to get divorced in.

<u>North Carolina</u>: There are only two grounds for divorce - separation for a period of one year and incurable insanity. Alimony can be reduced or barred to a spouse who committed adultery. Has not adopted the 1999 UMDA, but has permanent alimony. Does not recognize rehabilitative alimony. Now flirting with an alimony formula.

<u>South Carolina</u>: Lifetime alimony is present. Does not accept incompatibility as a reason to split. There has been an important 2015 House bill H3215 passed whereby Jan. 2016 there is to be a study recommendation report on what to be done with the broken divorce court laws.

<u>Tennessee</u>: Lifetime alimony present. Active alimony reform.

<u>Texas</u>: Still one of the **best** states, and is a community-property state. As of 2011, increased the potential amount of alimony from $2500 to <u>$5000</u> per mo., and increased the payment term from <u>3 years</u> up to a possible <u>10 years</u> based on the length of the marriage. Requires a 5-year marriage for post-divorce maintenance, except in the case of disability. For marriages that last for 10-20 years, the payments extend over a 5 year period. Marriages lasting for 20-30 years are eligible for **7 years** of alimony. Marriages that are 30 years or more are eligible for **10 years** of alimony. Cohabitation does not stop alimony. One unique distinction is a jury trial is allowed.

CHAPTER 4

ASSET PROTECTION

INTRODUCTION

This is a schematic as to how your assets can be "repositioned" to avoid later detection, and how your assets can safely be protected and cloaked with the legal entities you can use. If you have monetary assets secreted away where you think they won't be found, then you need to know how they can be discovered (outlined in Chapters 9 – 12). Knowing what the other side can do and what tools they can utilize, will help you to formulate your asset protection plan to protect what you have now.

A lot of business entity options are presented to be evaluated for an individual contemplating the route to invisibility. For most it is totally overwhelming. After all the presentation review, a single member LLC (disregarded entity) in New Mexico with invisibility is the recommendation, due to the simplicity, low cost, low maintenance, and ownership being hidden. Forming a multi-member LLC or corporation is more difficult requiring more than one person, with yearly meetings, stock certificates and corporate tax filing.

ASSET PROTECTION PRIVACY

The *Right to Privacy* is always a law issue, because there is no specific amendment to "The Right to Privacy" in the US Constitution or The Bill of Rights. The Rights to Privacy derive from common law and are cited by precedence from different cases and statutes.

Your asset protection planning with *The Right to Privacy* falls into the same situation. There is no ultimate right to your total privacy or the right to not report income and assets, and most governments and their statues offer options within these legal boundaries.

With a well-designed plan, one can find privacy. Think of it like this: A house may have a front door and a back door. The front door is visible to all the neighbors when compared to the back door. You enter the front door, all the neighbors know. When you enter the back door quietly and without commotion, very few people know. Either way, you have arrived at the same destination inside the house.

You can report your assets personally (the front door) or report your assets through a corporation, LLC, or trust (the back door). Regardless, <u>you have reported your assets</u>. Though asset protection plans are not for the purpose of reducing taxation, sound asset protection plan designs take advantage of these pathways for your assets. They don't necessarily hide them; asset protection devises the routes of ownership (title) and control, placing them on separate pathways. This in itself creates privacy.

With rampant identity theft and criminal schemes such as "phishing" and "pharming," it makes sense to keep your valuable assets away from your personal name and reported under your social security number.

When assets are transferred into a LLC (limited liability corporation), corp., trust or other similar business entity, the assets are no longer held or reported in an individual person's name. With such asset protection privacy, it is much more difficult for asset searches to either find or access account information or the assets themselves. This is critical to your invisibility.

WHAT DOES AN INVISIBLE LLC DO FOR YOUR ASSET(S) PRIVACY?

LLC without Owner(s) Disclosure
Find a state (New Mexico is the only state) without ownership disclosure, as 49 of the 50 states have limited liability company laws requiring that the names and addresses of LLC members must be disclosed in the Articles of Organization. Arizona as an example, provides that if the LLC is member managed, the names and addresses every member must be stated in the Articles of Organization. If confidentiality is your goal, you probably do not want to list your home, business or other address in the Articles of Organization, because it could be an easy way for somebody to discover that you are associated with the LLC.

First Get Your Business Employment Identification Number (EIN)
If it's single ownership, you need to elect the selected business type as entity "disregarded" for terms of taxes and to get a federal ID # (EIN), with the objective to not use your own SSN for the LLC, corp., or trust. Getting the EIN number is a simple online form, and you will have the number immediately. Then you can use this number for the establishment of the business bank account and whatever else you want for privacy.

Once obtained, you need to get a LLC business bank account that isn't an extension of you; it's a legal entity itself. You need to keep a clearly distinguishable line between your finances and actions and those of the LLC. It's the only way that you will maintain the invisibility and liability protection. You will need to follow essentially all the same basic procedures in terms of books and meetings if a corporation. Without these, the LLC can be declared null and everything fall back on to you.

Your liability protection is mainly in terms of legal liability. If properly configured with the appropriate operating agreement and following the required procedures for operating the multi-member LLC, you are legally protected.

Many people claim benefits of not having to personally pay the debts of the LLC, but this is a little bit misleading. Yes, if you maintain your LLC properly the LLC creditors cannot come after your personal assets to satisfy debts, but you will quickly find that most anyone that is willing to extend you credit will require a personal guarantee that will put you on the hook for the debts. This isn't at all uncommon, and it's not unique to an LLC. Even corporations have this situation, as it comes down to the lenders comfort with being able to recover their money.

YOUR CRITICAL HOME STATE ELECTION FOR YOUR BUSINESS LLC

State Registration and EIN
For reasons of privacy, you should register your LLC in a state that keeps your ownership private by not listing it. A secondary and very important factor to beware of before filing your LLC, is that your listed address may require you to pay LLC franchise fees if they think you are conducting business there, which can add to your annual fees. Some states like California are really aggressive, in that they demand a yearly $800 franchise fee for just having the LLC registered in their state, even though there was no active business or

sale of any kind conducted. Turns out New Mexico and Wyoming are the only states, that fulfill both the owner privacy and no aggressive yearly franchise fee requirements.

Generally you don't have to pay these LLC fees to the state unless it operates a storefront business. The best practice is to avoid meeting the state's definition of <u>transacting business</u> within the state. This will make the LLC exempt from the state's fee requirements. Basically if the LLC is simply holding property, holding title to real estate or automobiles, or doing "<u>limited business</u>," then you won't have to pay these fees or taxes. So there is a lot to think about when you register as a state LLC and want to keep a high level of privacy and asset protection.

What Is The Best LLC State?

One would think it would be one of these states. But after evaluation, it will be **<u>New Mexico</u>**, followed closely by **Wyoming**. Here's is why you might think otherwise:

- <u>Tax-Free Income States (7)</u>: Alaska, Florida, Nevada, South Dakota, Texas, Washington, and Wyoming.
- <u>No Sales Tax States (5)</u>: Alaska, Delaware, Montana, New Hampshire, and Oregon.
- <u>No Wage Income Tax States (2)</u>: New Hampshire and Tennessee - don't tax wage income, but do collect taxes on residents' dividend and interest income.

<u>Will I pay less LLC taxes overall in these states</u>? Not necessarily. States need revenue to function, and these states will have to make up for the lack of income tax somehow. New Hampshire and Texas, for example, make up for it in property taxes. Both states have some of the highest property taxes in the nation. The cost of higher property taxes, sales taxes, fuel taxes, and other taxes could amount to higher overall taxes in some of these states. If you generate income with a street address in these states, and file income taxes with their street address, expect the state revenue board to be giving you a call. Remember, your income tax revenue is based upon the state that you report the income tax to, so beware. Bottom-line, you do not have to live in the state that your private mail box (PMB) is located in.

- Arizona: Stay away, as limited liability company law requires names and addresses of LLC members to be disclosed in the Articles of Organization.
- California: <u>Stay away</u>. Do not consider this state for any reason, as the State's Franchise Tax Board charges a significant minimum $800 annual franchise tax or foreign LLC tax, and is extremely <u>aggressive</u> in collection.
- Delaware: A LLC leading state, but has <u>$250 annual franchise tax and reporting</u>. The business law and court structure is considered the most business-friendly in the nation, a factor that favors more important for larger and more complex businesses. If you register your small LLC, but do not reside there, you will <u>not</u> be subject to state corporate income taxes. Like California, not the best choice.
- Montana: No sales tax, but does have income tax. Very good state for vehicle registration with no sales tax, no inspection, and flat rate vehicle registration fee.
- Nevada: Being the best place to incorporate is a myth. Although famous for having no state income tax, expensive filing fees and the new $200 yearly business license fee are cost prohibitive. Corporations are required to hire nominees (typically law firms) to fill the director and officer positions, which can cost you thousands of dollars every year. Worse yet, LLCs are <u>not private</u> at all, as a list of the owners, members or managers must be filed annually and are found by internet search engines. Advantages: 1) No state corporate income tax. 2) Do not have to be a state resident to register an LLC there and take advantage of the favorable tax and fee structure.
- **New Mexico**: The **BEST** state. Has <u>no ownership</u> reporting, requires <u>no</u> annual report and <u>no</u> annual fee. Once the articles of organization are filed, they never have to be renewed. Doesn't tax out-of-state income, so you won't be walking into a <u>tax trap</u>. There typically is a nominal $100 annual fee to the resident agent and a small $50 franchise tax if the LLC pays federal tax. The most important factor - The identities of the members and managers need never be disclosed to the state, and ***you are invisible***. Has an unusual provision allowing creditors of the LLC to be cut off from making claims against it or its members, upon dissolution of the company in as little as ninety days. In most states when you dissolve a corporation, LLC or limited partnership, the owners of the company can be sued on its behalf for two to five years. If they decide to sue, they can only do so

within 120 days, which can make a dramatic difference for when you're ready to close up shop or protect your assets. The state requires a state tax identification number if you conduct an active business in the state.

- Wyoming: **A Close 2nd** State: Does not require the manager nor the members of an LLC to be listed on a public database. LLC laws and fees are geared toward small businesses, so fees are low, no franchise tax, but annual reporting is mandatory. Has a $50 annual renewal fee, no income tax, but does have a sales tax.
- Off-shore entities are under increasing pressure by the IRS and US Treasury. Most banks now turn over foreign client records, and withdrawals are now automatically subject to a 30% tax right off the top. Recommend stay away from offshore, as other US-based options are available.

New Mexico LLC - The Best State With Invisible Ownership
It is recommended that you set up your LLC in New Mexico for the following reasons:

- In most states where privacy is touted over and over again by promoters, a list of the members or managers must be filed annually that becomes public information.
- New Mexico adopted some of the most powerful Limited Liability Company (LLC) legislation making it a premiere choice for those seeking privacy and asset protection. The key decision factor is a LLC need not include the names of members, the mailing address of the principal office can be anywhere in the world, and unlike all other states, New Mexico LLCs do not require any annual reports.
- Asset Protection: Not all LLC state statutes are created equal, which is a point lost on most attorneys and CPAs. New Mexico has a well-written LLC statute that allows a tight operating agreement, and this is what determines whether or not you're going to secure asset protection. A single member LLC is not asset protection. A LLC is only an opportunity for asset protection, and whether or not you fulfill that opportunity is based upon how the LLC is set up.
- Resident Agent: The laws in all states require that both corporations and limited liability companies have a resident agent in that state who can receive official communications and send them on promptly to the owner or manager of the company. Example: If a lawsuit is filed against a New Mexico LLC, the documents will be sent to the NM resident agent. This must be a real street address, not a CMRA mail-receiving agency with a PO box (PMB is acceptable). Not having a storefront is not an issue. Use your postal mail box (PMB) street address as your resident address if necessary. Registered Agent fees typically run $100 - 150/year. If you don't have an active business or a storefront, one can forgo this agent requirement and utilize service by mail thru your PMB. I currently do not have a resident agent, but have an active PMB in my state of registration.
- A multi-member LLC takes the limited liability features of a corporation and combines them with the "pass through" tax benefits of a partnership, literally the best of both worlds. The low cost, minimal maintenance, no annual reporting, and total anonymity lifts the Invisible New Mexico LLC head and shoulders above any other state's corporation or LLC.
- The single-member LLC offers the same benefits at a fraction of the price with a much lower profile. Only the following is required for the Articles of Organization:
    - The name of the company and the address.
    - The mailing address can be anywhere in the world.
    - The name and address of the registered agent, and
    - The duration of the LLC, which can be limited or perpetual.
- It is not necessary to live in New Mexico to set up your New Mexico LLC asset protection plan. This state does not require the names of the owners, therefore your name does not show up on the public records! In fact, your name is not on any document other than your Private Operating Agreement which you control. Changes in ownership are also not of public record.
- The New Mexico LLC is most powerful when used as a holding company for your assets, bank accounts, and other business interests.
- Do not order your LLC from an online "incorporation mill," as they do not keep your name off of the public records, and they do not preserve your anonymity.

<u>Cost</u>: Can be as low as $300 - 400 for 3 years including the resident agent. This is something you can do yourself by going to the New Mexico governmental site (NewMexico.gov); Also Nolo.com and KeepYourAssets.net provide a lot of useful information.

LLC Advantages

- A structure easy to run by a single individual
- Personal information totally shielded from the public (only in a few states)
- No annual reporting
- Very low business start-up costs
- Little to no maintenance costs
- Very little record keeping
- The operating agreement is never filed or recorded
- No need to be a state LLC-filed resident
- Choice of being taxed as a sole proprietorship, partnership, C corp. or S corp. when engaging in "taxable activity"
- No double-taxation when doing business (unless taxed as C corp.)

LLC Superior Use(s)

- Your assets can become invisible
- Take assets out of your name but not out of your control
- Shelter your home, cars, family heirlooms and everything else
- Title and register automobiles
- Buy or sell property (including real estate)
- Open a business bank or <u>brokerage account</u> in total privacy
- Stop alleged creditors, private investigators and stalkers from finding you and your assets
- Hide legally large sums of money
- Run a prosperous business or become employed as an independent contractor with a thriving e-commerce website with full anonymity
- For total protection, use a "<u>friendly lien</u>" to further protect property from potential creditors

LLC Taxation

Business LLCs have what is called a "<u>pass-through" tax benefit like a partnership</u>. Any profits in a single-member LLC are counted as the member's personal income. However, as long as the LLC avoids "taxable activity," no business taxes will be due on Schedule C – Net Profit From Business. Any LLC investment Income you still report on the traditional federal Schedule B – Interest and Dividends and Schedule D – Capital Gains and Losses.

- <u>Single Member</u>: "<u>Disregarded</u>" for tax purposes and income and expenses are reported on the individuals Form 1040, as the single member is treated as a sole proprietor. If a corporation is a single member, the LLC income and expenses are reported on the corporation's return with <u>Form 1120 or Form 1120S</u>.
- <u>Multi-Member</u>: Taxed "pass-through" as a partnership and file Partnership Tax Return Form 1065. Income and expenses pass through the partnership directly to the partners. Each partner takes their share of income and expenses determining each individual partner's individual tax liability.

  Key <u>multi-member LLC's</u> minimum requirements:
  - Have at least two members.
  - Be taxed as a partnership.
  - Be managed by a manager, not the members. (Managers can be people or another business).
  - Have a <u>profit motive</u> (invest in real estate, CD's, stocks, businesses).

LLC's ASSET PROTECTION BASICS

Successful people think about litigation before it happens. Are you prepared?

A Limited Liability Company (LLC) has benefits in asset protection:
- Provide a level of asset anonymity guaranteed and protected by state law.
- LLC's have the pass-through taxation of a partnership and the limited liability of a corporation.
- Make yourself disappear from information databases and unable to be located.
- Make collection on judgments difficult.
- Reduces the incentive of getting sued in the first place.
- Then if you are sued, make sure your personal and business assets are protected.
- Insulate your assets from each other so they are not lost in lawsuits.
- Increases bargaining power with creditors.

Litigators accept cases contingent on the probability of winning the case, obtaining a settlement amount and upon the defendant's ability to pay. Attorneys assess the defendant's ability to pay after conducting an asset search using easy to find information such as the defendant's name, approximate age, and geographical location. Even when no assets are found, you may be automatically targeted due to your capacity to earn income. Attorneys and private investigators subscribe to online asset search services that list real estate, vehicles, planes, and watercraft in your name, and it takes about 15 minutes to run your report on the internet. Fortunately they cannot probe your bank and brokerage accounts even if they know your bank's name (if not hidden). Then after running a simple report, an attorney will decide whether or not to go after you or not. The merits of a case are a secondary factor compared to the ability to get paid. The attorney may take the case on their own nickel (contingency) if they locate a target with deep pockets.

Asset Protection Maxims
- Control your assets without owning them in your own name. An effective asset protection plan enables a person to control assets without linking them to identifiers, such as your name or social security number, that gives away the location and ownership of the assets. Assets can be owned by corporations and LLC's and controlled and used by you.
- Make your assets unattractive to the hostile litigator. You can make financial holdings, real estate, and other assets unattractive to the litigator. Making any judgments uncollectible also makes them a deterrence to the litigator. "Charging Order" protection can be combined with financial privacy for effective asset protection.
- Decrease Litigation Impact by Creating Multiple Entities. The best strategy for reducing litigation exposure is separating assets into multiple LLC's to protect each one from each other.

LLC Limited Personal Liability
When hostile creditors sue a corporation, typically they can only take the assets of the corporation. Generally, stockholders are not liable (have "limited liability") for the debts, liabilities and acts of the corporation. If a supplier or creditor comes after the multi-member LLC, they may not go after the member's house, car, or bank account, which limits the personal liability of the member.

The Multi-Member LLC Manager
You control the LLC that owns the assets. The key is to obtain a person to head the LLC as the manager. Because you're seeking privacy from the public record, this means that you (or your family members) should not serve as the manager. This role should be reserved for a person other than yourself or your spouse.
- Friends as Managers: Friendship and money do not mix. Most people have learned this lesson the hard way.
- Hire a Professional Manager: The professional manager works to protect the interests of the members and the LLC itself. This enables you to stay off state records and off the records of database resellers.

<u>What should the Manager do</u>?
- Sign the articles of organization in the state filing of the LLC.
- Is hired to perform a service. Does not own or control the company.
- Sign liens under your direction, against property and other assets.
- Is available by phone and email to answer questions and correspond.

<u>Multi-Member LLC - Charging Orders Frustrate Hostile Creditors</u>
- The <u>charging order</u> is the exclusive remedy by which a judgment creditor may satisfy a judgment against the member's interest in a limited liability company.
- Hostile creditors can take your LLC if proven you own it. Hostile creditors can take your economic interest through the courts by obtaining a <u>charging order</u>. When a judgment is awarded against an LLC, it may be levied, and the LLC's property seized or sold for payment.
- When a judgment is awarded against a member of a LLC to the extent that the operating agreement so states, distribution usually cannot be compelled to satisfy a member's judgment debt. This gives them the rights to any distributions made by the LLC to that particular member, but little else. Once the charging order is obtained, the hostile creditor is now first in line for any future distributions that are usually paid out to the member(s).
- A creditor of a member in an LLC is supposed to be limited to getting a charging order against the distributions of the member. As a result, the creditor cannot acquire the LLC interest of the debtor and therefore cannot acquire the assets of the LLC. As a result, the creditor traditionally has to wait until the manager makes a distribution in order to get paid. Of course, in most cases the manager has authority to delay distributions. In the meanwhile, the creditor has to pay the tax which would normally fall on the debtor (on income yet to be received).
- If a lawsuit against you is won and the hostile creditor obtains a charging order against your distributions, the LLC Manager may restrict distributions according to the operating agreement.
- Since the LLC's Manager may not make the distribution of the member's interest, all the hostile creditor has earned in the charging order process is a tax liability on "phantom income" (income never received). This will dampen the hostile creditor's motivation to pursue a charging order and they may either drop the case or settle for pennies on the dollar.

<u>Making LLC Assets Unattractive To A Creditor</u>
The multi-member LLC Manager can refuse to distribute the earnings (if provided for in the operating agreement). When a creditor enters a charging order against a member's earnings, the creditor is immediately responsible for taxes on the income distribution, whether the creditor receives the distribution or not. If no income distribution is made to the creditor, the creditor is still responsible for taxes on the "phantom income."

BEST TIME TO IMPLEMENT YOUR ASSET PROTECTION PLAN

When is the best time ...? Before financial or legal problems like your divorce is encountered. Asset transfers can be challenged and reversed under the fraudulent conveyance laws, if it can be shown that the transfer was done to hide your monetary assets and unfairly frustrate a legitimate creditor.

An effective asset transfer must be completed well in advance of an economic or litigious threat. For example, gifting assets to family members shortly after receiving notice of litigation may result in the undoing of the asset transfer. The hostile creditor could argue that the debtor intended to unfairly frustrate the creditor because of the timing of the asset transfer. Therefore, the timing of the asset transfer is critical to protecting assets from hostile creditors. To prevent such a risk, transfer assets into the asset protection structure prior to possible claims from hostile ex-spouses, collectors and creditors.

The asset transfer must also have the following additional attributes:
- Solvency hasn't changed after the asset transfer.
- The litigation was not foreseeable.
- The debtor did not abscond after the asset transfer.
- The assets were not transferred to a family member or friend.
- Assets were transferred for at least 70% of market value.

Don't think that your financial planner, CPA or attorney understands asset protection with LLC's, as they were never trained in college and are not in the asset protection business. Surprisingly, the vast majority of LLC's that are created are not formed by attorneys or CPA's, as most LLC's are created by individuals and asset protection professionals.

Asset protection isn't taught in law school. Although law schools offer classes on corporations, trusts, estates and wills, there is no specific curriculum for asset protection. Asset protection after all, is designed to put lawyers out of business and prevent lawsuits. So when looking to implement an asset protection plan the obvious question is, "Who is qualified to offer advice in the asset protection arena?"

Remember that making your friends and relatives the manager of your LLC destroy your secrecy, as attorneys, PI's, or asset searchers may be able to check on your friends and relatives to track down your assets. Hiring an outside individual as a Registered Agent will enhance your secrecy, and you maintain control and use of assets.

Do remember single member LLC's that are only owner managed offer little or no liability and/or asset protection from lawsuits. If you want a LLC with liability protection, the LLC must be owned by two or more members. So most of us caught in the alimony clutches will go with the single member LLC, as the invisibility is worth more than the liability protection.

Many ineffective single member LLC's are marketed on the internet today that meet only zero, one or only two of the IRS requirements. These ineffective LLC's walk around with a false sense of security, and are greatly disappointed when their LLC crumbles when challenged.

We live in a litigious society. If you own a business, own rental property or practice a profession, you have a chance of being sued. Real estate, large cash balances in your bank account or a healthy investment portfolio, get predatory lawyers foaming at the mouth. So how do you protect your cash, stocks and mutual funds?

Why LLC's or Corporations?
Under the law, a corporation is an artificial "person" completely separate from you. Because it is an independent entity, a corporation's liabilities and taxes are separate from the people who own and operate it. This is the reason why almost all successful people choose to incorporate. It permits you to keep you and your liabilities separate from your assets.

However, it is only in a carefully selected state that you can set up a LLC or corporation so that, your identity and ownership can remain completely private. Since the ownership of the LLC or corporation cannot be traced to you, your enemies will not be able to take your assets.

Critical Steps to Asset Invisibility
Once your private LLC/ corporation is formed, a new bank and/or brokerage account can be established for the business, and your cash and investment holdings can then be transferred out of your name to the business account(s) using a cashier's check (not a wire transfer, that can be traced). The best timing is to get your LLC established just before or after the divorce and just before you decide to stop paying alimony,

then immediately afterwards open the new business account. Leave a time allowance of 3 months to get the business account opening and the money transfers accomplished.

You will utilize your business checking account thru your business LLC/corporate checking account to pay for your day-to-day activities, and now all of your assets are out of your name and will not show up if an attorney or asset searcher conducts an asset search on you. This strategy will not only lower your lawsuit worthy profile, it hinders any future collection efforts.

STRATEGIES FOR EFFECTIVE ASSET PROTECTION

To be truly effective, all asset protection strategies must meet three criteria:

- Asset(s) Ownership: Must be totally anonymous and private. If assets can't be legally tied to you, then they can't be taken when someone comes after you. So to achieve this protection you have to set up your asset protection and privacy plan in a state jurisdiction that supports these criteria.
- Liability Protection: You should try to be legally protected from any liability, with a multi-member LLC or corp. However, most will elect the simpler single member LLC that gives you invisibility, but provides to asset or liability protection except the ownership invisibility.
- Plan Beforehand: The third and most important criterion for effective asset protection is that it must be done at the right time. You must act ahead of time to protect what you own before it comes under attack. Once a lawsuit is expected or has been filed, the law will not allow you to move your assets.

How to Achieve Asset Protection

What is the best way to achieve asset protection? It can be summed up in three words: *Don't Own* anything directly in your name.

Now you might think that this flies in the face of the American Dream which says you need to own your own car, home and everything else that is a prerequisite for a happy and successful life. Now we are not talking about not eliminating debt on those assets. It's great to be debt free. You just don't want to own those things in your own name because if you technically don't own the assets, but merely control them, then the assets are well protected, and you still have the use of them. You see, you don't want ownership. Ownership is a liability. What you want is use of the assets. In fact it was John D. Rockefeller who summed up this philosophy when he said, "Own nothing and control everything." So to really start to understand the mindset around asset protection you need to think like a Rockefeller.

One way to achieve this protection is through the formation of corporations to hold the assets. Why corporations? Under the law, a corporation is an artificial "person" completely separate from the people who own it and control it. This is different from an individual or sole proprietorship. With an individual or sole proprietorship the owner bears full and complete responsibility for his actions. But a corporation is an independent entity. A corporation's liabilities and taxes are separate from those of its owners, officers, and directors. Therefore a corporation gives you the greatest personal liability protection and this meets our first criteria we talked about.

Another reason corporations are advantageous is because they enable you to compartmentalize your businesses or assets. You can place different assets under separate corporations. Now you still have complete control over everything, but if one asset runs into trouble, it won't jeopardize the other assets. Without incorporation, all your eggs are in one basket and if something happens to that one basket you could be totally wiped out. For that reason some people choose to have separate corporations for their larger assets such as a home, rental property, boat, or RV, to separate out any liability.

Because of the corporate formation laws in certain state jurisdictions, you can form corporations that can provide total privacy. This is why almost many successful people choose to incorporate. It permits you to manage your assets anonymously. Your private corporate life is never made public. And there's only a couple of states in the U.S. and a few places around the world where a corporation can be formed, while you own and control your corporation, your identity and ownership can remain a total secret. This meets our second criteria mentioned.

You can use the LLC or the corporation to protect fixed assets such as homes, autos, bank accounts, boats, planes, and some liquid assets.

The other feature is nominee officers, which ensures your complete privacy and anonymity, the second criteria for asset protection. A nominee is simply a trusted person you appoint to stand in and provide their name and signature in lieu of yours. Use of nominee officers and directors in their corporations, so your name will never appear on any of the corporate documents if you so choose. Your identity can be kept completely private.

Here's an Example on Implementing Asset Protection
So now you have some understanding as to how a LLC or a corporation limit your liability and provide you with the privacy and anonymity you need for maximum asset protection. Let's now talk about how asset protection can work for you.

First let's look at an example: Their lawyer says great! We'll sue them, so let me do some research and we'll talk tomorrow. The lawyer then orders an <u>asset search</u> on you. When the report comes back, on the top of the page is your name, underneath is your date of birth, your home address, your phone numbers, listed and unlisted, any children you have and their names and ages. Also in the nationwide asset search listing is all property you own including any vehicles and tax information (but fortunately, no bank or financial asset info).

When this disgruntled customer returns to the attorney the next day, the attorney is going to say one of two things to their client:
- "Great, all their assets are right here, and they have deep pockets. Let's draft a complaint and garnish/sue them" - or,
- "I can sue this person, but there are no visible assets to go after. I can start proceedings if you want, but I'll need a $15,000 retainer to cover my initial attorney's fees and expenses."

Based on human nature, <u>99% of all litigation will stop right here</u>. Contingency fee lawyers or asset searchers need a pot of gold at the end of the rainbow, and they're not interested unless there is the potential for a big reward.

So you want to be in the second category where you are not at risk. So to start off, let's assume you have a home worth $500,000 and you have $150,000 in stocks and bonds in your brokerage account. On your home you have a first mortgage for $300,000. You have $200,000 in equity in the home and $150,000 liquid assets exposed. So what do you do?

First you need to form a LLC or corporation anonymously
Do you transfer title of the home into the corporation then? No, for a few reasons: One is you want the home to stay in your name, as it becomes the decoy. You see, the first things a competent attorney will ask are:
- Do they own a home?
- Do they have a job or own a business?

If you are living a six-figure lifestyle and don't own a home, they are going to assume your assets are hidden and may want to go looking for them. The other reasons you want to retain title to your home is for tax deductions on mortgage interest, capital gain tax exemption when you sell your home, and the protection you already get from homestead exemption in your home state.

So if you don't transfer title, what do you do? You can place a <u>friendly lien</u> on the home for $220,000 and record it in favor of your corporation. You may be asking, "What is a friendly lien?" A friendly lien is a legal lien placed on a real property and it doesn't necessarily represent a cash loan from the corporation you form. The corporation may have rendered professional advice or services creating the debt owed to the corporation. At any rate, it serves your purpose of encumbering any remaining equity in your home.

Now, you can then transfer the $150,000 in your stock and bond portfolio to your LLC or corporation in a brokerage account. You still retain control over all the assets yet any equity is now invisible to the predatory eyes of an attorney. You can also open a bank checking account and/or an online brokerage account under the LLC or corporation.

As powerful as these strategies are in protecting your assets from lame lawsuits, you must be put in place long before (2 years min.) any legal challenges surface. Any asset transfers you make after a legal challenge will be considered fraudulent conveyance and will be set aside by the courts. During the divorce this asset transfer will become difficult, so you need to make the transfer to non-interest bearing accounts with no income tax reporting to be successful.

The entire litigation process is predicated on the plaintiff's ability to collect. It costs a great deal of money in attorney's fees, court costs, etc. to pursue a court case. If they don't think you have assets to take, chances are they won't be interested in suing you in the first place. In other words, do you own anything of value that would make it worth their time and effort to sue you?

Cash in bank accounts, stocks or mutual funds in a brokerage account can be relatively easy to reach if they know the actual bank location, giving the plaintiff's attorney the green light to file their claim. So how do you not own these assets but still maintain control over them? The answer is by setting up a <u>private LLC or corporation</u> to be the owner of the assets <u>while you anonymously maintain control of them</u>.

ASSET PROTECTION WITH A FRIENDLY LIEN

A <u>friendly lien</u> is simply a lien against property that you own, that is held by a party or parties that is friendly to you. Some other terms used to describe this device are "friendly mortgage" and "friendly loan." The classic example of a friendly lien is as follows: If you borrow money from your parents, and they place a lien on your home to secure repayment of the loan, that lien is friendly. Friendly liens are effective asset protection tools, because a creditor that comes along after the friendly lien is in place will always be in a "junior position" to the lien holder. Some explanation follows...

Liens upon property work on the principal that "first in time is first in right" – so a prior recorded lien is always "senior" to a subsequent lien. Subsequent liens are always "junior" to the prior recorded liens, as these lien holders are arranged in an order referred to as "priority." This priority is important: if a sale of the property is ever forced, or if a creditor appears, the lien holders are entitled to receive the proceeds from the sale of the underlying property in the order of their priority.

In some cases, a piece of property can have 3, 4, or 5 liens on it. The lien holders thereby stand in priority in the order in which the liens were placed on the property. Bear in mind that a lien must be properly "perfected" to be legally effective, which means that the lien must be properly recorded so that the world has notice of the lien.

And so, a friendly lien achieves two important goals:
- First, it puts a friendly party in a superior position of priority to any creditor that comes along later. This means that the subsequent creditor (who may be aggressive or hostile) gets paid only if there are any assets left after the friendly lien is satisfied.
- The second important goal is simply that a friendly lien "encumbers" a property – it ties it up, and makes it look less attractive to an otherwise aggressive creditor. Encumbered property is always less attractive to creditors. A creditor always "runs the numbers" – the decision to pursue litigation or collections is always an economic decision.

Where Friendly Liens Go Wrong
The big question with friendly liens is the following: How friendly can the lien holder be? Can it be a relative? Can it be a corporation that I secretly control? Friendly liens must be independent – they cannot be mere shams meant to frustrate creditors.

Many asset protection websites claim that you can protect your assets by forming your own corporation and instructing the corporation to place liens on your otherwise-exposed property. They further instruct that you can disguise or conceal your ownership in the corporation through the use of appointed directors. Such a scheme will work only if undetected. If detected and exposed, the lien would be ignored, and the creditors could reach your property.

Creditors' attorneys know this trick. In fact, the surest way to raise suspicion of a flimsy lien is to use your own corporation to create a friendly lien. A creditor's attorney that discovers such a lien in an asset search, may choose to investigate further.

HOMESTEAD LAWS - *No Protection for Alimony or CS*

If you own your home, you may think you want to homestead it depending upon where you live, because homesteading can protect a portion, or even all of your home's equity from creditors. But how protected you are is largely dependent on what state you live in and on what kind of debts you have.

Homestead statutes are state laws protecting homeowners from losing their residences from creditors' forced sales. Many states have enacted homestead exemption laws to help their residents retain their primary residences against liens. Present-day state homestead laws emerged from the federal Homestead Act of 1862, as pioneers headed west to stake their claims to land. States enacted their own homestead laws after Congress completely abolished the federal law in 1976.

The law was specifically designed to protect the person filing the claim from creditors, who were forbidden from placing liens against homesteaded land. The law served several purposes. Among other things, it encouraged settlers to migrate to the western United States and thus encouraged economic development in that region. It also gave debtors a chance to get a fresh start, keeping them off of any form of public assistance. Because much of the supply of federal land was exhausted by the early portion of the 20th century, Congress largely ended the practice of federal homesteading in 1935.

It wasn't just the federal government that had homestead laws however. Many states also had them, and these laws are still in effect. And like the federal law, these laws are designed to protect certain assets from creditors in the event of bankruptcy or other financial problems.

State laws differ greatly, and they do have certain exceptions. For instance, homestead laws can't be used to protect your assets from the IRS. Many states will not allow you to use these laws to protect your assets, in the case of bankruptcy or if you stop making alimony payments. Generally the homestead exemption does not protect a person against liens resulting from child support or spousal maintenance arrearages. In a contempt proceeding brought to enforce the payment of any form of child support or spousal maintenance, the court may consider the debtor's homestead equity as a financial resource.

In some states, homesteading takes place as soon as you move into your home and without a need to file any paperwork. In other states, you may need to live in your home for six months, and you may have to file a homestead claim with your county recorder.

The dollar amount of protection also differs greatly from state to state. For instance, Florida allows you to protect the entire value of your home. Arkansas is on the opposite end of this spectrum, offering only $2,500 worth of protection. Many of these laws will not protect you from debts incurred prior to the time the homestead was filed. This means that the sooner you file a homestead, the more protection you will receive.

As an example, the Nevada Homestead Law provides residents with a way to shield up to $550,000 of equity in their homes from creditor collections. An equity creditor cannot forcibly sell a homeowner's real property if the property is valued at $550,000 or less. However, a creditor can file a lien and force a judicial sale if a homeowner's equity exceeds the $550,000 limit. The homeowner's equity is not the loan on the property. In other words, if a homeowner's principal residence is valued at $200,000 and $175,000 is owed, the equity is $25,000. Thus, a Declaration of Homestead would allow a person to protect their home from a creditor's lien.

One thing that is common to homestead laws is that they <u>only protect your principal residence</u>. In most cases, this means a permanent building that is a single family residence. Some state' laws will also cover trailer homes and the contents of the home (your furniture and other belongings).

Most homeowners are not aware that they can homestead their principal residence. This means that unless you live in a state that automatically offers homesteading, you may be needlessly exposed to debt collectors.

On the other hand, homesteading in states that offer little or no protection may be more trouble than it is worth. For example, if you are applying to refinance your home, you may be required to lift your homestead prior to getting that new loan you want.

<u>Legal Implications</u>
Under the Homestead Law, many types of property can be homesteaded including condominiums, single-family homes, mobile homes and manufactured homes. The law does <u>not</u> protect homeowners against certain types of debts, including tax liens, mechanic's liens, mortgage liens, and <u>delinquent alimony or child support payments</u>.

CHAPTER 5

CHANGE IN CIRCUMSTANCES - TRADITIONAL OPTION

POST START OF ALIMONY - REALITY OF CHANGE IN CIRCUMSTANCES (CIC) MODIFICATIONS

The traditional legal way to get your alimony reduced or terminated (like at your retirement) is with your filing of a Change in Circumstances (CIC), but you could also have a surprise CIC filing by your ex-spouse against you for more money. As more baby boomers are facing new problems from the economic downturn, some post-divorce ex-spouses are asking for an increase in alimony.

Let's say it now may be your turn post-divorce to get motivated to file your own CIC. Here is an epilog of what can happen to you:

- Example #1 – Job Loss: Most people do not realize that they must file a supplemental petition for modification or a CIC of alimony immediately after a job loss, and that's what gets them into arrears trouble, they don't. Consequently when you go into court, the court has the disposition you have "unclean hands." From there the unfortunate reality is the courts at best will only provide you with a downward CIC if your unemployment has been long term (over a year), and in the interim while you have been looking for another job, the alimony does not stop.
- Example #2 – Severe Loss of Income: I filed a CIC to modify alimony and child support due to a severe loss of income, and now my ex-wife and her attorney have deposed me. The deposition discovery required documentation on <u>every</u> bank account for the <u>last 3 years</u>, <u>every</u> credit card statement for the last 3 years, and a list of <u>everything</u> that I owned and its value. This is not freedom and is more like communist Russia or China! I have already offered my ex-spouse 100% of my business along with 100% of the residual (retirement) income I am receiving from it - but they flat out declined. They would rather have control and power over me with lifetime alimony. No crime was committed. I just simply got divorced, but have to pay for the rest of my life and be investigated!! First big mistake, gave them everything to come after your assets.
- Example #3 - Retirement: I am a permanent lifetime alimony victim, having been divorced for 10 years, and have paid the ex-spouse over $150,000 in alimony. I recently retired from my job after 33 years of very hard labor, long hours with declining health. I had no choice but to retire as my job, became too hard for me to continue due to my health. My understanding was that when I retired, my ex would get part of my retirement, and the alimony would cease. My ex currently earns about $3,400 per mo. (now including pension + alimony). My income from my portion of my retirement is now down to $2,500 per mo. It is totally unjust that I should have to continue to pay alimony to someone who is <u>grossing $900 more</u> per mo. than me, and that I should be enslaved to support an ex-spouse 10 years after our divorce! I cannot get closure, and now I have to go to court to attempt to get a CIC and pay again more money for legal expenses with no guarantee of the reduction outcome.

A wakeup call will happen when you realize the state courts generally will not let you be under-employed, either part-time or begin a career change, unless you can show a real documented medical issue. As ridiculous at it sounds, your working life is not your own once you are divorced and have an alimony obligation. You are not allowed to change a career to have your personal fulfillment if it pays less money. You can do it, but the alimony award won't be modified down. If you develop a real medical condition, get plenty of documentation from a medical professional to have good support for the trial. This is a rough road to take.

Attempting to get a modification before you move out-of-state or escape is an option, but it will obviously cost you legal fees to attempt the modification. If you go all the way thru a court decision (as opposed to settling for a lower amount with the ex during the process), it will probably run in the neighborhood of $10 - $30,000 depending upon how hard they fight back. The ex will probably only settle for a lower amount if you can show good evidence during the discovery time frame when the case is reopened for the modification. If you stay in the divorce state, lose the case and do not pay, you expose yourself to receiving a bench warrant followed by an ankle bracelet or being thrown in jail. If you move out of state and do not pay, you won't be thrown in jail in the other state, because domesticate of the judgment first is required. But if the ex-spouse finds you in the other state, they have to domesticate the alimony judgment to your new state, and then he judgment unpaid amounts will accrue there. If you return to your original state, you could have the outstanding bench warrant and the lien executed and then possibly be thrown in jail.

If attempting to modify alimony thru a Change in Circumstances, figure on close to a year or more to actually get to a judge to make a decision. Because of the legal courtroom monetary expense, statistics show family law cases have 70% of petitioners at filing self-represented and growing to 80% self-represented at disposition for dissolution. Change in circumstance filings are ridiculously expensive, drawn out, and in favor against you. More importantly, this will also be another big disruption in your life.

A reality check:
- Review of your alimony as a payer will only get a significant lower modification if you have no assets, and your income drops over a long term (3 years or more). So if alimony is still being paid, you literally do not have enough to survive on.
- Judges will make you sell your assets, bank and retirement accounts, stocks to keep paying the court order. All this is fact based and depends on the judge's mood and inclinations.
- So before seeking a modification, do the math... the fees and costs of deposition and hearings as an upfront cost, against how much and how long the reduction in payments.
- MSA settlement agreements are a big hurdle to getting a modification, especially if the agreement says "non-modifiable."
- End Result: Change in Circumstances is an illusion for most, so what do you do? You take drastic measures - *Invisibility*.

CAN YOU MODIFY ALIMONY THRU A CHANGE IN CIRCUMSTANCES (CIC) FILING?

A payer ex-spouse may request a reduction change in alimony payments after their divorce, but you will have to show an unexpected, long-term, involuntary change of circumstance. You cannot quit your job and expect to be awarded a downward modification of alimony, so be careful about getting fired. You may be accused of getting fired "on purpose," so that you can get a reduction in alimony.

You can attempt to reduce the amount of alimony if you have a certain negative percentage of financial change (usually over 10%). The not simple procedure will vary slightly in each state and according to the local county family court jurisdiction. First you must file your motion in the divorce decree state's civil court. This means if you have moved out of state, you get to travel back to the scene and rehash old memories, or possibly with a letter of power of attorney, your lawyer can do it for you without the costly travel.

In that court you file the supplemental petition for modification of alimony, or in the case of abatement, a supplemental petition for abatement of alimony. Depending on the local court's rules, filing a modification will either reopen your prior divorce case, or the court may require you to institute a new action. If you are reopening your divorce decree case, you will use the same style (pleading heading) and case number as the old case. If the local rules require you to open a new action, you are the petitioner and the ex-spouse is the respondent, and a new case number will be assigned.

For this post-divorce judgment action, you will need to serve the pleading to the other party, the ex-spouse. So get a summons issued by the Clerk of Court along with the pleading for alimony modification/ abatement, which notifies the ex-spouse they have some court time coming.

Your pleadings will be served to the ex-spouse via a process server and once served, you will receive a Return of Service that must be filed with the court, which gives you the date the other party was served. Then the ex-spouse has a certain amount of time to file their answer as outlined in the summons. If the ex-spouse also filed a counter-petition, you will be required to file an answer to their counter-petition.

The bad news - You will need to comply with mandatory disclosure rules and provide at a minimum, bank statements, pay stubs and any other proof of income as part of your filing financial affidavit. Try to minimize your disclosure info, as it will only be used against you and for future collections. You will want to include your written lay-off notice, if it exists. In your CIC modification request, you will also need to provide evidence documentation for the request for the alimony modification. Then you wait for an answer from the ex-spouse. If the ex-spouse retained an attorney, the attorney will file an answer on their behalf. The ex-spouse will also need to complete a financial affidavit and comply with mandatory disclosure for info up to 3 years backwards.

Beware your ex-spouse could be a no-show at these proceedings. What do you do then?

In almost all cases alimony is supposed to be modifiable, but you must have a valid reason for the modification. If you and the ex-spouse cannot settle or come to an agreement, you will attend a court hearing on the modification or abatement of alimony. The Court will review the financial circumstances of both parties, then make its ruling. This whole process can take 1-3 years, and cost you $15 – $50,000 in legal expenses, and at best you will get a reduction. The long odds against you are that your modification request will be turned down. Is it worth it?

LAST RESORT, A CIC WITH A COSTLY COURT PROCEDURE

If you go to court post-divorce for a change in circumstances (CIC) modification filing, here is what will happen. Judges generally try to help parties resolve their case before the trial date, but that is often simply impossible if after months and years of negotiations, conferences, and motions, you and your spouse or ex-spouse still have <u>not</u> reached an agreement, your last recourse is to have a <u>trial</u>. The trial gives the judge the opportunity to hear both parties' wish lists, substantiated by volumes of documents, possibly witnesses and any other information the contenders think will persuade the judge in their favor.

Some judges might give you a "<u>bench</u>" (oral) decision at the end of your motion or before trial, as though you had a jury. Your lawyer should be able to find out <u>before the trial</u>, if your judge makes bench decisions.

After the judge ponders all the issues, they will make their decision. Because the judge has heard all the evidence and witnesses, a decision made by the judge at the trial's conclusion is taken very seriously by the powers that be. This decision should put an end to motions and conferences called for modifying temporary orders or changes in visitation schedules without a change in circumstance. Everyone has spent a lot of time, money, and effort at the trial, and asking for subsequent modification might not do you much good, unless there's been a substantial change in circumstances that would warrant modification after the fact.

Your trial will be very much like those you've seen on television and in movies. If you are the plaintiff or petitioner, the ex-spouse who started the action — your lawyer presents your case first. They will probably call you to the witness stand, where you will be sworn in and asked to take a seat. After your lawyer has finished asking you questions (direct examination), your ex-spouse's lawyer has the opportunity to ask you questions (cross-examination). Your lawyer has the right to object to improper questions, so give their time to do that before answering. It's also a good idea to take a moment before you answer to collect your thoughts.

It is certainly possible for you as the pro se litigant to represent yourself at trial — but if there is enough at stake for you to get to this point, you might do best with a potentially-expensive lawyer involved.

After the cross-examination, your lawyer can ask you questions again; maybe your ex-spouse's lawyer interrupted you while you were trying to explain something. Your lawyer can now give you the chance to present your explanation (your re-direct examination).

After your re-direct examination, there can be a re-cross-examination. The questioning can go back and forth for as long as the judge will allow it. When there are no more questions for you, your lawyer can call a witness to the stand on your behalf, and the whole process starts all over again.

After you have presented all your witnesses (it's often just you, your ex-spouse, the court-appointed psychiatric evaluator, and expert witnesses such as an appraiser of real property or of a business), your side "rests." It is now your ex-spouse's turn to present their witnesses. The same questioning occurs, only the roles are reversed. Your ex-spouse's lawyer conducts the direct questioning, and your lawyer cross-examines the witness.

After your ex-spouse (the defendant) presents their witnesses, your lawyer can call witnesses to refute what's been said (called rebuttal witnesses). After you've called your rebuttal witnesses, your spouse can do the same.

It is the rare pro se litigant who has enough skill and experience to question an expert witness hired by the other side, particularly "experts" who have testified many times. When both sides have rested, the judge might allow each attorney (or if there are no attorneys, the spouses themselves) to make a short, closing speech. Alternatively, they might ask that memoranda be submitted to them by a certain deadline. Sometime later they make a decision.

Trials can be as short as half a day or as long as several months. The length of a trial depends on the number of witnesses, how long each examination takes, and what motions are made during the course of the trial. The emotional and financial costs rapidly add up.

THE REALITY OUTCOME OF MOST CHANGE IN CIRCUMSTANCES (CIC) FILINGS

One would like to believe that the state family law legal system will do you justice, if you file a legitimate change in circumstances (CIC): 1) against your ex-spouse who has been cohabitating and receiving financial support from the cohabitator, and you have evidence from a PI backing up your claim. 2) for a major life change - your retirement after working 45 years, and you are now 66-67 or beyond years of age. 3) or you are over 55 and have been out of work for over a year while seeking employment, but no luck. For the worse your finances are rapidly declining from your monthly living expenses and the alimony payments, and you have to get some relief.

Surprise, case after case examples have shown that a majority of cohabitation CIC requests are denied, even though some state family laws have clearly defined alimony is to stop upon cohabitation, or be automatic upon retirement, etc. The CIC end game, one spends a lot of money in court and ends up with nothing except a big legal bill, and you might get to pay your ex-spouse's expensive legal bill also.

A CIC retirement request example - A should-be-retired Dr. gave meaningful testimony during a state legislature alimony reform bill session, that upon reaching full retirement age at 65 and filing for a court CIC change in circumstance modification ... the CIC was denied and they had to return to continue working from

65 - 72, and ... Six years later after $70,000 in CIC legal bills and $100,000 in additional alimony during this time frame, he did not receive a curtailment in his permanent alimony. In fact was ordered to purchase a life insurance policy guaranteeing the permanent alimony for a term of 5 years after his death to his ex-spouse. What is being done for his retirement life expenses ...?? Lifetime alimony slavery.

This is the state legal system at work, clearly so one-sided even a blind judge should be able to see the unfairness. But it happened to a Doctor, a licensed professional, and perhaps you will be next.

The sad saga of CIC circumstance filings is that 1-3 years of your time will be involved. You will have to inventory and declare all your assets and lifestyle expenses once more for the courts and ex-spouses to scrutiny, a $15,000+ legal bill will be yours to pay, and the likelihood is your request will be denied. At best you will receive a partial reduction, but rarely elimination of your alimony. Better odds in Las Vegas.

So as the saying goes ... skip the CIC, time to move on with your life ... Plan B.

DOES RETIREMENT END PERMANENT ALIMONY?

The immediate answer is "*not necessarily.*" Many ex-spouses believe that retirement is their way out of the alimony obligation. Your retirement may be sufficient grounds to constitute a "change in circumstance" filing to reduce or terminate alimony, however, it must be noted that retirement alone is not an automatic ground to terminate alimony.

By law alimony automatically terminates at the death of the payee, the death of the recipient, or the remarriage of the recipient ex-spouse. If the above does not happen, the alimony will continue until modified by court order.

The key issue is whether the retirement is mandatory or voluntary, and whether the retirement was taken at ordinary retirement age (nominally 65 - 67) or at an early stage from a civil or military retirement, which must be taken into consideration when reducing or terminating alimony. In most states (unless automatic), you will have to go back to court to argue your retirement to suspend the alimony payments.

Permanent alimony termination laws from retirement vary from state to state, and only in a few states (2015 – only 3 states) may alimony be automatically reduced or terminated if the payee ex-spouse retires at the right age on the grounds of "change in circumstances." The catch is not in most states and you will have to prove it in court one more time. Even if not automatic by MSA decree, the major hurdle will be one more time, you will have to go back to court in your divorce decree state and argue your CIC case, and you might lose.

Each alimony case should be analyzed and studied separately, and decision for the annulment of alimony is taken after thoroughly examining the causes of retirement. If the payee ex-spouse retires before the normal retiring age and asked for reduction of alimony, then the court while granting alimony reduction takes into account whether the retirement was made in good faith or not whether the payee was planning their retirement at an early age in order to get rid of alimony obligation. Some other factors that a court considers when a person asked for termination of alimony after retirement are the age and health of the payer, their motives in retiring, their ability to pay and the financial sources of the recipient ex-spouse.

The real life circumstances, there is a lot of state case precedence that your costly retirement CIC filing may at best reduce the alimony payment, but not eliminate it as hoped. One may also have to go back to court more than once and still continue paying, so the legal costs may not be worth the gain.

COURTS FROWN ON EX-SPOUSES WHO QUIT JOBS TO AVOID PAYING

Many ex-spouses try to end-run the alimony system by quitting their jobs, as they often feel very resentful when ordered to pay alimony, and think that by doing this they are saving themselves money. Beware judges are very cranky with people who don't pay alimony or child support. They understand that you can be temporarily out of work, but do not accept the excuse that you can't find anything, even a job washing dishes.

Adding that even if you are out of work, in most cases you probably will still be forced to pay. If somebody has a job and they take themselves out of the financial game, the court does not look kindly on that. Do you want to play games with the court?

You may think the Change in Circumstances will lower significantly the amount of money you pay, but the judge can set it not at what you are making, but what you are <u>capable</u> of making. And people find all kinds of ways to end their employment such as faking an injury, creating bogus excuses why they can't work and even quitting outright. And people create situations to get fired.

But if they suspect that you are pulling a fast one, it all comes down to you proving it. If they have a suspicion that you are malingering which is what it is called, faking an injury, or pretending to be sick so you don't work, you have to prove why you can't work. They can ask for an independent evaluation, but be cautioned as pain sometimes cannot be proven. It's really hard to prove pain, and when it comes right down to it, it's always about what can you prove.

They can call in a third party to ask for evaluation, someone qualified who can come in and do a physical or mental, evaluation, or both. There are people who claim they can't work because of drug or alcohol addiction. There are things you can do about that such as go to AA, or go into rehab. Just because you have a physical injury, does that disable you from do all kinds of work? You might not be able to do construction work, but can you still talk on the phone?

The issue of support is one area that frustrates all litigators, since it usually is the arena where the most games are played. It is not about truth or justice; it's all about what you can prove according to rules of evidence. Unfortunately under penalty of perjury, people lie about their assets and what they earn.

The other problem that adds to the frustration is that even though a support order has been put in place, there is limited recourse for not paying alimony, particularly if one moves out of the divorce decree state. They can still order support from somebody that hasn't the ability to pay it. The court can serve an order on your employer to garnish your wages. For child support, the court combined with the child support agencies can make your life far worse.

LACHES AND EQUITABLE ESTOPPEL DEFENSE FOR LONG TERM ARREARS

<u>Question</u>: What should you do when you haven't paid a court-ordered child support or alimony for many years, with the arrears amount more than you could possibly pay, when suddenly you get a notice to appear in court and may be put in jail?

<u>Answer</u>:
There are few defenses to unpaid child support or alimony in certain situations. If a person who is due unpaid child support or alimony waits too long to go to court to collect, the person who was supposed to pay can plead defenses of <u>*laches and equitable estoppel*</u>. These terms basically mean that the recipient payee waited <u>too long</u> to pursue their rights to collect, and the payer had

a reasonable belief that the recipient wasn't going to go to court to try to collect or enforce the orders.

However, because child support is a right vested in the child, not the parent, the judge may order past child support to be paid, or for some past medical bills to be paid, despite any valid defenses that might be raised.

If past due alimony only is the issue, the affirmative defenses have merit as the payer is on stronger grounds, because there is no minor child involved. However, sometimes an elderly person who was supposed to receive alimony could have become of diminished mental capacity. Every case has to be looked at for the specific set of underlying facts that might create exceptions.

Note that *laches and equitable estoppel* are affirmative defenses that may be used as a defense against long term unpaid child support or alimony, but typically only works for 10-20 years of delay.

BANKRUPTCY CANNOT ESCAPE ALIMONY

Declaring bankruptcy during divorce or following it adds another wrinkle to a situation that may already include alimony. Bankruptcy and alimony do not work well together. Alimony is designed to limit any unfair economic impact of divorce on an ex-spouse who earns much lower wages than the other.

Courts have much discretion regarding the award of alimony, its amount, and its length. Many states base their spousal support statutes on the Uniform Marriage and Divorce Act (see page 13). This legislation recommends that courts consider aspects like the length of the marriage, standard of living, length of time the receiving individual will need to become self-sufficient, and ability of the payer to support him or herself and the recipient. Because of these factors, there are instances where bankruptcy can get rid of alimony or a portion of it depending on your circumstances.

Bankruptcy and alimony are tricky subjects. Alimony is <u>not</u> usually permitted to be discharged in bankruptcy. The payer must pay alimony in full, except under <u>two</u> circumstances;
- If the divorce decree classifies a financial obligation as an alimony payment, but this payment is really for something else like marital debt, it may be possible to discharge the payment in bankruptcy.
- The second exception occurs when an alimony obligation is assigned to a third party. For example, if the payer does not make alimony payments and the receiver assigns collection rights to another party in exchange for receiving the money from that third party, the payer may be able to have the alimony discharged due to this assignment. Therefore, alimony recipients should carefully consider assignment of this obligation to a third party.

The reality is an ex-spouse may be forced to file for bankruptcy due to their inability of nonpayment of daily living expenses. Others may try to use bankruptcy as a way to avoid obligations within the divorce decree. Though the automatic stay in a bankruptcy prevents creditors from demanding repayment of debt, it does not prevent a former spouse from filing or continuing a lawsuit to create or modify alimony awarded in a divorce decree. The courts may even be used to collect unpaid alimony. This is where a difficult situation occurs concerning bankruptcy and alimony.

Under the Bankruptcy Abuse Prevention and Consumer Protection Act of 2005, unpaid alimony and child support claims are provided <u>priority</u> over other creditor claims including taxes. An ex-spouse owed back alimony has to file a proof of claim with the bankruptcy court handling the case. The law also requires the bankruptcy trustee to provide this individual with written notice of the bankruptcy and its discharge.

BANKRUPTCY HAS LIMITED HELP WITH ALIMONY AND CHILD SUPPORT

Bankruptcy is a terrific way to take care of many kinds of debts, but you may have heard that not all debts will be discharged in a bankruptcy. As a result and depending on the kind of debt you have, you may be worried that declaring bankruptcy would not really help you. What you may not know is how bankruptcy can help you with your debts, even the ones you can't discharge outright.

Support obligations fall in this category of debt, and include things like alimony and child support payments. Because these are priority debts, you will not be able to discharge them outright with a Chapter 7 bankruptcy, and in addition, the automatic stay will not prevent collection efforts on past due support obligation payments. Nevertheless, a Chapter 7 bankruptcy will only help you get caught up and stay caught up on your support payments. So when your unsecured debt is discharged, all the money you were spending on things like credit card payments will be freed for use toward your support obligations.

The protected status of support payments can be a good thing in the event that your case is a Chapter 7 asset case. In this rare kind of case, some of your assets will be liquidated to pay creditors. You probably would rather see the proceeds of your liquidated assets go to something like child support, rather than sending it all to unsecured creditors. In that case, your attorney should file a proof of claim on behalf of the support recipient, and this will ensure that most of the proceeds from the liquidated assets will be put to use toward your support payments.

A Chapter 13 bankruptcy will be even more helpful to you when it comes to past due support payments. Say you are really behind on your alimony payments. Your ex is pestering you all the time about the past due amount and you need some relief. A Chapter 13 filing will allow you to work these payments into your repayment plan and allow you to catch up over the course of a 3 to 5 year repayment plan. Note that you must be careful to keep up with your ongoing post-petition payments; failing to make the new payments as they become due can put your case in jeopardy. However with the help the repayment plan, you buy yourself time to manage old debts and therefore keep up with the new ones.

If you've been struggling to catch up on your child support and alimony payments, bankruptcy can help you get back on track. Your debts that won't disappear in a bankruptcy, but can at least become manageable after a successful bankruptcy.

GREEDY EX-SPOUSE CAN FILE FOR A CIC AND INCLUDE YOUR 2ND MARRIAGE SPOUSE'S INCOME AS GROUNDS FOR INCREASED ALIMONY

In some states the new 2nd marriage spouses have been forced by state law to contribute some of their 2nd marriage wage earnings to a 1st marriage ex-spouse's permanent alimony, even there is no relationship. This occurs because of a successful court modification request by the other 1st marriage ex-spouse for more alimony thru an expensive Change in Circumstance (CIC) filing and subsequent court judgment award. It is unjust, but when the ex-spouse learns of your recent remarriage and then files for a CIC to increase their alimony, during the document discovery period you will be required to produce your last three years of income tax returns.

Say as an example during the initial discovery period you listed $80,000/year income and your new spouse's is $50,000/year, so now the total household income wages are reported at $130,000/year. The bad news is some state courts will say there is now additional $50,000 in discretionary income, which is what the Bar means by "pooled" income. Although the term is contradictive in nature, it means that the new spouse's income will be used for determining a new higher alimony award for your ex-spouse. This is true justice at work.

At a minimum it is recommended that the new spouse keep their prior financial assets separate in their name only (not joint), and despite the financial penalty, declare "married filing separately" income tax returns so that the financial assets do not give the appearance of being pooled. The downside, your tax rate goes up about 5% or roughly $5000 per year. A 2nd marriage pre-nup also solidifies the asset separation.

One 2nd wife even took it a step further. She not only kept everything of hers separate (income, bank accounts, assets, etc.), she also signed a prenuptial agreement that specifically outlines that her assets only belong to her, and that they are not for the benefit of her husband. She and her husband haven't co-mingled anything, which has kept her assets out of the courts. To further insulate her husband from his 1st marriage ex-wife, she revised their wills so that <u>nothing</u> goes to him when she dies. It is all willed to her children, who all know it is really for her husband and are happy to ensure he gets her estate after her death.

Another 2nd wife took it to a new high and in a different direction. She decided it was better to divorce her current husband, to keep the 1st marriage ex-spouse from ever staking a claim.

So it is not surprising this existing alimony law problem has become a stumbling block to some potential 2nd marriages, if the engaged couple becomes aware of their state law's loophole. Florida and Massachusetts are two states where this travesty occurs, but Massachusetts recently passed new legislation closing the door on this unjust money grab.

The long and short, if you stick around and get to go thru this replay of your divorce with the judge throwing out the ex-spouse's CIC motion, you still get to pay your side of the legal bills. Vote with your feet beforehand, avoid the legal bills, and go Plan B before the next request for your reappearance in court. Do not send the ex your tax returns as this asking for trouble. Remember always move out of your divorce decree state ... Then you don't have to look back. Best of all, you get to stay in the US.

CHAPTER 6

CONSIDERATION OF CONTEMPT - ALTERNATIVE OPTION

INTRODUCTION - CIVIL CONTEMPT

This is the alternative option, if the thought of traditional Change in Circumstances (CIC) court time at retirement age (66-68 or before) does not look favorable or affordable to you, and you need to move on with your life. For alimony non-payment arrears only, civil penalties are generally misdemeanors and <u>not</u> classified as felonies. So it is simply "*contempt of court*" for which you can be fined and occasionally jailed. Beware Florida, NJ and South Carolina are a few of the exceptions when there is a large monetary judgment, the civil contempt can be converted to criminal. Caution with a child support arrears violation over $5000 (see page 154 regarding CSRA violations), as it is far more serious.

The important factor is alimony non-payment is civil contempt (not criminal) and is <u>not</u> extraditable state-to-state. So generally they can't touch you in another state. What an ex could do if they have the money and dedication to pursue you, is domesticate their original judgment court order to the foreign state you are now residing, but they would have to first come up with a hefty retainer for an attorney in that state. If this were to happen to you, it's just a matter of relocating again. Consider the long term. Time to move on …

CONTEMPT OF COURT

How can a judge have someone imprisoned for contempt of court and not consider this a violation of their right to due process or unlawful imprisonment? If someone is jailed for contempt of court, how can they be held for an unspecified length of time, without this being cruel and unusual punishment?

The short answer is that a person facing imprisonment for contempt of court has likely received full due process of the law. Most people that face contempt charges have been fully advised on several occasions as to the consequences of their actions.

Contempt of court refers generally to any <u>willful</u> disobedience, or <u>disregard</u> of a court order or any misconduct in the presence of a court or action that interferes with a judge's ability to administer justice or that insults the dignity of the court, and is punishable by fine or imprisonment or both. A judge who feels someone is improperly challenging or ignoring the court's authority has the power to declare the defiant person (called the contemnor) in contempt of court.

There are two types of contempt - <u>civil</u> and <u>criminal</u>. <u>Criminal</u> contempt occurs when the contemnor actually interferes with the ability of the court to function properly - for example, by yelling at the judge. This is also called <u>direct</u> contempt because it occurs directly in front of the judge. A criminal contemnor may be fined, jailed, or both as punishment for their act.

Civil contempt occurs when the contemnor willfully disobeys a court order. This is also called indirect contempt, because it occurs outside the judge's immediate realm and evidence must be presented to the judge to prove the contempt. A civil contemnor may be fined, jailed, or both. The fine or jailing is meant to coerce the contemnor into obeying the court, not to punish them, and the contemnor will be released from jail just as soon as they comply with the court order. In family law, civil contempt is one way a court enforces non-payment of alimony or child support, custody, and visitation orders that have been violated. Indirect civil contempt is likely to be the charge. Don't get it converted to direct.

Contempt of court proceedings come with due process. Generally to comply with due process requirements under the Constitution, a person must be told what charges or allegations are facing them, and they have a meaningful opportunity to be heard and present evidence on their behalf. With regard to civil contempt proceedings, this is not really a problem because the person has already been ordered to do something, and has willfully refused to comply. That is, the person against whom the order was entered already had their opportunity to be heard on the issue. For example, if the contemnor has failed to pay proper alimony payments, they already had the opportunity to present evidence as to why they should not have to pay, or pay as much as the court required.

Further, the sanction for contempt is limited in its imposition for so long as the disobedience to the court's order continues; once the party complies with the court's order, the sanction is lifted. The contemnor is said to "hold the keys" to their own cell, so strict adherence to all due process requirements is not necessary.

With regard to criminal contempt, the contemnor will usually be given their opportunity to be heard after the fact, but they still get their opportunity to be heard. Recall that criminal contempt is more often imposed because the contemnor had actively disrupted court proceedings, and incarceration is needed for safety and the proper functioning of a court.

CONTEMPLATION OF STOPPING PAYING ALIMONY

If you are obligated to pay alimony, you may feel the ruling is unfair. It may be in the sense of fairness, but the state law prevails. The rules relating to revising the alimony payments status are both state-specific and case-specific. You can stupidly elect to appeal the divorce decree judgment, with the intention of stopping the payments. A failure to pay can be regarded as a charge of indirect civil contempt of court, or in some states as criminal contempt of court (over $5000 of arrears) if children are involved. The rules regarding contempt of court cases vary between states. Typically, you can expect to be fined and/or possibly incarcerated if you choose not to obey a judge's orders.

Typically, the act of failing to pay alimony is considered with facts specific to the situation. The most severe penalties are reserved for those who can afford, but intentionally choose not to pay alimony. If you can afford to pay, and appear to have missed one or more payments due to time issues or paperwork errors, you are more likely to be forgiven. Failure to pay or notify the court that you cannot afford your alimony payment indicates to the court that you lack credibility and are attempting to deceive your former spouse. By contacting the court and your former spouse about your inability to afford alimony payments, shows the court that you are honest and doing everything possible to avoid penalties.

If you want to stop paying alimony, look at your ruling. Is your MSA or judgment for non-modifiable spousal support? This means, does it contain language which says it cannot be changed? Also, if your judgment is for modifiable spousal support, did you sign away your right to request a modification after the initial ruling? If either of these two things is true, your only avenue to stop payment may be a successful CIC appeal or plan your escape. If your judgment can be modified, it is necessary to return to court to request either a lower or complete suspension of alimony payment obligations, but dream on.

If you return to court to request an original ruling modification, you will need to provide a good explanation and supporting documentation. The judge who rules on the modification of the original alimony may or may not be the same judge who initially issued the ruling, and may not be familiar with all facts of your particular situation. So it is even more important to establish a strong case for reduced alimony obligations, if you are attempting to show that "change in circumstances" have changed for either you or your ex-spouse.

Some of the circumstances in which a judge may consider ordering that you pay less alimony or no alimony include: 1) your former spouse has gotten a new job and become self-sufficient; or 2) your former spouse who used to earn less than you during the marriage, is now earning more than you.

The best way to deal with an unfair alimony ruling is to show the court in an efficient, responsible manner the facts, and hope that the judge rules that the facts are in your favor. Realistically, do not expect a good outcome in most circumstances. The typical outcome of an expensive CIC case is no change or a slight reduction.

CONTEMPT OF COURT ORDERS

Contempt means the willful violation of a Court Order.

What are the defenses to Contempt? Either that you did not violate the family law Court Order, or that the violation was not willful. The cases are usually about failure to comply with an Order requiring support payments (either alimony or child support), or can also be about the failure to follow Orders relating to custody or visitation.

What happens if the Court finds that someone is in Contempt?
The offender can be ordered to cooperate or face incarceration. The Court can even order incarceration until cooperation begins. This may mean payment of all or part of the support owed, or cooperation on terms of custody or visitation. The Court can also require the offender to pay the other side's attorney's fees.

Can the Court punish someone for Contempt?
Yes, the Court cannot only take steps to ensure cooperation, it can also hold someone in civil or criminal contempt and punish them by making them pay a fine and/or serve time in jail for each violation, as punishment (even if they decide to cooperate or pay all owed monies).

How long does a Contempt case take?
Typically contempt cases are quicker than divorce or other family law cases, since they focus on one or two straightforward issues - Was there a violation of an Order, and what should the Court do about it?

Is Contempt the only way to enforce a Court Order?
For arrears collection, there are collection methods such as garnishment of bank accounts, wages and other assets, and the property of the payer can also be attached.

If a party fails to pay child support or alimony, a judge can hold the person in "contempt of court" and jail them. In order to jail a person for non-payment, a judge will determine a "purge amount" which the person can pay to get out of jail. The judge must also determine after an evidentiary hearing that the person has the present financial ability to pay the purge amount. This type of contempt known as civil contempt, in effect gives the person a "key to get out of jail" (i.e., the purge amount).

A judge can jail a person for intentional or willfully disobeying any specific court order through a process known as "indirect civil or criminal contempt." This process does not involve a purge amount or a "key to get out of jail," but rather is used only for punishment. The judge can impose a sentence up to six months in jail.

There are other means available to enforce child support such as the state's driver's license or professional license suspension. If a person owes a large amount of child support or alimony, a court order will be obtained (reduce the arrears to a money judgment) and a certified copy of the order filed in every county in which they believe that you may own real estate. The money judgment which earns interest at the statutory rate (4 – 12% per annum), serves a judgment lien against any real property owned by the non-paying party. When this happens, there can be no property sale occur until the judgment lien and accrued interest is paid off.

In addition to the above-stated enforcement procedures, there are many other procedures available - writ of execution (for levy and sale), writ of attachment, writ of garnishment, or entry of an Income Deduction Order (IDO).

ENFORCEMENT OF COURT ORDERS

In general divorce court orders can be enforced in the same manner as any other non-criminal order. In most instances, an order can be enforced by filing a motion or petition with the court.

The Marital Separation Agreement (MSA)
Many divorcing couples work out the thorny details of alimony and other property divisions as well as other issues such as child custody in a contract known as a separation agreement. This agreement may be drawn before or after the parties file for divorce and even if they are still living together; it is simply spells out legal rights and obligations without taking any formal action in a court of law. However once this document is agreed to, it is enforceable as a contract should its terms be breached by either party.

If alimony is agreed to in the property settlement agreement, and the agreement is incorporated into the final decree, then the court doesn't have the power to change a dime of it except thru a CIC. But if the court sets the amount of alimony, it maintains complete control as to whether it can be raised, lowered, or halted.

Enforcement
Once the court orders that alimony is to be paid, failure to pay is disobeying a court order, otherwise known as contempt of court. Remedies available to the person seeking alimony include: wage liens, levies upon real and personal property, garnishment of financial assets and property, and garnishment of wages. It is possible that you will be imprisoned for failure to pay alimony, even though alimony is not considered to be a debt within the meaning of the Constitution which protects debtors from imprisonment.

The numerous ways to enforce an order for alimony or spousal support include:
- Contempt proceedings
- Wage garnishment
- Entry of a money judgment
- Writ of execution and sale
- Security requirement
- Sequestration
- Uniform out-of-state enforcement laws

Contempt
A party subject to a valid order who has knowledge of the order and the ability to comply with the order, and then fails to comply with the terms of the order is subject to contempt charges. Usually, contempt is quasi-criminal in nature, and the burden of proof of the moving party is typically "beyond a reasonable doubt." A party may be found in contempt for many violations, including failing to abide by custody orders, failure to pay support, and other violations. If the person cited is found guilty, they are subject to jail time as well as being fined.

Contempt is the disobedience of a valid court order. If an ex-spouse refuses to comply with court-ordered alimony, the other ex-spouse usually can file a contempt proceeding or action for contempt in which they ask the court to hold the payer in contempt of court. Because each failure to comply with a court order can be a separate contempt, when it comes to alimony, the payer ex-spouse can be charged with a separate contempt for each payment missed and can be punished for each offense. The penalties for contempt include a jail term, usually for no more than 30 days, a fine, or both. In a situation where the Court had ordered that alimony is to be paid and the order is not being complied with, a Complaint for Contempt may be filed with the Court. This option is to be used in a situation where there is reason to believe that they have the means to pay, but is refusing to do so.

The person who is in arrears will be called to defend themselves. The Court may order that the payments be deducted from the individual's paycheck or by direct withdrawal from a bank account if they can find either. A judge also has the power to order that the non-payer be jailed until they agree to make the payments as ordered.

Wage Garnishment Order
The court is required to issue an earnings assignment for all support orders. A garnishment order requiring the payer's ex-spouse's employer to directly pay the support to the recipient of child, family or spousal support is now mandatory whenever the court makes or modifies a support order. The only exception to this rule is where the parties agree otherwise. This tool can be particularly powerful where a party has failed to make regular payments, as the employer is required to directly pay the recipient the support out of the payer's pay check.

Spousal support payments generally are taken directly from the wages of the payer ex-spouse through wage garnishment and income withholding. Note federal and state laws limit the amount or percentage of the payer ex-spouse's wages that can be garnished, and some funds can't be garnished at all, like income tax withholdings and some federal retirement benefits. Social Security payments can be garnished. Generally for arrears, garnishment is 65% of the net wage, unless the individual has remarried, in which case the maximum that can be garnished is 50%.

Entry of Money Judgments
The recipient ex-spouse has to go to court and get a judgment against the payer ex-spouse in the amount of any past due alimony arrearage. Once there is a judgment, the recipient ex-spouse can attempt to collect the amount of the judgment through one of the enforcement methods such as wage garnishment.

Writ of Execution
Utilizing this procedure, a party owed support or other funds may petition the court for an order that assets be seized and sold to satisfy the obligation, but only if they can find you or the property. This procedure also can be used against your bank and brokerage house accounts to get obtain large sums of money that are past-due. A variation is a writ of execution and sale, which directs the local sheriff to take and sell specified property of the payer ex-spouse. That property is then sold by the sheriff (sheriff's sale), and the money from the sale is given to the recipient ex-spouse as payment on the arrearage.

Security Requirement
Many state laws allow courts to require a party to post security to insure compliance with its orders. "Security" usually refers to money deposited with the court. If you fail to make the required payments, the recipient ex-spouse can take the security to satisfy your debt.

Sequestration
After the recipient ex-spouse gets a money judgment for the amount of past due alimony, they file an application for sequestration, where the court will order that certain of the debtor ex-spouse's property be held until you pay the debt. Unlike the requirement for security, sequestration can be requested only after the payer ex-spouse is in arrears and has refused to comply with a court order to pay the debt. Sequestration is not a favored enforcement tool because of the impact on the payer. Not only are you deprived of property, but a third party called a "receiver," usually has to be appointed by the court to hold the property and is

Uniform Out-of-State Enforcement - Domestication

If one ex-spouse moves out of state, both the Revised Uniform Reciprocal Enforcement of Support Act (RURESA) and the Uniform Interstate Family Support Act (UIFSA) require the new state to enforce an existing order for spousal support from the divorce decree state. However, there are differences in the UIFSA and RURESA rules involving issues like registering support orders in a new state and asking the new court to modify or change those orders. Out of state divorce judgments can be enforced, but only with a lot of effort and expense. The ex-spouse has to have the divorce decree state judgment enforced by obtaining a certified copy of the judgment and filing a Petition to Register and Enforce Out-of-State Final Judgment locally in the foreign state. Once the court entered a final judgment registering the divorce final judgment as an out-of-state decree, the foreign state judge then can enforce the out-of-state judgment as if it had been entered there.

Child Support Agencies

Some state's child support enforcement agencies will provide assistance to enforce an order for alimony spousal support, but only if there is also unpaid child support from the same individual. Note that some states (like New Jersey) comingle CS and alimony, so it is impossible to be "paid up" on child support but not the alimony.

Private Support Collection Agency

A last resort option to enforce an alimony order is to retain a private support collection agency, as independent support collectors provide services to ex-spouses who are owed alimony and/or child support payments. There is no upfront fee to retain support collectors, but they withhold 30-80% of the support payments they collect as a fee.

CIVIL CONTEMPT CONSEQUENCES

A Motion for Contempt is a common occurrence in family law proceedings, and here are the possible punishments for being found in contempt.

What Happens if an Ex-Spouse Refuses to Pay Alimony?

If the payer ex-spouse fails to pay alimony in a full or timely manner, possible avenues of recourse include:
- Retain a lawyer to file a motion for contempt for court-ordered payments.
- Or the recipient ex-spouse can file their pro-se motion for contempt using the proper state forms.

Once the court orders that alimony is to be paid, failure to pay is disobeying a court order known as contempt of court. The following remedies are available to the person seeking arrears:
- Wage liens
- Levies upon real and personal property
- Garnishment of property
- Garnishment of wages
- Court may order the paying ex-spouse to pay the delinquent amount plus interest.
- Willful failure to pay may lead to a possible imprisonment (dependent on the state)

A significant tactical situation occurs if you have moved out of the divorce decree state. A judge will only issue a divorce decree state judgement and instruct the recipient ex-spouse that they must domesticate the judgement to the foreign state.

What are the consequences of being found in contempt?

Time to reach for that get out of jail free card you've been holding onto. You might be thinking, "Really?, they're going to send me to jail just because I missed a couple of monthly payments?"

If the court has determined that there was a valid order you knew about and failed to comply with, and you have the present ability to comply with that order, you are now in contempt.

The first thing the court will do is give you the opportunity to cure your contempt, which typically is done for financial contempt. If you are able to pay some or all of the back support you had been withholding or pay off the debt assigned to you in your dissolution judgment, then it is unlikely the judge will send you to jail. You may have to pay a portion or all of your ex's attorney's fees for having to take you to court to enforce the order.

Remember that civil contempt was initially set up to coerce compliance of the parties, not punish them with confinement. If the contempt action can get you to do what you're supposed to do, then it is unlikely jail time will be involved.

If you on the other hand have the ability to pay, and the court gives you the opportunity to cure your contempt but you refuse, the court may sentence you to some jail time. While this may seem counterproductive, the idea here is that you are not being sent to jail because you can't pay, but because you can and just don't want to pay. You will likely want to post bail, and the court can use that money to repay the debt owed.

Again, civil contempt is meant to coerce compliance, and most people will be willing albeit begrudgingly to comply with an order when their wallet starts taking a beating.

INDIRECT CIVIL CONTEMPT PROCEDURE

No general procedure rules are available to follow, but state Family Law Rules of Procedure governing civil contempt proceedings apply in family law support matters:

1. Motion And Notice Required:
    *   Service by mail is sufficient. Service by publication is not permitted.
    *   Notice must be reasonable, so a notice received the morning of contempt hearing is not sufficient notice. Motion and notice must specify acts claimed to be contemptuous. Must specify time and place of hearing.
2. Hearing:
    *   Court must inform respondent of allegations. Moving party has burden of proof.
    *   Once noncompliance is established or admitted, the burden shifts to you, the respondent, to show inability to perform or excuse.
    *   Respondent is <u>not</u> entitled to court-provided counsel, because proceedings are remedial and <u>not</u> criminal.
3. Fines:
    *   A compensatory fine may be imposed, and be based on evidence of the injured party's actual loss.
    *   A coercive fine may be ordered to coerce compliance.
    *   Coercive fines must have <u>purge provision</u>.
    *   Attorney's fees may be awarded as sanctions.
4. Incarceration:
    *   Incarceration may be ordered, but only if a purge provision is provided, and court finds that contemnor has the present ability to perform the financial purge. Period of incarceration can be <u>indefinite</u>, as the contemnor "carries keys to their cell in their own pocket."

WHAT HAPPENS WHEN YOU STOP PAYING ALIMONY?

Alimony awards require one ex-spouse to pay the other spousal support maintenance for a defined period or permanent until death. Typically, the alimony payment obligations terminate upon the death of either ex-spouse or when the recipient remarries or cohabits with a nonfamily member of the opposite sex. When an ex-spouse who has been ordered to pay alimony does not pay, courts can order garnishments and hold nonpaying ex-spouses in contempt of court.

Contempt Requests

Ex-spouses can request "show cause" or contempt orders against former spouses who are delinquent in their alimony payments by filing a Motion for Civil Contempt and Enforcement to initiate a contempt proceeding against the nonpaying ex-spouse. Once the ex-spouse completes the form and files it with the clerk's office in a local circuit court with jurisdiction over the matter, they must serve the motion and accompanying summons on the defendant-nonpaying ex-spouse through personal service from the attorney by a process server or sheriff.

Garnishments and Security Bond

Courts can issue garnishments attaching personal property of ex-spouses who fail to pay their monthly alimony payments. To obtain a garnishment, the recipient ex-spouse must file an attachment or garnishment for past-due alimony in court and request service of the salary garnishment on the defendant and the defendant's employer. Once the employer receives the notice, then the employer must withhold portions of all future paychecks until the delinquency is settled. To prevent subsequent delinquencies, judges may require the obligated ex-spouse to pay to purchase a security bond, providing a personal pledge or guarantee to continue paying future payments. This bond scenario is one you really want to avoid.

DOES LOSING OR CHANGING YOUR JOB/ EMPLOYER STOP THE GARNISHMENT?

Yes! When you stop working or get laid off by your last employer, that employer following the terms of the employer's garnishment notice will send a letter notice to the alimony recipient and perhaps the state disbursement unit that your employment has stopped on your last day. It will also list your new employer as "unknown." This presents an opportunity – the moment that your next employment can become invisible to future garnishments.

Adding to the task while you are looking for a new job, it would be strategically advisable for you at this point to get a PMB postal mail box, move, and change all your financial institution locations. Make this a high priority in the first stage of your unemployment. You can buy yourself some additional time by writing a few interim personal checks and sending the money to the ex-spouse or the state agency that collects the money Then when you are ready at the conclusion of this job loss and life changing event, you can terminate the alimony payments, implementing your Plan B and become invisible.

MOVING OUT OF STATE IMPACT UPON JUDGMENT ENFORCEMENT

As laws differ from state to state, many alimony payers believe that relocation is their way out of the alimony obligation, but alimony cannot be stopped on the grounds that the receiving ex-spouse or payer spouse has moved to some other location. It just makes alimony collection more difficult.

Typically any divorce decree that is ordered by the court is binding on the payer ex-spouse unless the court formally amends or reverses its decision. Divorce decrees are binding court orders, and the payer ex-spouse has a legal obligation to abide by them so long they are in effect irrespective of the location. The bottom line is that once ordered by the state court, a person cannot simply change their mind and run away from an alimony obligation. Fortunately for alimony only, the consequences are less and much harder to enforce.

If the you, the paying ex-spouse has left the divorce decree state in which you owe child support or alimony, the recipient ex-spouse can still enforce the order after obtaining domestication in that foreign state. However, this is not a simple process. In the interim until the domesticated judgment is registered, you will not be arrested, receive an asset lien, or be garnished in the foreign state.

If you elect this route and move out-of-state, you may have a divorce decree state judgment entered against you and be found guilty of indirect civil contempt in that divorce decree state court. This is the decision point you need to come to terms with yourself, as you may end up with an alimony misdemeanor or child support misdemeanor/ felony record if they proceed beyond the initial motion and domesticate the judgment to your foreign state.

URESA & UIFSA DOMESTIFICATION ENFORCEMENT ACROSS STATE LINES AND JURISDICTION

America has become a nation of transients, with many people having the same name moving to a different state, and having multiple location addresses if the resident address is sought. A recurring problem is that after child support or maintenance alimony is awarded in the divorce decree state court where the parties resided at one time, and then one or both parties move to other state(s). Enforcement becomes more difficult.

URESA (<u>Uniform Reciprocal Enforcement of Support Act</u>) provides two important rights. First, if a person owing support has moved to another state, whether it be in a divorce, separation or paternity proceeding, then the act provides an enforcement mechanism. Under URESA each state designates an office (either the prosecutor's office, city/county/state's attorney, the public welfare office, or a special office for support administration; where the ex-spouse presents their problem. The Court or officer in the divorce decree state (without filing fees or court costs) then forwards the petition to the Court where the person owing the support might be found. Then that Court enforces the obligation by contempt, installment payments, liens on property, arrest, or other court action. This enforcement is conditional providing that the person who is delinquent can be found, (which is usually the problem), then the Courts of the other state will try to get all or some of the arrearage, and will try to enforce compliance with the Orders for Support in the future. Plan B is obviously the defense to this scenario.

The second important right that URESA provides is that child support orders (but not alimony) will be registered from state to state, so that a public record exists of the support and arrearages. In virtually all child support cases a properly recorded order that finds that an arrearage is due acts as a lien on the property of the delinquent party. If the delinquent party wants to get a loan, buy a car or engage in any financial transaction where a credit check will be run, the child support arrearage will show up. Usually this results in some action being taken, and remember unpaid child support always shows up on a credit report.

One further difference between spousal support and child support is that the power to modify spousal support awards generally <u>stays with the state where the divorce is granted</u>. The code does <u>not</u> authorize the court to transfer jurisdiction to another state and neither does the <u>Uniform Interstate Family Support Act </u>(**UIFSA**), which many states have adopted. This can be inconvenient if everyone has moved away from the state where the divorce was granted, and one of the parties wants to have the spousal support amount modified.

Enforcement in the foreign state can occur, as the order to pay spousal support can be <u>enforced in any state after domestication</u>, but only with significant cost and time expenditures. The normal procedure is to register the decree in the paying ex-spouse's foreign state by filing certified copies of the judgment with the local court. That court can then take the action necessary to collect the money.

Payment can also be enforced in the state that granted the divorce, as the court there can order wage-garnishment and hold a delinquent party in contempt. Often it is more cost-effective to do the enforcement in the state where the paying ex-spouse lives. It is easier to have a party held in contempt and sent to jail in the state where they live, for the simple reason that the local sheriff can go to their house and arrest them. The sheriff from the state where the divorce was granted on the other hand, cannot cross a state line to arrest someone who hasn't paid their support, so extradition in these cases is extremely rare.

So the key here, UIFSA is applicable because all states have adopted it, but not easily enforceable. The key is that if you run or hide, <u>make sure you cannot be found</u>!

DOMESTICATION OF A FOREIGN STATE JUDGMENT - UEFJA

Approximately 47 of the 50 states have adopted the <u>Uniform Enforcement of Foreign Judgments Act (UEFJA)</u>. Under this Act, they can convert the foreign (i.e., sister state) judgment into a judgment. A Notice of Filing (in lieu of a complaint) is prepared and filed with the Circuit Court of the County where the judgment debtor was last known to reside or to have their principal place of business or employment. What is required from the creditor or the person seeking to have a judgment enforced is the following:
- An exemplified or authenticated copy of the judgment from the divorce decree state;
- An affidavit that the judgment is from your divorce decree state court and has not been satisfied; and
- Filing costs to cover filing of the Notice with the affidavit, and the copy of the exemplified judgment.

Once the arrears are reduced to a judgment, the ex-spouse has the same collections options available to other creditors, for example a credit card company that sued and won in court. They can use that judgment to attach the non-payer's bank account, or to seize their car or other assets for sale. If you can't find the non-payer's assets, they can force the non-payer to tell them under oath, what and where they are under threat of contempt of court.

The "recognition" of a foreign judgment occurs when the court of one state or foreign country jurisdiction accepts a judicial decision made by the courts of another "foreign" country or jurisdiction, and issues a judgment in substantially identical terms without rehearing the substance of the original lawsuit.

Once a foreign judgment is recognized, the party who was successful in the original case can then seek its enforcement in the recognizing country. If the foreign judgment is a money judgment and the debtor has assets in the recognizing jurisdiction, the judgment creditor has access to all the enforcement remedies as if the case had originated in the recognizing country, e.g. garnishment, judicial sale, etc.

This is frequently referred to as <u>Foreign Judgment Domestication</u>. Once they file these items with the clerk's office, the court sends a copy of the judgment and an affidavit prepared on the plaintiff's behalf to the debtor. The collection firm armed with the judgment generally sends a copy directly to the judgment debtor and files a certificate of service with the court as further proof that the Notice has been properly served on the judgment debtor in accordance with the Act. The debtor then has 30 days to object to the domestication of the judgment. No execution or other post judgment enforcement of the foreign judgment can occur prior to the expiration of the notice period. The collection law firm will then go to work to collect the judgment, and frequently issue a garnishment or lien against the debtor's bank account and otherwise attempt to identify and locate debtor's assets within the foreign state.

WHY THEY MUST DOMESTICATE A JUDGMENT TO A FOREIGN STATE - UEFJA

When a judgment has been issued in another state and the debtor resides in a foreign state, it is necessary to domesticate the judgment so that it can be enforced in the foreign state, and then collection can begin on the judgment. The term "foreign judgment" means any judgment, decree of order of a court of any other state or of the United States if such judgment, decree, or order is entitled to full faith and credit in this state.

<u>The foreign judgment must first be recorded in the actual state and county where the debtor lives or owns property</u>. After the judgment has been properly recorded, the Clerk of Court will notify the debtor that the foreign judgment has been recorded. In most state counties, one cannot initiate any collection action until 30 days after the notice has been sent to the debtor by the Clerk. The procedure on domesticating a foreign judgment varies somewhat within the state and in different counties. Most counties only require that the fee is paid to record the out-of-state judgment, and the notification sent.

Executing the judgment will also vary, based upon the county in which it is filed. Typically <u>they must execute the judgment In each county to collect upon the debt</u>. There is also the legal option to file a new lawsuit against the creditor, in which case it is unnecessary to undertake the other domestication process.

Now assume they have successfully obtained a judgment against a party (you), and you owe them money. The problem is, the jurisdiction in which they obtained the judgment is not the jurisdiction in which you the debtor/defendant have assets. Was their judgment obtained in vain?

The answer is no. Under the <u>Uniform Enforcement of Foreign Judgments Act (UEFJA)</u>, they can seek to enforce the hard-earned judgment in the jurisdiction in which the debtor/defendant has assets. The law refers to any judgment obtained outside of the state in which the law is sought to be enforced as a "foreign" judgment. The process is known as "<u>domesticating</u>" a judgment. For example, a judgment you obtained in Ohio can be domesticated in Kentucky through the process spelled out in the UEFJA. Instead of going through the process of once again filing a complaint, waiting for the answer, and filing motions for summary or default judgment, all they have to do under the UEFJA, is file the original authenticated judgment in the county in which the court would have jurisdiction over the debtor/defendant.

The UEFJA allows the debtor/defendant time to respond to the filing, in order to claim any defenses against the judgment they would have had under the jurisdiction under which they obtained the judgment. After the time has passed, or after the Court has overruled any potential defenses, the judgment is then enforceable under the foreign state law as if they had actually obtained the judgment in that state in the first place. Then they can file notices of judgment liens in the appropriate County Clerks' offices, attempt to seize personal property for a sheriff sale, attempt to garnish any accounts belonging to the debtor/defendant, and possibly arrest you.

STATE LICENSED MEDICAL PROFESSIONALS – WHAT DO YOU DO?

As a state licensed professional you are in a difficult spot if you want to become invisible. Here is why, if this is your scenario:

<u>Medical Doctors, Nurses, and Dentists</u>: Physician and other medical licensure is looked at very closely. There's a National Practitioner Data Bank, and there's immense cooperation between states and hospitals to keep track of doctors. Insurers and health insurance companies who receive bills in your name, and medical malpractice insurance companies keep track of you. There is also a "NPI Number." National Provider Identifier. A National Provider Identifier or NPI is a unique 10-digit identification number issued to health care providers in the United States by the Centers for Medicare and Medicaid Services (CMS). To practice, any medical professional who prescribes medication needs not only a state license, but a Federal DEA (Drug Enforcement Administration) number, - that's essentially licensure from the US Government DEA which permits you to prescribe narcotics.

In 2013, NPDB and HIPDB merged into one database referred to as NPDB - National Practitioner Data Bank. The NPDB is a federal data bank which was created to serve as a repository of information about health care providers in the United States. The Medicare and Medicaid Patient and Program Protection Act of 1987 led to the creation of NPDB, a data tracking system designed to protect program beneficiaries from unfit health care practitioners. The NPDB was implemented in 1990 and required reporting of adverse licensure, hospital privilege and professional society actions against physicians and dentists related to quality of care. In addition, the NPDB tracks malpractice payments made for all health care practitioners.

So for a practicing medical professional, there is no easy way to be "off the grid" while in the U.S. A good or avid lawyer or PI would have extreme difficulty to find you, even supposing they know how to look thru the NPDB databank.

CHAPTER 7

PLANNING YOUR ESCAPE

THE STEPS TO INVISIBILITY AND DISAPPEARING

What does this mean for those of you who need to get away from the alimony remarriage, and keep a wide berth from a former spouse, garnishment, the courts, and private investigators? As they have several ways of getting to you, here is how you start to slow or stop them, and make it expensive and not worth the time and money investment to come after you. The essentials are:

- Get a <u>new</u> job stopping the current employer wage garnishment. Court time with a judgment and discovery of your new employer are required to reinstate the garnishment. So the game plan evolves into the next critical steps.
- Establish a <u>new</u> alternative private mail box (PMB) separate from your residence using your <u>new</u> business name.
- List your private PMB postal mail box address for all your employer, insurance info, and bank/401K accounts. Bottom-line, never list your actual residential address in any potential database. To get an acceptable private postal mail box (PMB) with a street address, see page 94.
- Never file a change of address with the USPS. Bottom-line, never list your residence address associated with your name on anything including your tax returns as you can be found.
- Establish a LLC.
- Establish <u>new</u> banking and investment relationships utilizing only your business LLC or corporation name (not your own name) with your PMB street address and get a debit card only.
- Move, preferably out of the divorce decree state.
- Switch to using debit cards and shut down all credit cards except one (to maintain your credit basis).
- Re-title all items of property ownership like bank accounts, brokerage accounts, houses, autos, motorcycles, and boats with the <u>new</u> business name and PMB address.
- Get a <u>new</u> phone number with a <u>new</u> non-contract wireless carrier in the business name only. Do not list the phone in your name; use the business name.
- If you have a 2nd spouse after the divorce, remember they will need to become involved in the same steps of invisibility.

Take it slow, doing your homework to create invisibility and perhaps cause peripheral confusion, as every misstep can lead to someone finding you. So study this prep carefully.

1. *Shut Down Your Current Identity Profile*
This is the act of taking all information that currently exists about you and changing it, or making it obsolete by moving on and becoming invisible. Move from your current residence, establish an alternative private mail box separate from your residence, establish new banking and investment relationships utilizing a business LLC or corporation with anonymous or invisible ownership, get a new phone number with a new non-contract wireless provider, and then get a new job. Also prepare for the need to lose your current internet and data miner identity.

Then look at your wallet plastic cards, as any one of your membership cards or signup registrations can assist a private investigator/ skip tracer in finding you: 1) Grocery and drug stores, bookstores etc. that keep track of every item you buy thru their card. 2) Thru your frequent flyer account name and zip code, someone can learn about your travel records. 3) Car rental companies list your account by phone number, that can tell them where you last rented a car, and 4) Rebate cards and warranty registrations. The list goes on and on. Stop using them, and make them become obsolete.

You can take your personal info one step further and create multiple false leads. Submit USPS change of address forms to locations (that are undeliverable), but which will be picked up by the multiple robotic data miner search engines receive the USPS change of address submission info and that scan all internet websites. Or consider when flying out-of-town to wherever, rent a car and actually go to a realtor and apply for an apartment, to trigger the agent running an abbreviated credit header report (not a credit report) but generating a hard inquiry on you. Then later the PI/skip tracer looking for you may run your credit record or credit header report (if they have legal third party access) and see your new undeliverable address or an inquiry from a rental company in Phoenix and start looking there. Your goal is to eat up their budget and time.

Repeat the process until it is a confusing mess to the potential asset searcher/tracer.

2. *Maintaining Your Invisibility*

The final act of taking your present identity scenario to your future with invisibility and no follow-up leads will depend on your skill. The big realization that: 1) Most importantly, never provide your residential home address on any documentation that can become a database. 2) Any prior contact with friends/relatives must now be maintained only through new throwaway email accounts and/or non-contract prepaid cell phone plans. Phones list "caller ID", so beware anyone you call has your phone no. linked to you. 3) For address listings with your employer, banking, health/ dental insurance, auto insurance, driver's license, and tax returns, use only your private postal mail box (PMB) with a street address (not your residential address). You need to stay invisible. Don't ever get comfortable and feel safe.

PLAN AHEAD

Many people have an idea perhaps from reading a book, and then pick up and go leaving no forwarding address, after only simply disconnecting their utility services. Big mistake, as with your present alimony factor and particularly with child support (CS) involved, someone may come looking for you. So take your time and follow the steps below to make your escape last:

- Develop your plan at least six months before you hit the road and begin to reformat yourself in your current location.
- Establish a business LLC or corporation with your ownership anonymous or invisible to the public.
- Close out and move all your current bank and financial accounts to new undisclosed locations, reopening the new business accounts in the new business name (not a personal account). Closing out the old accounts is important, so there is no impact on your credit report.
- Get a new cell phone carrier and a new number thru a non-contract provider using your business name only.
- Establish a couple of throwaway email accounts at Yahoo or Google. Provide minimal or no profile on-line information about yourself. Make up your birthdate.
- Do not use any of your current pre-escape debit/ credit cards to purchase anything in the place you are going to escape to. Get a new business debit card from a new financial institution, using your new LLC business address and the PMB box. Most importantly, no new credit cards. Keep one credit card to maintain your credit rating and to be able to rent a car. After the move, formally close out the old debit card accounts thru the institution.

- For any future new rental or utility account applications, start using your business name if you can, along with your middle name and your last name. Long term, lose your first name. The catch is they will want your social security no. to check your credit status.
- Do not file any USPS change of address forms.
- If there is CS involved, get your 10-year passport renewed, so you have a clean slate.
- The objective – no useful info is to be found, or if you leave any behind - create confusion.

The key here is to provide your data miner and credit report(s) database with no new useful info about your plan enroute to becoming invisible or afterwards.

Is it possible to buy someone's identity? The answer is simple – no, as one never knows whose identity you are assuming. Does that person have a warrant or a tax lien you do not know about? What skeletons dwell in their closet? What if you take this unknown person's identity, and tell your new friends you are from Hoboken, NJ. Now you're sitting at the beach sipping a gin and tonic and a couple of tourists show up and start talking with you about the place you just told them you were from. Call it the fluke factor, as you have no control over something when the fluke factor comes into play.

The reality of life is you have zero control over the people you meet or the situations you walk into. When you are on the road, you will meet acquaintances in the most remote place as well as their acquaintances in places like London and San Francisco. It is difficult to avoid other Americans when you are in a foreign country, as Americans overseas tend to gravitate towards each other like teenagers in a mall on Friday night.

New identities are a red light shining, blaring trouble. New identities usually have the word felony standing behind them.

If you are looking to disappear, leave your alimony life behind, or just start over and not have people from your past find you, it can be done with a few steps of privacy initiation and then maintaining your invisibility.

Some people believe that they can just pick up and go. The problem does come if someone comes looking for you, they have your whole past and present to search. They may have your family and friends to contact, banks, credit card application info, IP addresses, the list is as long as the person's imagination and budget.

Remember investigative firms actually work for the ex-spouse, and their best interest is not yours. Armed with a judgment if they know where your assets are, your things are attachable. Judgments last for 2-10 years and accrue interest (4-12% dependent upon the state) with additional penalties for arrears.

Now educate yourself on how to become *invisible* for your privacy, and how to escape from your legal family court alimony obligation.

INTERNET - YOUR COMPUTER'S IP ADDRESS LACK OF PRIVACY

Here is how it starts. The majority of Americans suffer significant ignorance of how their personal information is released online. It is important to know that every time you click on a link and request a web page, your computer gives out a numeric code known as an IP address (like 24.124.180.96) to identify your computer to another computer (a server). There is no other way for a server to know where to send back information.

When you surf the web, your computer stores tons of data about where you have been on the internet, what you have been doing, and what information you have entered when surfing the web. Over time, this information builds up on your computer. If someone gains access to your computer, they will have a treasure trove of personal data that could cause you serious problems. Things like credit card information, bank account information, passwords, social security numbers, all can be accessed by these kinds of hackers.

The key to protecting your privacy is knowing how to protect your personal information. Individuals concerned about their online privacy need to learn how they share personal information online, and to take actions to protect personal information online. To prevent this, you need to regularly remove information (cookies) from your computer so that it does not pile up like a digital fire hazard.

There are 3 privacy options available:
1. Go totally wireless using your cell phone internet connection and it's associated IP address
2. Go to an Internet café and use the wifi with their IP address, or to a public library with their hardwired connections. The downside of wifi public locations is beware of possible key-stroke scanners.
3. Utilize a virtual private network (VPN) connection, hiding your IP address and possibly encrypting your data, and maybe using an anonymous onion-router web proxy (TOR as an example).

Option #3 is the recommended option for the simplicity, function, and low cost.

Or one other simple privacy software product and move your IP if you utilize multiple computers:
*   Portable Mozilla Firefox: Free – Keep your browser on a flash drive minimizing information stored and shared, doesn't put or leave information on the PC you use.

CAN SOMEONE FIND YOU THRU YOUR INTERNET IP ADDRESS?

Possibly, but most likely not without a subpoena to your internet provider. In most cases all that can be easily determined is your ISP, the state and a close proximity of the actual city or location you reside in. In big cities, that is probably a 2 mile radius, in small towns closer, but not exact. Is that close enough?

In some cases with static IP address or business services, the ISP provides IP allocation records to the American Registry for Internet Numbers (www.arin.net), the non-profit organization responsible for managing Internet numbering resources in North America. As an example SBC used to include customer information in those allocation records, but due to privacy concerns now use their own information with a customer reference number. Read about internet anonymity, proxy servers, and how to hide your IP address. To find out what is broadcast about your IP address, there are on-line tools to look up your IP address. As an example, try WhatIsMyIPAddress.com shows your general location complete with a map.

How can someone find out who you are?
A little background first. IP address allocation is handled by The Internet Assigned Numbers Authority (IANA). IANA in turn delegates authority to Regional Internet Registries (RIRs). The RIRs, in turn, further delegate blocks of IP addresses to their customers, which include Internet Service Providers (ISPs) and end-user organizations. Each of the RIRs handles a specific geographic area:
*   ARIN (North America and portions of the Caribbean)
*   AfriNIC (Africa)
*   APNIC (Asia and the Pacific region)
*   LACNIC (Latin America and portions of the Caribbean)
*   RIPE (Europe, Middle East, Central Asia)

Each of these organizations allow lookups to their data. Different ISP's segment their blocks of IP addresses by region and you can see that in the lookup. The lookup provides the name and address of the organization the block of IP addresses was allocated to. The ISP's can name these blocks if they choose. The naming often indicates a geographic location, for example, IRV-CA, aka Irvine, California.

There are many websites where you can look up an IP address. (One good one is WhatIsMyIPAddress.com that provides complete info with a location map – see page 90). In general, start by looking up an IP address with ARIN seeing what geographic location information can be learned from the results. From there do a reverse DNS (rDNS) lookup to see what hostname the ISP provides. A hostname is something like www.example.com, or can be more specific to include regional information.

From there do a trace route which displays the hostnames many of the machines in between two points on the internet. Sometimes the rDNS/hostname of a specific IP address will not reveal any location, but the rDNS/hostname of the machine next along the path will reveal some.

That's about all the information that can be obtained without a subpoena, which is only given and complied with by the internet providers in criminal cases. Your IP address says a lot about you providing your general location, etc. and can be used to identify you personally. It can also be used to track you around the internet to figure out what you are doing, even if you have used other software to prevent your internet history from popping up.

USE A VPN (VIRTUAL PRIVATE NETWORK) SERVICE - GET SECURE INTERNET & HIDDEN IP ADDRESS

Applicable to private individuals (not just businesses), a VPN is a <u>secure</u> way of connecting to a <u>private</u> Local Area Network, using the Internet or any unsecure public network to transport the network data packets privately using encryption.   The VPN uses login authentication to deny access to unauthorized users, and <u>encryption</u> to prevent unauthorized users from reading the private network packets. The VPN can be used to send any kind of network traffic securely including voice, video or data. VPNs are frequently used by companies as a means of allowing their employees to access the company Internet network when they're logging in remotely.

When it comes to free Wi-Fi, often you'll need to sign in which means creating an account. Avoid these places, instead go to Starbucks, Barnes & Noble, and AT&T Wi-Fi with no sign-in, and they don't require anything more than clicking to refresh every couple of hours. Once you're online, however, put a VPN to work for you to help prevent wireless snoopers from seeing what you're doing. <u>Hotspot Shield</u>, a VPN service proxy, will do this and it's free (or pay $ to avoid seeing their ads). Or you could set up a router with VPN support at a remote location and link to it direct providing another hop.

<u>Use your own Virtual Private Network</u>
If you want to encrypt your web activity from home or wherever you go, a virtual private network (VPN) is the best route. There are hundreds of free and paid VPN options online, so it's pretty easy to use a VPN. Not only is the information sent over a VPN encrypted, but depending on which kind you use, it's protected from hackers and potential malware with added layers of security. And because VPNs allow you to log in via a private connection no matter where you are, they've become a favorite work-around tool for travelers who want to stream content from home (since you're logging into a U.S.-based network, you're basically treated like an American wherever you go online).

If you don't want to be tracked thru your IP address, use a VPN service that turns your web surfing into <u>anonymous web browsing</u> using their web-based proxy server software tools. The downside is slight, as all VPN services slightly slow your response time, as there are intermediate proxy servers.

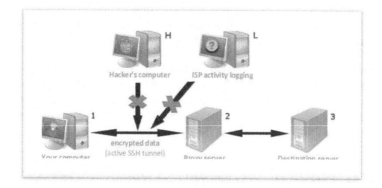

At the very least, use one of the inexpensive VPN services to do your internet searches:

- Anonymizer: $80 one-time, US-based.
- BTGuard
- Cryptohippie: $275/year, at least two intermediate proxy servers, US-based.
- Free Hide IP: $20 one-time; no encryption, ISP hide only.
- IdentityCloaker: $10/mo., encryption included, international-based.
- IPVanish
- IVPN
- MullVad

- PRivatVPN
- PrivateInternetAccess
- Proxify: $10/mo; ISP hide, US-based since 2003.
- PRQ
- Privacy.IO
- Real Hide IP
- Tiger VPN
- Tor: Free but slow, as their onion router bounces your web traffic around through different servers.
- TorGuard; $4 – 10/mo.
- VikingPN; $120/yr.

WEB SPIDERS, WEB CRAWLERS AND SEARCH ENGINES

What are Web Crawlers? Ever wonder how your internet search engine comes back with endless information when you hit the search button for just about any topic? Web crawlers, also known as web spiders, bots, and web roots is the answer to that one. So what is a Web Crawler? It's a program or script that methodically browses the web and gathers information from web pages and indexes all of the information on the page and drops it in a main dispensary.

Web spiders can:
- Provide up-to-date data (If you change a phone number etc.)
- Check links
- Validate HTML code
- Help market search engines and researchers find the most up-to-date info

Web crawlers are crucial for collecting data on the ever expanding web. With so many web pages being added daily, and all of the information that is constantly changing, search engines like Google, Yahoo, and Bing would be all but useless without them. Search engines wouldn't work at all in fact. The dark side, web crawlers can be used for evil as well. Some choose to use web crawlers maliciously - hacking servers or gathering info for spamming.

So, how exactly do they work? When a web crawler visits a page, it reads visible text, hyperlinks, tags, and keyword rich Meta tags. Using the info that it just "read," the web crawler will determine what the web page is about and index it. This can include info about you. So don't have a web site with your contact info.

INTERNET, HOW TO ENABLE "DO NOT TRACK"

Most web browsers have started to implement <u>Do Not Track</u> (DNT) technology which intends to allow users to opt out of third-party web tracking including tracking of information for behavioral advertising. Currently if available, users can only opt-out of tracking by third-party trackers such as web analytic services and advertising networks by setting an opt-out cookie, and the cookie cannot be deleted or else the tracking will start again.

Do Not Track adds a "Do Not Track" request to the HTTP header sent by your browser to the web server that notifies the third-party that you as the <u>user wish not to be tracked as a privacy preference</u>. It instructs the site not to plant any trackers which normally in the kind of tracking cookies on the browser. And mostly important, end-users just need to configure or enable Do Not Track setting once to opt out of all web tracking.

Once enabled, Internet Explorer (IE) will also start to automatically generate a list of blocked third-party operators in the Personalized Tracking Protection List based on third-party contents hosted on the sites you visit. IE monitors if a third party is delivering content to more than a few websites, which indicates it may tracking the web users. As a result, the third party will be added to the block list. Thus the "Do Not Track" in IE does more than simply sending the DNT header to the third-party websites, in that any sites been added to the list will not be "called" at all, which means IE will not send any HTTP requests to the blocked third-party websites, instead of just not allowing them to install trackers locally. In other words, <u>Tracking Protection List</u> is a blunt tool similar to popular <u>Adblock Plus</u> as it not only blocks trackers, but also blocks third-party content serving.

HOW TO FIND AN IP ADDRESS OF AN EMAIL SENDER - IDENTIFY THE ORIGIN OF EMAIL MESSAGES

Internet emails are designed to carry the <u>IP address</u> of the computer from which the email was sent. This IP address is stored in an email header delivered to the recipient along with the message. Email headers can be thought of like envelopes for postal mail. They contain the electronic equivalent of addresses and postmarks that reflect the routing of email from source to destination.

Concealing a Secret Identity?

Finding IP Addresses in Email Headers
Many people have never seen an email header, because modern email clients often hide the headers from view. However, headers are always delivered along with the message contents. Most email clients provide an option to enable display of these headers if desired.

Internet email headers contain several lines of text. Some lines start with the words **Received: from**. Following these words is an IP address, such as in the following fictitious example:

Received: from teela.mit.edu (**65.54.185.39**)
by mail1.aol.com with SMTP; 30 Jun 2014 02:27:02 -0000

These lines of text are automatically inserted by email servers that route the message. If only one "Received: from" line appears in the header, a person can be confident this is the actual IP address of the sender.

Understanding Multiple Received: from Lines
In some situations, multiple "Received: from" lines appear in an email header. This happens when the message passes through multiple email servers. Alternatively, some email spammers will insert additional fake "Received: from" lines into the headers themselves in an attempt to confuse recipients.

To identify the correct IP address when multiple "Received: from" lines are involved requires a small bit of detective work. If no faked information was inserted, the correct IP address is contained in the last "Received: from" line of the header. This is a good simple rule to follow when looking at mail from friends or family.

Understanding Faked Email Headers
If faked header information was inserted by a spammer, different rules must be applied to identify a sender's IP address. The correct IP address will normally not be contained in the last "Received: from" line, because information faked by a sender always appears at the bottom of an email header.

To find the correct address in this case, start from the last "Received: from" line and trace the path taken by the message by traveling up through the header. The "by" (sending) location listed in each "Received" header should match with the "from" (receiving) location listed in the next "Received" header below. Disregard any entries that contain domain names or IP addresses not matching with the rest of the header chain. The last "Received: from" line containing valid information is the one that contains the sender's true address.

Note that many spammers send their emails directly rather than through Internet email servers. In these cases, all "Received: from" header lines except the first one will be faked. The first "Received: from" header line, then will contain the sender's true IP address in this scenario.

WHAT IS IN AN EMAIL FULL HEADER?

An email consists of three vital components: the envelope, the header(s), and the body of the message. The envelope is something that an email user will never see since it is part of the internal process by which an email is routed. The body is the part that we always see as it is the actual content of the message contained in the email. The header(s), the third component of an email, is perhaps a little more difficult to explain, though it is arguably the most interesting part of an email.

Header
In an e-mail, the body (content text) is always preceded by header lines that identify particular routing information of the message, including the sender, recipient, date and subject. Some headers are mandatory, such as the FROM, TO and DATE headers. Others are optional, but very commonly used, such as SUBJECT and CC. Other headers include the sending time stamps and the receiving time stamps of all mail transfer agents that have received and sent the message. In other words, any time a message is transferred from one user to another (i.e. when it is sent or forwarded), the message is date/time stamped by a mail transfer agent (MTA) - a computer program or software agent that facilitates the transfer of email message from one computer to another. This date/time stamp, like FROM, TO, and SUBJECT, becomes one of the many headers that precede the body of an email. An example of a full email header (below) that should always be read from bottom to top.

```
Return-Path: <example_from@dc.edu>
X-SpamCatcher-Score: 1 [X]
Received: from [136.167.40.119] (HELO dc.edu)
    by fe3.dc.edu (CommuniGate Pro SMTP 4.1.8)
    with ESMTP-TLS id 61258719 for example_to@mail.dc.edu; Mon, 23 Aug 2014 11:40:10 -0400
```

Message-ID: <4129F3CA.2020509@dc.edu>
Date: Mon, 23 Aug 2014 11:40:36 -0400
From: Taylor Evans <example_from@dc.edu>
User-Agent: Mozilla/5.0 (Windows; U; Windows NT 5.1; en-US; rv:1.0.1) Gecko/20020823 Netscape/7.0
X-Accept-Language: en-us, en
MIME-Version: 1.0
To: Jon Smith <example_to@mail.dc.edu>
Subject: Business Development Meeting

Fortunately, most of this information is hidden inside the email with only the most relevant or mandatory headers appearing to the user.

Header Characteristics

A single email header has some important characteristics, including perhaps the most important part of an email - this is the KEY:VALUE pairs contained in the header. Looking at the above, you can tell some of the KEY:VALUE pairs used. Here is a breakdown of the most commonly used and viewed headers, and their values:

From: sender's name and email address (IP address here also, but hidden)
To: recipient's name and email address
Date: sent date/time of the email
Subject: whatever text the sender entered in the Subject heading before sending

Headers Provide Routing Information

Besides the most common identifications (from, to, date, subject), email headers also provide information on the route an email takes as it is transferred from one computer to another. As mentioned earlier, mail transfer agents (MTA) facilitate email transfers. When an email is sent from one computer to another it travels through a MTA. Each time an email is sent or forwarded by the MTA, it is stamped with a date, time and recipient. This is why some emails, if they have had several destinations, may have several RECEIVED headers: there have been multiple recipients since the origination of the email. In a way it is much like the same way the post office would route a letter: every time the letter passes through a post office on its route, or if it is forwarded on, it will receive a stamp. In this case the stamp is an email header.

When viewed in their entirety, these multiple recipient headers will look like this in an email:

Received: from tom.bath.dc.uk (**138.38.32.21** ident=yalrla9a1j69szla2ydr)
    by steve.wrath.dc.uk with esmtp (Exim 3.36 #2)id 19OjC3-00064B-00
    for example_to@imaps.bath.dc.uk; Sat, 07 Jun 2014 20:17:35 +0100

Received: from write.example.com (**205.206.231.26**])
    by tom.wrath.dc.uk with esmtp id 19OjBy-0001lb-3V
    for example_to@bath.ac.uk; Sat, 07 Jun 2014 20:17:30 +0100

Received: from master.example.com (lists.example.com **205.206.231.19**])
    by write.example.com (Postfix) with QMQP
    id F11418F2C1; Sat, 7 Jun 2014 12:34:34 -0600 (MDT)

In the example shown above, there are three Received: stamps. Reading from the bottom upwards, you can see who sent the message first, next and last, and you can see when it was done. This is because every MTA that processed the email message added a Received: line to the email's header. These Received: lines provide information on where the message originated and what stops it made (what computers) before reaching its final destination. As the example shows, these Received: lines provide the email and IP address of each sender and recipient. They also provide the date and time of each transfer. The lines also indicate if the email address was part of an email list. It is all this information that is valued by computer programmers and IT department associates when making efforts to track and stop SPAM email messages. And it is this information that arguably makes headers the most important part of an email.

EMAIL - FULL HEADER EXPOSURE OF YOUR IP & LOCATION

Be careful here also, and abandon usage of **all** prior email accounts. Remember most email programs will divulge your IP address and general location. Instead establish a new throwaway email and a new password. It is noteworthy that web-based Google or Yahoo email services do not display your IP in their full headers (because they display their IP addresses of their web proxy centralized servers, which masks your location). So as a golden rule, remember any email sent or received can reveal your IP address and general location thru examination of the full header. Thus beware your email is one of the most notoriously unprotected forms of communication.

See this sample below. If they find out your email name, they can send you an email and thru the full header get your ISP address, that gives them a general area where you are located.

Sample Email Full Header Info

Return-path: <person@email.com>
Received: from mac.com ([10.13.11.252]) by ms031.ma om (Sun Java System Messaging Server 6.2-8.04 (built Feb 28)) with ESMTP id <0JMI007ZN7PETGC0@ms031.mac. n> for person@email.com; Thu, 12 Sep 02:18:50 -0700 (PDT)

Received: from mail.dsis.net (mail.dsis.net [**70.183.59.5**]) by email.com (Xserve/smtpin22/MantshX 4.0) with ESMTP id I79BOnNS000101 for <persTrust FundsTrusemail.com>; 12 Sep 2014 02:18:50 -0700 (PDT)
Received: from [192.168.2.77] (209.239.114.234) by mail.dsis.net with ESMTP (EIMS X 3.3.2) for <person@website.com>; 12 Sep 2014 02:18:50 -0700
Date: 12 Sep 2014 02:18:50 -0700

From: Some Person <sender@email.com>
Subject: Test Email
To: This User <person@email.com>
Message-id: <61086DBD-252B-46D2-A54C-263FE5E02B41@email.com>
MIME-version: 1.0 (Sample Message framework v752.2)
X-Mailer: Sample Mail (2.752.2)

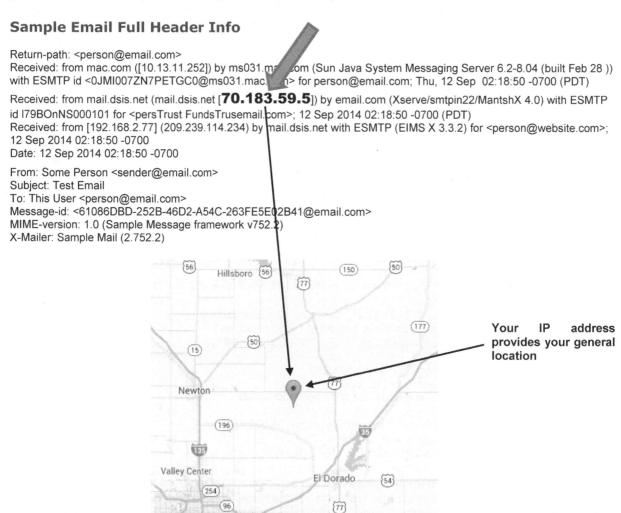

Your IP address provides your general location

This is this IP's address location (near Witchita, Kansas) -
This is how you can be found!

EMAIL ENCRYPTION

It is possible to collect and analyze all plain text emails (that is emails that you have not taken steps to encrypt. To prevent intrusion by unscrupulous identity thieves, use email encryption services.
- <u>PGP</u>: Protect the security of your emails.
- <u>Hushmail</u>: Free – Encrypt your emails as they bounce around the internet.

HOW TO KEEP DATA MINER COMPANIES FROM TRACKING YOU - DO NOT TRACK

These days, it's nearly impossible for the average consumer to expect anonymity online or off — at least not without a significant bit of legwork first. Data brokers companies that specialize in gathering information about consumers and selling it to third parties — have turned the collection and sale of publicly available personal information into a multibillion-dollar industry.

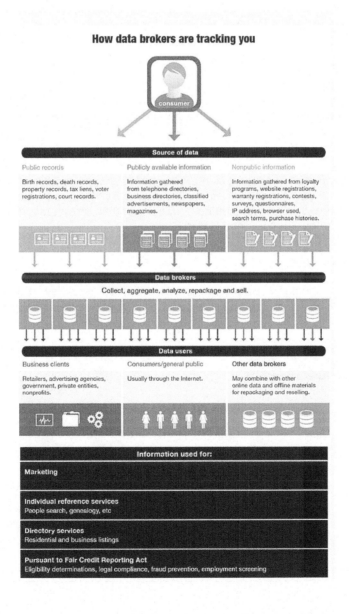

At any given moment, hundreds of these companies are analyzing everything from our ZIP code, income and ethnicity to our taste in music, our driving record and how often we search for funny cat videos. They then take that information, sort us into groups and make a fortune selling it to marketers, employers, charities, government agencies, and other businesses. As to what they do with this information, the details can be hazy. Some data are sold to marketers, but other information can be used to screen prospective employees, run background checks, detect identity theft, or come up with a dubious alternative to traditional credit scores. There's little we know about data tracking and the companies that do it. Neither regulators nor lawmakers have managed to wrap their heads around data brokers quite yet.

First start with your search engine - Cookie Elimination
You may think of your search queries as a private conversation between you and the boundless realm of the Internet, but the opposite is often true. Search engines can and often do keep a log of everything users search for. When you click on links that turn up in search results, the corresponding website will often get a blurb of data telling them which search term led you to their site, along with a log of your computer location and IP address.

To prevent search engine tracking, make a habit of deleting your search history and cookies (the little bits of code that attach themselves to your computer when you browse online). One problem with this strategy is that deleting your cookies can undo all of the shortcuts you've created (such as passwords and specific website preferences).

Then Enable the "Do Not Track" feature
In response to revelations about NSA spying and the federal government's ongoing collection of consumer data, a group of Internet heavyweights including Google and Apple, have rolled out a feature called "Do Not Track." DNT lets consumers opt out of third-party web tracking, and it's one of the simplest ways to keep third-party trackers at bay.

To initiate "Do Not Track" on your browser, go into your browser preferences and look for the tab labeled "Privacy." Check the box to enable the DNT feature. You can get the same protection on your mobile phone by enabling DNT via your browser privacy settings. Most popular browsers offer a DNT option including Google's Chrome, Mozilla Firefox, Explorer and Safari.

Find and block data trackers yourself
If you really want a window into the seedy world of data brokers, all you need to do is download a browser plugin like DisconnectMe or Ghostery. Both tools give you a bird's eye view of the potentially hundreds of data tracking sites that may be "watching you" online at any given moment. Here's a peek below at how many sites are tracking you.

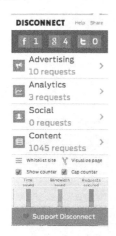

Disconnect Me (Tracker Program)

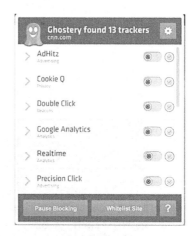

Ghostery (Tracker Program)

PASSWORD MANAGEMENT PRIVACY

No matter how secure your networks, encryption, anti-virus and computer habits, the weakest point of all security systems is the password. Good password habits go a long way but with increasing computing power, it is becoming increasingly easy to break simple passwords by brute force. Using password generators helps you keep track of more passwords and make those passwords more complex to prevent brute force attacks.

- KeePass: Free – Keeps track of all of your passwords, so you only have to remember one password to unlock the secure database where they are stored.
- RoboForm: Enters your passwords automatically. Can be very helpful when strong passwords are long, complicated and easy to misspell.

PHONE/ CELL PHONE

Under no circumstances have a land line phone, as you become listed with your number and name in phone directories and then in internet people search directories and data miner databases. Similarly when opening your cell phone account, don't use your name either; use your business name only. Here is why and how.

First off, one needs to change their cell phone no. and their service provider. The most practical approach is to go with a cell phone from one of the no-contract companies - Virgin Wireless, StraightTalk, Net10, or similar buy-your-own phone, and then list the phone account in the name of your business LLC or corp. Do not use your own name. The area code selected for the no. does not have to be in the area where you give the address from, as they require no proof of address or name (only minimal information) to get a working phone account. You don't have to present or list any personal ID info. Stay away from the big name storefront companies (AT&T, Verizon, etc.)

If you are really hardcore, go buy a pre-paid cell phone and prepaid card. With the pre-paid cell-phone get a phone number that has an area code in another state. Dump that phone number every 6 months, and get a new one different number and a different area code from the original phone. This hardcore approach is not really necessary as cell phone records are privileged, and logs can only be gotten by illegal pretexting.

The next touchy issue is Caller ID when calling family and friends. Remember when calling anybody your number shows up on their caller ID, unless you punch in first "*67" to block the caller ID no. from displaying. If you make one call, that is all that is needed for a PI to locate you, and all your effort and hard work will be thrown out the window. So if you need to get in touch, get a pre-paid cell-phone or card from a different provider and call those you need through the prepaid cell-phone. You can change your phone no. every so often as a precaution.

As a prevention to your phone no. being displayed, one can punch in "*67" before entering the phone number to restrict your phone no. being transmitted when making a call. But if you dial *67 when calling a collection agency or some other sophisticated co. or agency, you may be wasting your time, because these commercial (800 or 900) numbers utilize ANI (Automatic Number Identification) which overrides the *67 block. For these delicate calls, use a pay phone.

There must be a clean break between your old and new phone service and address. The telcos sell your info including cell phones #'s to data mine aggregators, and sites like zabasearch get it from them. My bank sent me an email requesting me to verify my wireless cell phone no. that I had never given to them, but I had listed the phone with my last name and current address. So when you go into a wireless phone store and apply for new wireless service, put a dummy initial in your name to make it more confusing for the aggregators (and to let you know when the telco has sold your name after you've already opted out). Don't give them your social security #, or if you have to, an incorrect one (why not?).

<u>Google Voice</u> will obscure your real phone number, and get you numbers for almost every state, screen/block calls, as well as many other handy things.

TELEPHONE RECORDS PRIVACY

Telephone records are private, and third party access is restricted by a host of state and federal statutes, including the <u>Telephone Records and Privacy Protection Act of 2006</u>. The Act prohibits pretexting to buy, sell or obtain personal phone records, except when conducted by law enforcement or intelligence agencies. The bill threatens up to 10 years in prison to anyone pretending to be someone else, or otherwise employs fraudulent tactics to persuade phone companies to hand over confidential information about their customers.

If an investigator finds out your phone no., they can use legitimate tools to try to identify the telephone carrier and your general location. There are a number of online tools that allow one to input the phone number to determine the carrier and location (e.g. www.phonefinder.com). However, those cannot be completely relied upon for accurate information, particularly in today's age of portable cell phone numbers, Skype, and Voice over Internet Protocols (VoIP).

YOUR MAILING ADDRESS - THE CMRA PMB (Postal Mail Box)

"*What is your address*?" or "*What city do you live in*?" When asked, you simply need to start thinking like a lawyer, so your address (without a second thought) has to be "the address <u>where you receive your mail</u>."

So get a Postal Mail Box (PMB) mailbox within once-a-week driving range of where you live at a small <u>non-franchised</u> or private progressive <u>Commercial Mail Receiving Agency</u> (CMRA) with mail forwarding and email scanning options. 2nd choice is a larger UPS Store (similar to Earth Class Mail). Open this PMB in a business company name using the same PMB address, so as to <u>not</u> use your home address on the USPS Form 1583 (Application for Delivery of Mail thru Agent) application. Use your passport (has no SS #) and some other frivolous ID for the 2 ID pieces with the form they will ask you to fill out.

For ID use your passport - ironically your passport has nine digits - the same as a Social Security number. So add to the confusion, and use your passport ID (not your driver's license) for opening the bank and CMRA accounts.

Next you will need to establish your LLC or corporation using this postal mail box (PMB) mail address, and make that PMB address your mail address for all accounts. It is against Post Office rules to use the words "Post Office Box" or "P.O. Box" in your address unless your box is at the Post Office. The Post Office requires each individual receiving mail through an agent to be properly registered with that agent, and since you have the box key your ID is never checked.

You may wonder what the CMRA advantage is, since CMRAs cost more than a PO Box rental at the USPS.

<u>CMRA Street Address or USPS PO Box</u>?
- A CMRA's street address (provides more services than a USPS PO Box).
- Many merchants will only ship to a street address.
- The advantage (and a big one!) is that CMRAs accept envelopes and packages from courier services such as UPS, FedEx, and DHL. Non-USPS Express carriers (FedEx, UPS, DHL, etc.) will only deliver to a street address (such as a CMRA).
- Many financial institutions require a street address (<u>not</u> a PO box) for a credit card or a merchant account issuance.
- To maintain your hidden residency ... use a private PMB postal mail box. Never fill out on any form your true residential address. Never!!

For hard core privacy advocates, have a nominee open a CMRA mailbox for you, and have all mail delivered in either their name or the name of a company. On a positive note, a CMRA will allow you to use a company name with no proof of existence. Pay your bill in-person with cash.

<u>FedEx and UPS ID Example</u>
How can FedEx or UPS store locate your actual street address, even though the package or letter was addressed to their PO Box? The UPS and FedEx have nationwide databases accessible by their company owned and franchised stores everywhere. Put in a phone number or maybe even just a name, and there you are. So never use your real name or your residential address here either. Here is how it happens:

I went to send something to a friend at a UPS store franchise. Of course, I gave my alternate name and address, and no phone number. I did of course have to give the actual contact info for the person to whom I was shipping the package. The first thing the clerk asked for was the recipient's phone number. They then read off to me the person's name and address. Using my How to Be Invisible (HTBI)-honed curiosity, I asked them how they knew this info. The clerk said, "Oh this person must have used our services before" - but mind you, this person lives thousands of miles away from the store at which I was shipping the item!

Moral of the dilemma - Be very careful of associating your phone no. with your name and actual residence address.

<u>Keep Your Residence Address Private</u>
One option is to become a renter, as tenant names are not public record, and so long as you can find a trustworthy landlord, you should be all right. If you are a real estate property owner, reposition or re-title your property to your LLC or corporation. For your invisible privacy protection the ownership needs to be hidden, possibly thru a New Mexico LLC and the PMB address.

STOP JUNK MAIL AND THE DATA MINERS

The major junk mail harvesters of your name and address are thru:
- Land line telephone
- Creditors (credit cards, mortgage)
- Charitable organizations

<u>To Stop Junk Mail, Start Online</u>
There are ways to stop receiving mail that you don't want, by contacting many of the mass mailing marketing agencies that keep track of you and send junk mail to you. The first step is to eliminate all important mail like bank statements, credit card bills, etc. by switching these account statements to email delivery.

The next step to stop junk mail is where it starts, in your mailbox. Alternatively if a self-addressed envelope is enclosed, mark it, and return the section that shows your name and address crossed out with this separate message:

MOVED. NO FORWARDING ADDRESS.
DELETE THIS NAME AND ADDRESS
FROM YOUR FILES.

If no envelope is enclosed, just return the unopened mail to sender, or reseal it and send it back. For this, you need some blank address stickers and a black marker that makes a thick line. Put the sticker below the first line to cover just the address. Then <u>black out the postal code that looks like a bar code</u>, because otherwise the letter will come back to you. On the blank sticker, use a rubber stamp or print by hand:

MOVED. NO FORWARDING ADDRESS.
RETURN TO SENDER

Notice that many database vendors want personal information to remove you from their database. Further if you read the opt out policy, many hedge and state that removing you is entirely at their discretion. Usually it's a partial removal, as they often have multiple records, followed by your data re-appearing within a year or so. Do not ever give them SS, DOB, age or other non-public information. Just because they don't display, it doesn't mean the info is not entered into their database, which may be shared with others who will. They can change their privacy policy tomorrow, and there isn't a thing you can do about it.

Here is what you can do to combat your predicament:

- Change of Address, Temporary: File a USPS temporary change of address (USPS Form 3575 – Change of Address Order) from the last place you lived to another random new address that is out-of-state, vacant, and undeliverable (Vacant land with an address, no mailbox, and not for sale). Use Google Map's satellite view to identify and select the site. Recommend a vacant not for sale lot as the best choice, as the mail truly is not deliverable. Then three months later change it again to another random undeliverable location. Make certain you can lose all your old mail sent to your new temporary address. This false trail sends your decoy change of addresses back electronically to all those that will be sending mail to you and to who will be looking for you in the future. The major point is these decoy addresses will automatically show up on future credit reports and data miner databases.
- Change of Address with PMB Mail Box, Temporary: Alternatively, rent a Commercial Mail Receiving Agencies (CMRA) postal box in another state (you don't ever have to visit the CMRA site except by email), have all your credit cards and other bills sent there and then forwarded by the CMRA back to you. After 3 months, move the bills back to your original address and abandon the CMRA box. This will add a new and current address to your credit report. Even though you re-pointed your bills back, most credit bureaus will still list the new PMB address as your current one. The best part is they refuse to correct them unless you send in a copy of your driver's license (like that will ever happen).
- Spam: Fill the databases with useless junk. Send in subscription cards for catalogs, coupons and every marketing spam request with new variations on your name including your initial with undeliverable addresses in other parts of the country and so on.
- Donations: Using your full name and initial and a made-up address, donate $5 to each and every candidate, Republican, Democrat, Green, Tea party, Libertarian and every other party there is. All will be dutifully reported and picked up by the data miners.
- End Result: Once there is enough junk in the data miner databases and search engines, anyone searching for you will have a real hard time unwinding it all and figuring out who you really are or where you are.

AVOID THE USPS NATIONAL CHANGE OF ADDRESS (NCOA) DATABASE - Stay Out of It!

Don't file a USPS Form 3575 - Change of Address. Here is why:

National Change of Address (NCOALink) is a secure dataset of approximately 160 million permanent change-of-address (COA) records consisting of the names and addresses of individuals, families and businesses who have filed a change-of-address with the USPS. It is maintained by the United States Postal Service and access to it is licensed to service providers and made available to mass mailers. The National Change of Address Processing Systems has helped direct mailers maintain a clean mailing list for decades.

There are six licenses available including Full Service Providers (48 months) and Limited Service Providers (18 months). The use of NCOALink is required in order to obtain bulk mail rates, as it minimizes the number of UAA (Undeliverable As Addressed) mail pieces saving the mailer money and reducing the USPS's processing of this type of mail.

<u>How It Works</u>
NCOALink is a product of the United States Postal Service, USPS, and is used to provide updated and accurate addresses for individuals, families, and businesses. <u>It will also indicate foreign moves and people who have moved with no forwarding address</u>. The USPS offers licenses for Interface Developers and Interface Distributors and all NCOALink interfaces are certified by the USPS. The addresses in the database are specifically designed to match the USPS requirements. Each entry is matched against other entries to ensure that there are no repeated addresses. The software will update old addresses through the information provided by the postal service. Consumers have the option of changing their address online or filling out the "Change of Address" form at the Post Office when moving.

For mailers who want to update their mailing lists with the most current addresses, they would submit their file to a company that offers the NCOALink service. These can be licensed NCOALink providers or third party companies that submit the files to a licensed NCOALink provider. The NCOALink process also includes CASS (Coding Accuracy Support System), DPV (Delivery Point Validation), LACSLink, and SuiteLink.

USE A PRIVATE CMRA PMB MAILBOX ADDRESS FOR OPENING YOUR BUSINESS LLC/CORP.

One of the most effective ways to protect your privacy is to <u>remain anonymous using a company name and a PMB address</u>. There are many legitimate reasons one may want to hide their actions and whereabouts, an example - victims of stalking. The regulations of Commercial Mail Receiving Agencies (CMRAs, like Mail Boxes Etc.) make it illegal to receive mail anonymously or under an assumed name. Good news, the USPS has promulgated regulations that limit the availability of the names of CMRA customers.

Unlike post offices, CMRAs have convenient business hours and accept deliveries from private carriers such as Federal Express, UPS as well as from the USPS. They also give small enterprises a professional aura, since those businesses can list an address as a number or suite, such as "123 Main St. #401." The acronym <u>"PMB" (Private Mail Box or #)</u> should precede the renter's box number on a separate line in the address, because the USPS state they will not deliver mail to CMRAs without this code, but they do. In actuality the PMB mail is sorted by the PMB operator.

Private mailbox services can be extremely convenient, as most provide copier and other office machines for your use and sell basic office supplies. They will also sign for registered and certified mail and overnight deliveries addressed to your mailbox, so you don't have to sit around all day for fear of missing an important UPS, DHL or FedEx delivery. More importantly if needed, they can forward your mail to your other pickup mailbox address.

The USPS has adopted some regulations regarding their use. If you use a private mailbox service, you should designate your box number either with the number sign "#" (123 Main Street, #456) or the letters "PMB" for "Private Mail Box" (123 Main Street, PMB 456). But you can also use Suite, Apt. or Unit if that is the terminology the CMRA uses.

In the name of fighting mail fraud, the USPS will deliver only to CMRA customers who have filled out a Form 1583 - Application for Delivery of Mail Thru Agent and produced two forms of identification including a photo ID. Copies of each ID will be kept by the CMRA and the USPS. <u>CMRAs must forward this information to the postmaster</u> and maintain copies of it on their premises. The trick is to provide <u>minimal information</u> on the Form 1583. The address you list can be your former residential address. Filling out the paperwork is not a big deal, so don't make it into one. Use your passport for the photo ID, as it has no address.

MONEY – BANKING AND INVESTMENT ACCOUNTS

Do all your banking online (email statements without any mailings) so your privacy is maintained, and the bank will be happy not to mail your statements. This also cuts down on the weekly trips to your PMB box. Banks do a good job of maintaining your privacy as long as you stick to debit cards (no credit cards).

CHECKS

Get them from your bank or order them printed from Checkworks.com or Deluxe.com with only your business LLC/Corp. name, but use your PMB address or <u>no</u> address. The agenda – have minimal ID info on the check with no phone number or residential address listing of yourself. The checks when circulated are run thru bank barcode scanners, and the banks can enter your address into a database (unconfirmed). Don't chance the bank scan, and that database being distributed. Fortunately, the check manufacturers have strict privacy laws, and do not distribute your info to the mass mailers.

CREDIT AND DEBIT CARDS

Credit card application(s) info is traceable thru your credit reports. The credit card application request listing your address immediately shows up on your credit report, and the active credit card usage shows up on an abbreviated credit report or credit header. Cash and debit cards are king, as they don't show up on your credit report or credit header. So stick to debit cards only, but keep one credit card active to maintain your credit rating, and revise the mailing address to your PMB. Don't cancel all your credit cards as 3 – 5 years after doing so, you will be surprised to learn you have <u>no</u> credit rating and have to start over.

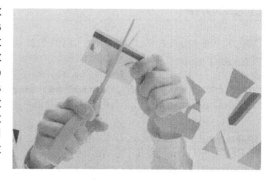

<u>Credit Card Application Forms</u>: While there is little you can do to make references useless on credit that has already been extended, there is a lot you can do to make any future references useless if requested. Look at the wording of the request - "*close relatives not living with you.*" The typical consumer will go through their address book and provide just that - close relatives who are not residing with them - the perfect skip tracer's reference. But the statement "*close relatives not living with you*" can be broken up into some components that will make the references totally useless. Break it up like this:
- "close relatives" - who is closer than your parents?
- "not living" - both deceased
- "not with you" – you are in AZ, one is in FL and the other in NH.

So feel totally safe knowing that you can list both your dead parents as references, with your father buried in Florida and your mother in New Hampshire - and since you live somewhere else, they certainly meet the qualifications. No one will check the references except a future debt collector.

ARE CASHIER'S CHECKS TRACEABLE?

The Federal Reserve designated cashier's checks as a valid mode of currency remuneration. As such, their popularity and use has increased when cash or a personal check is not possible or convenient. Like other non-cash modes of payment, lost or stolen cashier's checks can be tracked. What about the transfer between two of your accounts or you have to open/pay an important bill that could be later traced back to your financial institution holding your money?

<u>Why Cashier's Checks Are Traceable</u>?
Cashier's checks are unique in that when they are purchased, the financial institution <u>programs the payee</u> directly onto the check. Therefore, the most complete data of all the forms is instantly available directly from the issuer. When a cashier's check is lost or stolen, contact the bank with at least the check number and date shown on your receipt, and they can immediately confirm not only that it was you who purchased it, but also that it is a legitimate check and not a forgery.

<u>Tracking Procedures</u>
All financial institutions use some kind of clearing house (organization) or internal department to track and verify payments. This department verifies the cashier's check is still outstanding by searching their data bases for the check number. If not found, the cashier's check has not yet been presented for payment or it hasn't yet cleared the process.

The clearing house can <u>track</u> the cashier's check to its last known point, even if that is only the point of purchase. If the check number appears to still be outstanding, they will periodically recheck the data bases, and if the number doesn't pass through the system, they can issue a stop payment, and the cashier's check can be replaced.

If the cashier's check has been cashed, the purchaser can obtain a copy of the front and back of the check, normally for a fee, and if not cashed by the correct recipient, the bank can initiate action to recoup funds and file criminal charges against the entity who illegally cashed the check.

If the correct recipient cashed the check but doesn't have record of the cashier's check, present a copy of the receipt and a second copy of the front and back of the cancelled or cleared cashier's check. The organization or person can investigate and determine the location of the payment, crediting the purchaser's account.

<u>Can a Lawyer, PI/Asset Searcher Track You and Your $$ Down Thru a Cashier's Check</u>?
This possibility is highly unlikely, but on the random chance they came across one of your cashier's checks, they now would know your financial institution from which the cashier's check originated and the institution location with your money. The important item is they still don't have access to your account number. So next there would have to be a court motion, and then they would need to get a subpoena. At best a cashier's check provides you some protection, but it is not foolproof.

AVOID OFFSHORE BANKING ACCOUNTS

<u>IRS Reporting Tightened with FBAR Regulations</u>: All U.S. taxpayers are required to file an annual reporting form called a <u>Report of Foreign Bank and Financial Accounts</u>, if they have a financial interest in any bank accounts maintained in foreign countries. The failure to file this form annually is a <u>felony</u> and can also subject non-filers to substantial civil penalties. Both the U.S. Justice Dept. and IRS have stated that foreign bank account reporting and compliance is a top enforcement priority. In 2009 the Justice Dept. entered into a Deferred Prosecution Agreement with UBS AG, Switzerland's largest bank, in which UBS agreed that it had assisted thousands of U.S. taxpayers in committing tax evasion by maintaining secret bank accounts in Switzerland for decades. Since that time more than 20 criminal prosecutions have been filed against UBS account holders, bankers, and investment advisors. Also in 2009 the IRS conducted a highly successful amnesty program for holders of undeclared foreign bank accounts, and more than 15,000 individuals came forward and admitted that they had secret bank accounts in Switzerland and other foreign jurisdictions.

In 2011 the IRS initiated their Offshore Voluntary Disclosure Initiative, a second amnesty program designed to encourage U.S. taxpayers with undisclosed foreign bank accounts to come into compliance with U.S. tax laws and avoid possible criminal prosecution. Shortly thereafter, the Treasury Dept. announced new regulations governing foreign bank account reporting, that made substantial changes to the foreign bank account reporting requirements.

The <u>Foreign Account Tax Compliance Act (FATCA)</u> is a 2010 US federal law that requires United States persons including individuals who live outside the US, to report their financial accounts held outside of the US, and requires foreign financial institutions to report to the Internal Revenue Service (IRS) about their U.S. clients. Congress enacted FATCA to make it more difficult for U.S. taxpayers to conceal assets held in offshore accounts and shell corporations, and thus to recoup federal tax revenues.

End summary, don't utilize offshore banking, as the risk and complications <u>far</u> outweigh any benefits.

ACCOUNTS, REGISTRATIONS, SUBSCRIPTIONS, AND MEMBERSHIPS

- Do everything through the name of your new business LLC or corporation without your personal name. Bottom-line, make sure your new LLC/ corporation has no similarities to your name or anything from your past. Use your PMB address as your listed business address.
- For all banking including receiving any type of direct deposit such as retirement money, do it through the LLC or corp. business account you opened.
- Do not register to vote, as this personal information ends up in data miner databases.
- Don't get a library card in your new location.
- Cancel all your retail, grocery store or similar memberships. Get new CVS, Safeway, Costco, or similar cards, and do not register or associate your name, address or phone no. with these new cards.
- Do not transfer or change of address any of your magazine subscriptions. Allow all to lapse with your name and former address, as these end up in data miner databases. If you want to continue, resubscribe in the business name and use the PMB address.
- Don't use your airline frequent flier account; use up your miles.
- Beware that when you request a new service connection for any gas/elec. utilities or TV-internet cable service, they require your name and social security $. They do this to check out your credit reliability, as if the utility bills happen to become unpaid, they get posted to your credit report or credit header report. Your alternative is to post a deposit in lieu of them checking out your credit status, or rent from a private individual with the utilities included.

AVOID SWEEPSTAKES, RAFFLES AND WARRANTIES

When you fill out a sweepstakes or raffle entry to get that free vacation weekend, a product warranty card, the frequent buyer club card to get discounts at the pharmacy or supermarket, or just about anything else, remember you are providing valuable information that will eventually get into a "Data Mine." This is a company database that wants to know literally everything about you. In turn, they will sell this information to whoever wants to purchase it. One of the purchasers will be ultimately a PI/skip tracer coming after you. The eagerness of a Data Mine to accumulate information without regard to its accuracy is its Achilles Heel.

AVOID PUBLIC MESSAGE BOARDS AND ON-LINE CLASSIFIED ADS

Stay off Facebook, Twitter, LinkedIn, Myspace, Instagram or any similar social networks. There has been an increase in the number of divorce cases using social networking evidence during the past five years. Facebook holds the distinction of being the unrivaled leader, with 66% citing it as a <u>primary</u> evidence source, while Myspace follows with 15%, Twitter at 5%, and other choices listed by 14%. So if you don't want to be court blind-sided, don't put anything up on Facebook or any other social network site, you would be ashamed of hearing when the opposing counsel makes their court presentation. One soon-to-be divorcee even had the husband legally served in 2014 with the divorce notice papers thru Facebook, because he could not be found. So if you have existing accounts delete all profile data and close the accounts.

Similarly, beware of your ad posting listings on EBay, Craigslist or similar, as search engines scan the ads, and your phone no. and name can be picked up. Now LinkedIn has joined the fray. The golden rule is never associate your name with your real address or your phone no.

AVOID DATA MINER TRACKING AND BEING FOUND BY A PI OR SKIP TRACER

The Collection Trade conventions are chock-full of seminars and information teaching a skip tracer or private investigator the latest tips, tools, techniques and scams to help locate skipped debtors such as you. With the advent of the Internet, some people are posting ways for people to skip - giving a potential skip some ideas on how to "pull it off." Studying them gives some interesting insights into the age-old cat and mouse game of Skip and Tracer. Some of this advice comes from the skip tracers themselves, who are now being retained to actually help people become skips.

A conversation with a private detective progressed to the following question, "If you were to try to become a Skip, what would you do knowing what you know about how PI/skip tracers work?" Their answer was most revealing:
- The Data Mine eagerness to accumulate information without regard to its accuracy is its Achilles heel. The more erroneous data in your file (about half of what was in mine was simply wrong), the harder it will be for the skip tracer to find the correct information. Since almost all of the information in your file gets there because you put it there, the answer is simple - live your life so that no correct information gets in, and make sure that plenty of incorrect information gets in there. Here's how:
- Whenever you apply for credit, you are asked certain questions all the time. Those questions are: Name, Social Security Number and Address. You want your Data Mine file to be filled with as much incorrect information as possible, but certain things must be given correctly so as to ensure that the incorrect information finds the right file (yours).
- The solution is simple. Always provide your correct name and Social Security Number. You don't have to mess around with this - the Data Mine will do it for you (as they did with mine - with ten different names and two different Social Security Numbers attached to my file, and I did nothing to create that). It's the multiple addressees you will be feeding into the Data Mine with great regularity that will constantly change.

The detective confided that this technique is sometimes used in the Witness Protection Program to throw people who would assassinate witnesses off the track from finding the witness. Obviously the witness is given a new identity. But in our less dramatic circumstance, it is recommended you not take on a false identity. Your name and your Social Security number can remain yours, but your mailing address can change often, and this fact of life is the weakness in the searcher's digital arsenal and your strength.

There is no reason to be concerned that the addresses you choose to bombard the Data Miners with be accurate or even exist. Once again, the system weakness here is that all addresses fed into the Data Mine are presumed to be accurate, and the Data Miners make no effort to verify them. LexisNexis's programs are geared to identify obvious false addresses like Private Mailbox companies (PMB's) or the UPS Store. LocatePLUS is not so programmed. Even so, LexisNexis will still accept the address and merely identify it as "suspect." Nonexistent addresses can be fed into the system ad infinitum. Therefore the following addresses while totally fictitious will be accepted by the Data Mine as true:
- 1352 E 45 Street, New York City (in the middle of the East River)
- 2284 W 84 Street, New York City (in the Hudson River)

- 1313 Mockingbird Lane, Lake Wobegone MN (Street Address of the Munsters, fictitious town made up by Garrison Keilor)
- 135 W 35 Street, Chicago IL (approximately 3rd base at US Cellular Field)
- What was the address of Barbie's house?
- You get the idea...

Addresses can be generated by using a site like Zillow (www.zillow.com), a homes for sale website. Generate them by logging onto Zillow and look for an empty residential lot in another state with an address but no mailbox (no mail delivery possible), and without a For Sale sign on it. The chosen site needs to have no internet link search that pops up when an address search is conducted. Then you will want to go to the USPS website and fill-out an USPS Form 3575 - Change of Address Order form for yourself for 3 months, then do it again for another undeliverable site.

Recommend you download and print the Form 3575 – Change of Address Order and then mail or deliver a paper copy in person to your local post office to change your address for free. It is recommended that you don't submit your address change online, because as part of their confirmation process, you have to incur a USPS $1 fee from your debit/credit card and produce a valid e-mail address. There goes your invisibility. Not so with the paper version that you hand deliver to the USPS.

After changing your address, the U.S. Postal Service will attempt to forward your mail to your new address for up to one year, but beware your mail all goes to the shredder as it will be undeliverable. The address change will not be reported to the three credit bureaus, as the credit bureaus only have your addresses that are reported by your creditors like credit cards, car loans, etc. However just as bad, the change of address will go to the data miner databases.

Do not apply for credit using any of these interim decoy forwarding addresses with your correct name and social security number. Instead rely upon the credit bureaus and the asset searchers finding your new false locations thru the USPS temporary change of addresses. Do this change of address every three months using all different addresses, and the asset searchers will find a mountain of useless information on top of whatever is in your data mine file.

As stated, some of the best and most valuable information an asset searcher can use is provided by you - the person wanting to escape. When you list references on a credit application, keep in mind that the only person who will contact these references is a future bill collector/ asset searcher hired by the lender. That is why the lenders almost universally request relatives - because while friends come and go out of your life, your relatives stay.

DO NOT UTILIZE FALSE IDENTIFICATION DOCUMENTS

Law enforcement agents who work undercover have false I.D.'s supplied by the government. Plan B or escape candidates can also have an alternate set of I.D. documents and learn to travel under an alias, but you'll have to make your own. You would have to learn the tricks of the trade of recognizing, making, and using false I.D., and understand the U.S. identity documents (birth certificates, driver's licenses, Social Security cards, passports, etc. Beware it is a major criminal offense if caught by law enforcement with false ID. So don't go this route.

CHAPTER 8

LLC OR CORP. FORMATION ISSUES

First step, review and select the state you are going to get your LLC or corp. business in, and then get the private PMB postal mail box in the same state. Do not use your residential address. Remember if you are not an active business, your business license (additional fees) does not need to be registered with the state. This initial step is vital as you really just need the LLC or corp.'s Articles of Incorporation generated from the state license and then this vital paperwork is used for the next step of initiating your business account banking.

Your business entity choice will probably be a single member LLC, as it is easier to establish and maintain, and achieves your objective of invisibility. A multi-member LLC or corporation adds complexity that is not necessary.

WHICH STATE?

This arena is really confusing and everyone has advice, most of it well-intended but not to your purpose or gain. Here is why. You initially might want to consider a tax-free state, if your LLC/ corp. is to have income. The most important factor is you will be tracked by your tax returns, both state and federal. So beware!

Remember the most important factors are: 1) the ownership's privacy needs to be totally hidden, 2) no state annual reporting by you, or/and 3) no annual registration fee/ franchise tax to the state. To find out the state annual registration and franchise tax fees, you will need to go to the state site and look for business license fees. This is something you can do yourself by going to the New Mexico governmental site (NewMexico.gov); Also Nolo.com and KeepYourAssets.net provide a lot of useful information. See page 50 for a more detailed state listing of the fee and franchise requirements.

- **New Mexico – Best State – Total Privacy:** The two most important factors – the business ownership (your identity) is totally hidden, and no annual state franchise taxes. NM is the only state with these beneficial factors. Now add safety and obtain your private business PMB postal mail box in the same state with mail forwarding (paid by you), and avoid the state franchise tax from the state you reside in.
- **No State Income Tax:** Seven states (Alaska, Florida, Nevada, South Dakota, Texas, Washington and Wyoming) have no state income tax, which means your pension or your business income won't be taxed. Sounds great, pay no income taxes, but expect the state sales tax for purchases to be higher.
- **Avoid State Franchise Taxes:** States with expensive annual franchise taxes like California, bad news. You may be currently considering either buying a piece of CA real estate or opening a brokerage account with a CA mailing address with your new NM LLC. Although it may be easy to put the loan and the property title in the LLC's name, this innocent decision has a price. According to the CA tax code, owning property in CA is equivalent to doing business in CA. That's the pitfall, of course. By simply listing your LLC address in CA which requires the members' names, addresses, etc., you will be subject to the hefty

$800/year state franchise tax, and this state will come after you aggressively for the money. This is the reason to get your PMB in the same state as the business license avoiding the franchise tax. Watch out for the other states.

OBTAIN A BUSINESS EMPLOYMENT IDENTIFICATION NUMBER (EIN) - THE SS-4 FORM

The second step after your business is legally established, is to get your business EIN number thru a simple IRS on-line filing whereby you get your number. You will need the business EIN when you open the business bank and/or investment, with the intent that the ownership listing and the financial income generated from your investments is reported to the IRS using this EIN number and the business name, and not your social security number. This adds an additional level of protection against an asset search possibly finding your investments when only searching for your social security number. Here is the simple one page form:

Some explanation on the IRS's EIN application jargon when you begin the on-line application:

<u>EIN Form</u>:
Although a single member LLC with no employees does not need an Employment Identification Number (EIN), <u>get one for the business investment reporting to the IRS using your EIN number</u> and protection of your privacy. This is obtained by filing an IRS Form <u>SS-4, Application for Employer Identification Number (EIN)</u>, which can be done online. Beware some states will also require you to obtain a state tax identification number.

<u>Filling out IRS Form SS4 - Question 9(a)</u>:
There is one important point to remember when filing out the Form SS-4 to obtain your tax federal identification number. Question 9a asks you to check the box that best describes the type of entity you are seeking a tax ID number for. The popularity of LLCs is due largely to the fact that they are taxed as a partnership, have limited liability for corporate indebtedness, and have more flexibility than S Corporations.

If your LLC has only <u>one</u> member, you cannot check the "<u>partnership</u>" box, so check the box for "<u>Other</u>" and write next to this box: "<u>disregarded entity</u>." If your LLC is taxed as a multi-member partnership (i.e., so there is no corporate level income tax), you must check the box for "partnership" in response to question 8a. The IRS will accept your classification on the SS-4.

One form issue that may come up when applying for a tax ID EIN number, if you have a private mailbox service and use the term "PMB" to designate your mailbox, the IRS computers are not currently set up to use the number sign (#) only. If you use the # sign on an IRS form, the IRS will disregard your box number entirely, so you must use the term PMB without the # sign. Not a big deal.

On the EIN application line 7b and 9a you will have to give them your Social Security no., there is no alternative. As it shows up on your tax returns, <u>don't dwell on this issue</u>. Just get your EIN as a first step toward your invisibility.

HOW TO FILE YOUR LLC WHEN YOU GET YOUR SS-4 EIN

A LLC limited liability company formed in any US state that generates a profit from its operations must file a federal income tax return and pay a tax on the profits. Here are the four methods of income tax available to an LLC under the Internal Revenue Code that can be setup by a professional or you with some further study and analysis of the options.

- <u>Sole Proprietorship – Single Member LLC</u> **(Typical Filing Status)**
  If the LLC has only one member or only two members who are married and who own their interest in the LLC as community property, the <u>LLC can be taxed as a sole proprietorship</u>. This is the IRS's default method of income tax for a single member LLC. An LLC taxed as a sole proprietorship is treated by the IRS as if it does not exist, as the IRS treats the LLC as a **disregarded entity**. The advantage of the proprietorship of federal income tax is that the LLC does not have to prepare and file a separate tax return. Everything goes on the member's IRS <u>Form 1040, Schedule C</u> (Profit Or Loss From A Business).

- <u>Partnership – Multi-member LLC</u>
  If the LLC has <u>two or more members</u>, it can be taxed as a partnership. This is the IRS default method of tax for every multi-member LLC. An LLC taxed as a partnership must prepare and file a partnership tax return. The LLC then issues each member a K-1 with the member's tax information. The members enter their K-1 information on their IRS Form 1040s.

- C Corporation – Double Taxation Entity – **Not Recommended**
Every LLC has the option to file an election to be taxed under subchapter C of the Internal Revenue Code. This method of tax is commonly called being taxed as a "C corp." or "C corporation." An LLC that elects to be taxed as a C corporation must prepare and file an IRS Form 1120. Do not elect to cause your LLC to be taxed as a C corporation without first consulting with an experienced business tax lawyer or CPA, because this method of taxes can result in two levels of federal income tax. A C corp. is a taxing paying entity. If it has $100 of profit at the end of the year, it must pay the federal income tax on that profit. Corporate tax rates are: 15% on the first $50,000; 25% on the next $25,000; 34% on the next $25,000; 39% on profits over $100,000 up to $335,000. The total tax on the first $100,000 of C corp. profits is $22,250, which is 22.3%. This means $77,750 is left after tax to pay to the members who then pay a second tax. Definitely don't election the "C" corp. option.

- S Corporation - **LLC Alternative with Multi-Members, No Double Taxation**
If the LLC is eligible, the members may file an election with the IRS and cause the LLC to be taxed under subchapter S of the Internal Revenue Code. The general rule is that all of the members of the LLC must be people who are U.S. citizens. The primary reasons LLCs elect to be taxed as an S corporation are: 1. To avoid the double tax applicable to an LLC taxed as a C corporation. 2. To reduce the amount of payroll taxes payable to the members (whether this will apply to your LLC depends on the facts and circumstances of your LLC's situation year to year). An LLC taxed as an S corporation is not an entity that pays tax. The LLC does file a tax return on IRS Form 11020S, but it does not pay federal income tax, as the LLC's profits and losses are passed through to the members pro rata based on the percentage ownership of each member.

What are the Eligibility Requirements for an LLC to be Taxed as an S Corporation?
An LLC may not be taxed as a S corporation unless it meets all of the following requirements set forth in Internal Revenue Code Section 1361: 1. It may not have more than 100 members. 2. It may not have a member that is not an individual (no companies) unless the member is an estate, a trust described in Section 1361(c)(2), or an organization described in Section 1361(c)(6). 3. It may not have a member that is a nonresident alien. 4. It may not have more than one class of membership interests.

Do You Elect Multi-member LLC or a S/C Corporation?
Partnership if your LLC wants to be taxed under the default method, it finalizes that method by filing the appropriate tax return on time. If the LLC wants to be taxed as a C or S corporation, it must file the appropriate form with the IRS per the following: An LLC that desires to be taxed as a C corporation must file an IRS Form 8832. New entities that want to be taxed as a C corporation from the date of formation must file the Form 8832 with the IRS not later than 75 days after formation. An LLC that desires to be taxed as an S corporation must have all members who own an interest in the LLC sign an IRS Form 2553 and file it with the IRS not later than 75 days after formation to be taxed as an S corp. from day one.

This is too complicated; avoid it.

Recommendation – Keep your life simple and cost low, so select a single member/ sole proprietor LLC.

YOUR LLC BUSINESS TAX INCOME REPORTING

If the account holder is a business, the interest, dividends and capital gains earned is business taxable income and is reported as pass-through income to the LLC business owners. The IRS considers business bank account interest as earned passive income that is taxable income to the account holder.

<u>LLC Structure</u>

A limited liability company is a legal structure that does exactly what its name implies. It provides a legal barrier of liability protection between the company's business transactions and the personal <u>assets</u> of the owner or owners. The IRS does not consider the LLC a separate legal entity for purposes of taxation, unless the LLC elects to be treated as a corporation. Instead all income and expense of the LLC flows through to the owner or owners, who then report the net profit or loss on their individual tax returns as either sole proprietorship income or partnership income.

<u>Business Tax ID Number, EIN</u>

To obtain an account using the LLC name, you will need to first obtain a tax ID <u>EIN</u> number by filing the federal SS-4 form. Banks and brokerage houses will use the <u>business EIN tax identification number</u> (not your SS #) to report interest and capital gains/losses earned to the IRS in the business name. If multi-member, it is important to keep LLC money separate from the personal funds of the owner, as co-mingling of business and personal funds may cause loss of the liability protection that the LLC provides.

<u>Tax Reporting of Income</u>

- The single member LLC profit and loss pass through to the <u>sole proprietor</u>, so you as the owner report the business profit or loss on Schedule C (Profit Or Loss From A Business) of your personal federal tax return. You will also need to list your EIN # investments on Schedule D (Capital Gains and Losses) next to your SS # on your business account investments. Don't be alarmed, only the IRS will have this information, and their data bases are not available to any asset search, except those affiliated with child support enforcement.
- If the LLC is a partnership, the partnership issues a K-1 to each partner containing their proportionate share of the profit or loss based on their ownership percentage in the LLC. Each partner then reports their K-1 income on Schedule E (Supplemental Income and Loss) of their personal tax return.

THE DIFFICULTY OF OPENING YOUR BUSINESS BANK ACCOUNT(S)

Here lies the challenge, but it can be done. One has to switch from your social security # basis to your new business LLC or corporation with its Employment Identification No. (EIN #), and finding a small friendly bank to open your business checking/ debit card account will take a little effort. Beware that because of the Patriot Act, this apparent simple task will be more difficult to implement than opening a personal account. The issue will be, your business has no background or existence prior to the opening of this business account. The bank will also question you about documentation with utility bills to prove you have a real business. A big bank like Citibank that is paranoid about the Patriot Act and international money laundering is a waste of time. Also do not do this at the same financial institution you used during your marriage, as it is imperative you find another reputable institution. For your LLC or corp. business account opening, you need your EIN # (obtained thru the SS-4 filing), the LLC Certificate of Authorization, and your passport for identification (no address or social security #). They still require your S. S. # on the application (because of the signature authority and secondarily due to the Patriot Act), but remember the S. S. # is also listed in the EIN application.

When you have all your LLC/corporate information together, go to the bank as a walk-in to open an account. Ask them on the spot what they need and if they give resistance, immediately walk back out. Otherwise sit down and proceed. If it seems workable, have the bank person fill out the business application. Give the person your CMRA postal mail box address for the account, and only use your passport for identification. Do not proceed the way I did, like fill out the business application first, and mail or take it in. Do it on the spot, and have the officer fill out the application for you.

The bank officer opening the account will go online and check either ChexSystems or TeleCheck, both service banks used to search whether or not you have any overdrafts left over from other banks. They will run your business LLC with your name, and there will be no record of any bank account for your new business in any state. You will state, that is why you are opening the business account with that bank, ala ... the cart and the horse. This is the tough part – proving you are a credible business. So intelligently tell the bank financial institution your business purpose. They may need to be persuaded you are a real business with a copy of your payment to a utility or a wireless phone bill with the company name and the address matching the bank application. A copy of your professional license can work if your profession matches the business name, or you have something else to prove you are a viable entity.

Some will even follow-up with a call to your cell phone, so sound professional. Bottom-line, banks and brokerage houses do not facilitate the opening of a business account, so it will take time, and you have to play by their rules. They will check you and your business out under the Patriot Act. Do not deposit any money with the application until your account has been opened (one more reason not to mail in the application).

Under the requirements of the 2003 Patriot Act, all banks must now do an identity check on all new customers. They use "Customer Identification Programs" (CIP) that compare your name, address, date of birth, and other facts to the information contained on your credit report. This identity verification process does not count as a hard inquiry and probably isn't even recorded as a soft inquiry either. Your credit score would not be damaged by that step.

The CIP regulations require institutions to implement reasonable procedures for:
- Verifying the identity of any person seeking to open an account, including a business account.
- Maintaining records of the information used to verify the person's identity, including name, address, and other identifying information.
- Determining whether the person appears on any lists of known or suspected terrorists or terrorist organizations provided to the financial institution by any government agency.

Business owners who have incorporated or formed an LLC are usually able to open a business bank account if listed in ChexSystems. Typically banks do not use ChexSystems when opening a business checking account, however a new trend is emerging, as some banks now run a ChexSystems report not only the business, but also the signors on the account.

In the past sole proprietors were the only businesses that may have been subjected to ChexSytems; but now partnerships, limited liability companies (LLCs) and corporations may be subjected to ChexSystems as well. If the bank does not use ChexSystems for signors on the account, they may pull a credit report. Bank of America is one such bank. While they do not use ChexSystems for business bank accounts, signors on a business account have a personal credit report pulled.

It no longer matters whether you are a sole proprietor, limited liability partnership or corporation. If you have questionable credit, you may not be allowed to open a business account. If you wish to open a business account, corporations and LLCs are required to have an EIN (employer identification number). This number will be used by the banks when opening a business checking account, not a social security number.

Lastly at the business account opening, turn down any offers for a business credit card, as your PMB address shows up on your personal credit report even though it was applied for in your business name (and not you).

So stick with business debit card(s) only, which stay off your credit reports. You will receive a debit card from the institution with both the company name and your name on it. Don't worry about that, but be certain the account has been established in your business name and EIN #, no exceptions. The checks can be formatted any way you want, but keep your name off the checks, and only use the business name and the PMB CMRA address.

Step 2 will be opening a sister brokerage account with your EIN # only for your large investments, thru the same financial institution as your business checking account. The timeline can be 1 – 2 months, as a multi-page application will again be filled out, and you will be asked a lot of questions to see if your business is real. It is tough to get validated for a newly formed business. Recommend spreading your money across two or more institutions using your business name (in case one is found thru an asset search, and a writ of attachment is applied). The trouble will be with your tax-deferred IRA/401K accounts, as they cannot be transferred out of your name. You must first cash out these assets, pay the tax penalty, and then relocate them to your hidden brokerage accounts. Recommendation – keep the IRA accounts intact, but transfer them to a new institution in your name (not the business) where they still cannot be found.

401K/ IRA AND ANNUITY ACCOUNT(S) TRANSFERS

The one exception to maintaining your privacy will occur when you transfer your IRA/401K or annuity investments to a new bank or brokerage house. You will be told that your desire to have the account in your business name and EIN number cannot be done for this investment tax-deferred account opening, as they have to stay in your name with your SS. One way around this stumbling block is to receive a cash out, thus losing the tax deferral and then put the money into the business account, paying taxes on the year of the cash out.

Instead, my recommendation is to move all your tax-deferred money in IRA/401K accounts to another undisclosed bank or investment firm using your name and social security number, your PMB address, and then don't worry about it. When you retire, these tax-deferred accounts should be the 1st ones you start drawing the dollars out of.

Don't be stupid and leave these tax-deferred investments in the same financial institution. Instead in the 1st year after the divorce, transfer them to new undisclosed location. Here is why. Years after the divorce or sooner when the ex runs out of money, they can get a Change in Circumstances (CIC) and a QDRO court order, and get these assets garnished with the account # if they know where they are.

USE YOUR BUSINESS NAME FOR ANY ON-LINE SHOPPING

When filing out business account applications for conducting on-line purchase forms like Amazon, PayPal, Netflix, Costco, etc., or even paying for a travel reservation, only use your business name, business debit card, and your PMB address. Never list your name or residential address. What is most critical is that the purchaser billing address must match the debit card business account address. The business name really does not matter, as the address and zip code must match. If a personal name is required, put the business name as the first name and some acronym for the last name. It does not matter, just fill in the blank. Generally, keep your name and residential address off the internet, any on-line purchases, and out of the hands of the data miners. There are some exceptions when you purchase an airline or cruise ticket, as these items have to utilize your matching ID name with driver's license or passport verification. Chapter 9 explains how your privacy is easily invaded by the data miners.

DO NOT GET A BUSINESS CREDIT CARD FOR YOUR NEW LLC/ CORP.

Now that you've formed your LLC or corp., you might want to establish business credit for your company. But don't do it, as this card application info quickly ends up on your credit report and credit header report with your reported address, allowing it to get into the data miner databases. This is the primary reason to stick with debit cards, to stay off the grid.

Not All Credit is the Same
Here is the 2nd reason.   Once your LLC or corp. is established, you may start receiving all kinds of credit cards solicitations for your business, however this credit card is not business credit. If you read the fine print carefully you will find that you are personally liable on this credit card. This means that if the company doesn't pay the bill, then you will have to. It's crucial for you to know the difference between true "business credit" and business loans that you're personally liable on. True business credit is a loan, line of credit, credit card, etc. to which you owe <u>no</u> personal liability.

CHAPTER 9

HOW TO MINIMIZE YOUR DATA MINER & CREDIT REPORT INFO

HOW YOUR PERSONAL INFO IS OBTAINED

Your personal information — everything from your shopping habits to your health history — can be available to asset searchers, private investigators, lawyers, creditors, employers, landlords, insurers, law enforcement agencies, and of course, criminals. All they need to do is tap into the public and private databases that gather, buy, and sell your vital statistics.

Demand for your personal information has exploded in recent years, and its availability has also raised privacy concerns. When users buy and compile various pieces of information about you, they can paint a very complete picture of your activities.

Whether the data are accurate or not, misinterpretations can lead to higher costs for credit and insurance, or the denial of a job. They can also prevent you from renting an apartment or opening a checking account, and even from returning unwanted merchandise to stores.

Here's what Big Brother, the Credit Reporting agencies and the multiple Data Miners have on you, and how it starts. You need to stop this info trail from being compiled by them and become invisible.

Your Credit History
Credit reports are compiled by the big three credit bureaus: Equifax, Experian, and TransUnion. Each has some 200 million files, which help form the credit scores used to measure your creditworthiness. Almost everything about your use of credit, including amounts borrowed credit lines, opened and closed accounts, application inquiries, and how well you've honored your obligations on mortgages, credit cards, car loans, and other types of credit. Bankruptcies, foreclosures, liens, and collections are also here. Public record information like court judgments might also appear. Other basics include your Social Security number, date of birth, and past addresses.

The federal Fair Credit Reporting Act (FCRA) allows companies to buy your credit information if they are considering transactions with you related to credit, employment, insurance, investing, government licensing, or other legitimate business need. The purpose, in general, is to assess your past financial responsibility, but insurance companies have stretched that to include predicting the likelihood that you will file an insurance claim, based on confidential credit-based scoring models.

Under the FCRA, you're entitled to a free credit report from the big three credit bureaus annually and to dispute errors. To maintain oversight of your credit reports, get one from each credit bureau. Go to www.annualcreditreport.com, the only authorized site for obtaining your free reports.

Federal regulations limit the time that negative information can stay on your report (seven to 10 years) and let you opt out of receiving preapproved credit offers.

Your Insurance Claims

Reports offered by LexisNexis, a data broker in Georgia, are based on claims information reported by insurers to the Comprehensive Loss Underwriting Exchange (CLUE). A-PLUS reports, sold by the Insurance Services Office in Jersey City, N.J., are based on information reported by over 1,400 insurers to the Automobile - Property Loss Underwriting Service. Both companies' reports reveal information about you and your automobile and homeowners insurance loss claims filed with reporting carriers over the past three to seven years.

Insurance companies use your claims history to assess how much of a risk you are, which can affect premiums or coverage eligibility. They can also use the claims history of a given property to determine how much of a risk that home presents. LexisNexis promotes its CLUE reports to home buyers and sellers, warning that a home's past can come back to haunt you in the form of higher premiums for your homeowners insurance.

Since LexisNexis and ISO are consumer reporting agencies as defined by FCRA, you're entitled to one free report a year. In some reports, negative information will remain for up to seven years. Go to *www.*choicetrust.com for information on how to obtain a CLUE report.

Your Health and Drug History

The MIB consumer file database is maintained by the MIB Group, a consortium of 470 U.S. and Canadian companies that sell life, health, disability income, critical illness, and long-term-care insurance. Two other companies, Milliman and Ingenix, compile your prescription drug history from databases maintained by pharmacy chains and prescription benefit managers, and sell IntelliScript and MedPoint reports to insurers.

Information significant to your health or longevity is reported to the MIB database in coded form. It includes medical conditions that you reported on insurance applications for individual (not group) coverage, and test results from medical underwriting exams. Potentially hazardous hobbies and driving records may also be there. Your actual medical records are not reported. The IntelliScript and Med Point reports contain information about the prescription drugs you've used over the last five years, including dosages, refills, and doctors.

When you apply for individual life, health, and similar coverage, you may sign a waiver that lets a prospective insurer check your MIB report, and IntelliScript or MedPoint reports to see if you've omitted significant information.

Your Checking and Saving Accounts

ChexSystems provides information on mishandled checking and saving accounts, a service used by about 80 percent of U.S. banks. TeleCheck assesses the risk of accepting paper checks at 350,000 retailers, financial institutions, grocery stores, and other outlets.

ChexSystems and TeleCheck collect information on mishandled checking accounts, such as overdrawn accounts closed by you or your bank. The reports can include your driver's license number, unpaid amounts, and who was stiffed. The reporting company is not required to remove information unless it's incorrect, but it does have to report any payback. Negative information can stay on your report for five years at ChexSystems and seven years at TeleCheck.

Banks can check mishandling data to decide whether to open a new account for you. Retailers can use TeleCheck to assess the risk of accepting your checks.

ChexSystems is an eFunds check verification service and consumer credit reporting agency like Innovis, Experian, Equifax and TransUnion. While most credit reporting agencies broker data about how a consumer handles credit relationships, ChexSystems provides data related to how a consumer has handled deposit accounts at banking institutions. It is owned by Fidelity National Information Services.

Eighty percent of all commercial banks and credit unions in the United States use ChexSystems as a step in the consumer checking or savings account application process. eFunds claims that their services are used in over 9,000 banks, including over 100,000 individual bank branches in the United States. The ChexSystems products offered by eFunds are DebitBureau, DebitReport, FraudFinder, Identity Theft, ID Verification, ICMS, ProspectChex, QualiFile, and Transaction Monitoring.

A consumer's ChexSystems report typically contains banking irregularities such as check overdrafts, unsatisfied balances, depositing fraudulent checks, or suspicious account handling that other banks have reported in the past five years. The majority of banks using ChexSystems will not open a new deposit account for a customer that has a negative item reported. In 1999 ChexSystems was successfully deemed a consumer reporting agency, and therefore governed by the Fair Credit Reporting Act. Consumers are now able to retrieve a free ChexSystems report annually.

Your Background
LexisNexis is one of the more prominent background-check companies and provides Person Reports. Their reports include a smorgasbord of dirt: auto and homeowner <u>CLUE</u> reports; pre-employment background checks; an "<u>Esteem</u>" report if you ever admitted to or were convicted of shoplifting; results of a national criminal records search; evictions; and public-records search results. Employers, landlords, insurers, governments, and volunteer organizations use background checks to measure the reputation and character of applicants.

Your Rental History
Core Logic <u>SafeRent</u> maintains a landlord-tenant database of 34 million records and a subprime payment history database of 40 million records to screen prospective renters. Another company, Experian <u>RentBureau</u>, includes nearly 6 million records nationwide.

Rent-payment history, references, credit ratings, criminal records, and scores designed to predict an applicant's risk of defaulting on a lease. Landlords who operate multifamily apartment complexes use the information to screen tenants and reduce losses that result when tenants skip out without paying, write bad checks, require an eviction, or cause significant property damage.

Your Utility History (NCTUE)
National Consumer Telecom and Utilities Exchange (NCTUE) is a consumer reporting agency, a subsidiary of Equifax based in Atlanta, that maintains customer data reported by utility service providers that are members of NCTUE. These providers include <u>cellular, local, and long distance phone companies, cable and pay TV services, internet service providers, and electricity, gas, and water utilities</u>. The data includes information about a consumer's account history, unpaid closed accounts and customer service applications. Consumers may obtain their free NCTUE Disclosure Report showing your history.

Your Purchase Returns
The Retail Equation maintains information on merchandise returns made to an undisclosed number of national retailers. Before customers are allowed to return goods, participating stores ask to run their driver's licenses through a reader to check their return history. The database info can include a record of your past returns at participating stores, the purchase prices, and whether or not you had receipts.

Retailers are on the lookout for certain fraudulent and abusive practices, which include returning shoplifted merchandise, "renting" (buying, say, a video camera to use temporarily for a wedding before returning it), and "wardrobing" (buying a dress, then returning it after wearing it). If your pattern of returns at a particular store raises red flags, you might not be able to get your money back the next time you try.

Avoid Product Warranty Registrations

So-called "product registration cards" are one of the more deceptive data collection practices in existence today. Consumers are led to believe that filling out the entire form is necessary to activate the warranty and/or to register the product, whereas they need only save the receipt to do so. The opt-out notices on such cards are vaguely written and hard to read. Consumers are not aware that the majority of such cards are mailed not to the product manufacturer, but to a data aggregation or data miner company such as Equifax. So definitely, never send the warranty cards in.

Mailing Lists - What To Avoid?

This is the Wild West of databases. Two major players are USADATA, which has delivered more than a billion names to over 100,000 companies and InfoUSA, whose databases contain 210 million consumers.

The primary information sold is your name and address. The lists allow salespeople to focus on consumers who are more likely to buy their products. But the real value for buyers comes from prescreening the names by certain characteristics — for example, people known to be affluent, homeowners, mail-order buyers, investors, people who have specific diseases or are disabled, new parents, older people, donors/contributors, and so on. Some companies develop lists of people who have fallen for get-rich-quick scams or investment frauds.

- Bottom-line, don't fill out any surveys or warranty cards.
- Address Change: When you move, stay out of the U.S. Postal Service's National Change of Address database. Do not file a temporary or permanent change of address using USPS Form 3575.
- Phone Lists: Put your phone number on the Federal Trade Commission's *"Do Not Call"* phone registry by going to www.donotcall.gov.
- Stop unsolicited preapproved credit card offers at www.optoutprescreen.com.
- Mailing Lists: To get your name off mailing lists, go to the Direct Marketing Association's consumer Web site at www.dmachoice.org.

DATA MINERS COLLECT YOUR INFO - GOOD LUCK FINDING OUT WHAT THEY KNOW

Every time you use the internet, you leave a huge trail of information in your wake – and it's not just your browser history full of cat videos. Companies called data brokers or data miners are constantly collecting a thousand little nuggets of information behind you, adding them up into a profile of you, and selling the profiles for lots of money. Data brokers still move in mysterious ways, leaving unanswered questions: how are they getting their data? Who's buying it? And perhaps most importantly, can you, the consumer, do anything about it?

Those are the key questions that the US government is trying to find answers to. It turns out though, that the companies that collect mountains of personal information about everyone online are quite hesitant to divulge meaningful information about themselves. The 2013 Senate Commerce Committee recently published a report delving into the details of data mining, but even the United States government had trouble tracking down some of the answers they were looking for. The committee report sought to answer four major questions about data brokers:

- What data about consumers does the data broker industry collect?
- How specific is this data?
- How does the data broker industry obtain consumer data?
- Who buys this data and how is it used?

The data collection companies were cagey at best when it came to revealing how they obtain data and discussing to whom it is sold. The report found data brokers currently operate with minimal transparency and behind a veil of secrecy.

Data brokers typically amass data without direct interaction with consumers, and a number of the queried brokers perpetuate this secrecy by contractually limiting customers from disclosing their data sources. Three of the largest companies – Acxiom, Experian, and Epsilon – to date have been similarly secretive with the Committee with respect to their practices, refusing to identify the specific sources of their data or the customers who purchase it.

The report also adds that the respondent companies' voluntary policies vary widely regarding consumer access and correction rights regarding their own data, with many companies providing virtually no rights for the consumers who are, in this case, the product being sold.

There is no comprehensive list of companies operating as data brokers, and because data brokers operate in the business-to-business world, most of their activities are not covered by existing consumer protection laws.

Being the subject of ever-more-targeted marketing doesn't necessarily sound scary or problematic, but the level of detail that a person's profile can hold is startling. The report cites the now-famous case where Target figured out a girl was pregnant before her own family did, sending coupons to their house. It also raises concerns about price differentials from shopper to shopper, based on profile information.

Acxiom claims it has data on 700 million consumers globally, and another company, Datalogix, claims its information includes almost every US household. Another company provided the committee a list of almost 75,000 different data points it tracks in its system. About the only way not to be a collection of information in a broker's database is to live completely off the grid, never use the internet, and use only cash you earn under the table and keep stuffed under a mattress. Even the paranoid among us are fairly simple to profile at least to a basic level.

The data collection industry naturally feels that voluntary self-regulation is sufficient to treat consumers fairly and make sure data privacy is properly maintained. The Senate report doesn't go as far as saying that voluntary self-regulation doesn't help anyone, but it does point out that opt-out policies and requests for deletion of personal data are essentially toothless in the real world. Opting out of data collection from one company doesn't help a person in the real world, where literally hundreds of other companies are still gathering the same data, and clamoring to sell it.

Ultimately the conclusion drawn in the report is that consumers should expect that data brokers will draw on this data without their permission, and at this time consumers have minimal means of learning or providing input about how data brokers collect, analyze, and sell their information.

DATA MINERS OR DATA BROKERS

Commercial data brokers and consumer reporting agencies have your number - actually make that numbers -- and do a brisk business compiling and selling reports about everything from your health to your wealth. It used to be that LexisNexis was the only legitimate company one could access to seek this kind of information. You had to be a corporate subscriber from a legitimate business, and it was very expensive. Now for a relatively low fee, any anonymous schmoe on the internet can get your entire financial history, everywhere you've lived, all of your relatives, your criminal record, and much more.

These high-tech trash-pickers - names such as Acxiom, Aristotle, ChoiceTrust, Claritas, KnowX, LexisNexis, LocatePLUS, and Pallorium do their homework. They scour public data from courthouse files, property deeds, marriage certificates, and even delve into credit reports, driving records, magazine subscriptions, and product warranty registration cards. Intelius and Acxiom are the two big address and telephone number data aggregators, and are the biggest source for most other websites that share sensitive information on the internet. This information is gathered by these professional search firms. They do not provide credit reports, but they have your credit card info. Bottom-line for the good, the data miners do not have access to your bank accounts or debit card info.

This is an introductory summary as to who the major data miner players are. This is why you need to avoid their databases:

Acxiom - Marketing-focused, not for the public.
Dubbed as the premier source of addresses and telephone numbers for telemarketers and mass mailers, has a reputation of collecting data better than anyone else. Boasts records on millions of Americans including drug test and criminal histories, education data, and the popular "Suspected Terrorist Watchlist" available at a premium price. Claims this data is to help employers weed out untruthful applicants and illegal employees, but often the information is used to create targeted ads by advertisers.

Aristotle - Political Campaign-focused.
For more than a decade, a leader in the field of political data and fundraising and instrumental in convincing the Federal Election Committee to drop its opposition to processing credit card contributions in a way that made it more cost-efficient for candidates – a turning point which helped enable campaigns online fundraising.

Intelius
One of the most sought after background check services out there, and hard to beat when it comes to services for Background Check, People Search, and Criminal Check.

LexisNexis
- One of the largest data aggregators and resellers in the country, as they compile, store, and sell information about virtually every U.S. adult. Its customers include employers, debt collectors, loan officers, media organizations, law offices, law enforcement, among others. A Georgia-based company that sells information in three markets - insurance, business and government, and marketing. They sell: claims history data, motor vehicle records, police records, credit information and modeling services, employment background screenings and drug testing administration services, public record searches, vital record services, credential verification, due diligence info, Uniform Commercial Code searches and filings, DNA identification services, authentication services and people and shareholder locator information searches, print fulfillment, tele services, database and campaign management services.
- Wins the coveted George Orwell award as the company most likely to be watching you right now, as they maintain more than 17 billion records on 220 million people with topics ranging from social security numbers to DNA samples. The majority of their information is sold to the highest bidder

which more often than not happens to be a representative of the US government, a leading American company, or a Nigerian fraud group.

- ChoicePoint, a former large data miner co. was purchased in 2008 by Reed Elsevier (parent corporation of LexisNexis) and disappeared. Had modules for bill collectors and legal professionals.
- LexisNexis Risk Solutions**:** A consumer reporting agency and reseller of credit information, that is compiled and maintained by the three national credit reporting agencies.
- Accurint: A division of LexisNexis for the collection industry with 37 billion data records. See page 119 for sample report.

LocatePLUS

The **leading** public information provider for law enforcement, private investigators, and skip tracing professionals with 30,000 subscribers. The investigative database cross-references millions of records to deliver results in real-time. With no annual contracts, sign up fees, or cancellation fees, is a flexible alternative **($50/mo.)** to expensive private investigation software or other skip tracing tools.

Search Systems

Was the first in 1997 to establish a directory of hard-to-find public record databases with access to over 36,000 databases containing billions of public records. Can access a directory of criminal record databases, verify contractor and professional licenses, check out corporations, property records and business permits, marriage and death records, and much more.

US Search

Founded in 1994, search for people's current addresses, phone numbers, background checks, criminal records and more.

SELF-DIRECTED ASSET SEARCH - CASE EXAMPLE

As an experiment an individual conducted research on themselves, and here is their outcome dialog and the confusion that ensues from all asset searches. From this example one will learn a productive asset search is not easy. In fact any valuable info is really hard to find. So here goes with the searching assessment tools:

I tried to skip trace myself for Stage #1, subscribing to one of the well-advertised online search engine sites. The results were dismal as I could not locate myself using that site. Not a single link or resource would show my current address (which I had been living at for 8 months and I know was on all three Credit Bureaus, as well as the County Recorder and several other sites). In all fairness, I was able to find myself at my previous address, as well as over two dozen people who shared the same name as I do. I do not use a middle initial, so a skip tracer using this tool would not be able to narrow the search down using that information. For an additional fee I could get more information on all these people including myself. To say that this method of skip tracing is useless is an understatement, since the costs and time involved in looking at all the "hits" would have been prohibitive for a skip tracer trying to find their targets quickly and cheaply. This economic fact of life is the skip tracer's Achilles heel.

As a further experiment for Stage #2, a private detective was engaged to use whatever tools a skip tracer would have available to them (meaning no government or law enforcement databases). The detective used two Data Mines companies - LocatePLUS and LexisNexis/ChoicePoint.

While the private detective did in fact locate me thru public information at my present address and indirectly identified my business, and found the fact that I own an airplane, the results weren't all that much better. This is considering the private detective asset search cost was around $400 and took over two hours of their time. For that type of investment to be worthwhile to a PI or a debt skip tracer, the debt amount would have to be huge. Here are the results – this is how the data miners work:

LocatePLUS

Using their service with the search criteria of my name, County and City of residence, LocatePLUS found 7 people who share my name. Close reading of the time lines would show that three had moved to other cities (two in 2005, one in 1996). In my listing there are 5 variations of a prior address, three variations of their incorrect present address and an address in a state I have never lived in. Following my instructions to only zero in on the correct "me," the detail on the correct target revealed an address obsolete by 8 months and a telephone number obsolete by 4 years. The residents at the address consisted of myself, my wife, one of or two sons and someone I never heard of. Another address showed me with a different name and a different spouse, and five other people I never heard of. The address mining went back at least twenty years, including the address of my business in New York - which I had sold fifteen years earlier. Listed at that address was the buyer of my business, his wife, their child and a half a dozen people I never heard of. The residence address in New York (which I left ten years prior) showed eighteen people I never heard of living there. PI/Skip tracer - enjoy yourself - all these leads lead to dead ends.

To their credit, LocatePLUS at least told the PI my gender and race, by pulling up a six year old traffic ticket. This wealth of misinformation and no information cost the PI a $50/mo. subscription.

LexisNexis/ChoicePoint

Works a bit differently - it charges the PI/skip tracer each time they seek more information. The search results yielded 15 names of which none were at my current address and 9 were at my previous address. The reason for this is the way ChoicePoint gives results - it lists each type of hit individually. Information from each of the three Credit Bureaus accounts for three of the 9 hits.

Once the PI/skip tracer zeroes in on a likely target, they are charged additional fees each time they "drill down" to get a better look at the actual information. The detective spent $100 in these "drill down" fees - far above what any skip tracer would spend except on the largest debt or arrears balances. What did the detective get for all this money?

To be fair ChoicePoint did find me, but let's see what they found. It had my current address, but not my telephone number or Social Security number. ChoicePoint truncated the last 4 digits of the Social Security Number, which will create problems for the skip tracer. In more detail …

- Name: My middle initial is either A, H, S or O or I don't have one. ChoicePoint also blended my professional designation (EA) onto my last name, and adding to the confusion had my older son's name listed as mine also.
- Social Security Number: Take your pick - mine or my son's, as we both share each other's. Keep in mind I have never done anything that would blend my son's credit file into mine. We do not share the same first or middle name, and I have not cosigned nor have any joint accounts with him. Making the issue even more cloudy, two other people's names come in sharing both our Social Security.
- Address: Correct for 25 years, along with the same addresses LocatePLUS had me in states I have never lived in.
- Telephone Number: Had my correct number, but listed to my business name (which it is not).
- Real Estate Transactions: Had the full details of the sale of my prior home and purchase of my current one.
- Pilot's License: Found it, but did not find my airplane.
- Business Affiliations: Four out of nine were mine.
- Relatives: Found my father who died seven years earlier. It also found his wife (who I have not seen or spoken to in over 20 years), my wife, both our sons, someone who I presume is my stepsister who I have never met and my brother (but at an address he has not lived at in over 15 years). Not particularly useful since my immediate family and I share the same address.
- Neighbors: At my current address, provided the names, addresses and phone numbers of six people who I have never met. At my immediate past address there were six names and phone numbers, only one of whom I know.

DATA MINER REPORT - *(LEXISNEXIS ACCURINT) (Not a Credit Report)*

SAMPLE
Comprehensive Report

Date: 11/28/15

LexisNexis Accurint

Subject Information

Name: **WILLIAM DOE**
Date of Birth: **4/11/1955**
Age: **59**
SSN: 444-44-xxxx issued in **Ohio** between **1962** and **1972**
Others Associated with SSN: none

AKAs (Names Associated with Subject)

DOE, WILLIAM A
DOE, BILL
DOE, W A

Indicators

Bankruptcy: **Yes**
Property: **Yes**
Corporate Affiliations: **Yes**

Address Summary:

123 MAIN ST DAYTON, OH 45440, MONTGOMERY COUNTY (Oct 2003 - Apr 2014)
Average Age: **45**   Median Household Income: **$136,658**   Median Home Value: **$416,200**   Avg. Years of Education: **19**

200 ELM ST DAYTON, OH 45429, MONTGOMERY COUNTY (Jun 1999 - Oct 2003)
Average Age: **34**   Median Household Income: **$19,167**   Median Home Value: **$67,600**   Aveg. Years of Education: **11**

Summary:
Bankruptcies:
 1 Found
Liens and Judgments:
 2 Found
UCC Filings:
 None Found
Phones Plus
 None Found
People at Work:
 1 Found
Address(es) Found:
 1 Verified and 0 Non-Verified Found
Possible Properties Owned:
 1 Found
Watercraft:
 None Found
FAA Aircrafts:
 None Found
Florida Accidents:
 None Found
Professional Licenses:
 None Found
Voter Registration:
 1 Found
Possible Associates:
 5 Found
Possible Relatives:
 1st Degree - 2 Found
 2nd Degree - 1 Found
 3rd Degree - None Found
Neighbors:
 1st Neighborhood - 7 Found

Bankruptcies:
UNITED STATES BANKRUPTCY COURT, NORTHERN DISTRICT OF OKLAHOMA - TULSA
Petitioner: DOE WILLIAM A
Case Name: In Re DOE WILLIAM A
Case Number: 000XXXX
Filing Date: 04/11/2000
Type: CHAPTER 7 FILING (NEW/REOPEN)
Status: Dismissed

Liens and Judgments:
Jurisdiction: OH UCC RECORD
Secured Parties: WILLIAM DOE
Debtor(s): 123 COMPANY INC
Type: INITIAL FILING
Filing Date: 09/07/1999
Filing Number: 0000000

UCC Filings:
[None Found]

Phones Plus:
[None Found]

People at Work:
Name: WILLIAM DOE
Title: ICE CREAM SCOOPER
SSN: 444-44-XXXX
Company: COOKIE DOE & CREEM
Address: 6543 CENTER DRIVE, DAYTON, OH 45401
Phone:
Dates: May 14, 2000 - Mar 18, 2008
Confidence: High

Address Summary:
123 MAIN ST DAYTON, OH 45440, MONTGOMERY COUNTY (Oct 2003 - Apr 2008)
200 ELM ST DAYTON, OH 45429, MONTGOMERY COUNTY (Jun 1999 - Oct 2003)
345 MAPLE DR FLETCHER, NC 34512, HENDERSON COUNTY (Jan 1999 - Jun 1999)
654 MARTIN LUTHER KING DR #200 CORPUS CHRISTI, TX 78412, NUECES CO. (Jun 1999 - Oct 2003)

Previous And Non-Verified Address(es):
WILLIAM DOE - 123 MAIN ST, DAYTON, OH, 45440, MONTGOMERY CO. (Oct 2003 - Apr 2008)
Property Ownership Information for this Address
Property:
Parcel Number - 11-11-11-111-111
Owner Name 1 - DOE, WILLIAM
Address - 123 MAIN ST, DAYTON, OH, 45440, MONTGOMERY COUNTY
Owner's Address - 123 MAIN ST, DAYTON, OH, 45440, MONTGOMERY COUNTY
Land Usage - GENERAL RESIDENTIAL
City Transfer Tax - $1,387.50
County Transfer Tax - $203.50
Total Transfer Tax - $1,591.00
Sale Date - 01/14/2003
Sale Price - $166,000
Sellers Name 1 - AARDVARK, ANAKIN
Seller's Address - 123 MAIN ST, NEW YORK NY 12345-1234
Brief Description - SHELBYVILLE COUNTY LAZY LAKE
Loan Amount - $136,000
Loan Type - FANNIE PAC
Data Source – B
Neighborhood Profile (2010 Census)
Average Age: 45
Median Household Income: $136,658
Median Owner Occupied Home Value: $416,200
Average Years of Education: 19

Possible Properties Owned by Subject:
Address: OH
State: OH
County/FIPS: MONTGOMERY

Seller: SMITH, JOHN A SMITH, SUSAN M
Assessor's Parcel Number: NXX-XXX-XX-0021
Sale Date: 11/21/1995
Sale Price: $189,600
City Transfer Tax - $1,387.50
County Transfer Tax - $203.50
Total Transfer Tax - $1,591.00
Title Company: ABC TITLE CO

Watercraft:
None Found

FAA Aircraft:
None Found

Florida Accidents:
None Found

Professional License(s):
None Found

Voter Registration:
DOE, WILLIAM A
123 MAIN ST
DAYTON, OH 45440-1234
COUNTY: MONTGOMERY
DOB: 03/XX/1944
Registration Number: 1 5544332
Registration Date: 08/07/1991
Party Affiliation: DEMOCRATIC

Possible Associates:
123 INVESTMENTS, INC, 123 MAIN ST, DAYTON, OH 45440
ABC, INC, 123 MAIN ST, DAYTON, OH 45440
COOKIE DOE & CREEM , 6543 CENTER DR, DAYTON, OH 45401
HAPPY ABC PRODUCTIONS , 645 MARTIN LUTHER KING DR #200, CORPUS CHRISTI, TX 78412
XYZ ENTERPRISES , 200 MAIN ST, TULSA, OK 74137

Possible Relative Summary: *(Click on name to link to more details - No Charge)*
SHEILA DOE, Age 62
HALLE DOE, Age 48
TAYLOR DOE, Age 38
WILLIAM DOE, JR, Age 33

Possible Relatives:
SHEILA DOE   DOB: 01/01/1946 Age: 62; 123 MAIN ST, DAYTON, OH, 45440 MONTGOMERY CO. (Feb 2003 - Feb 2012)
HALLE DOE   DOB: 07/12/1960 Age: 48; 123 MAIN ST, DAYTON, OH, 45440 MONTGOMERY CO. (Feb 2003 - Feb 2011)

Neighbors:
EDWIN SMITH, 115 MAIN ST, DAYTON, OH, 45440 (Oct 1999 - Apr 2012)
JOHN HARMAN, 121 MAIN ST, DAYTON, OH, 45440 (Mar 1990 - Jun 2011)
JANET WHITE, 122 MAIN ST, DAYTON, OH, 45440 (Jan 1989 - Apr 2012)
JOSEPH BROWN, 128 MAIN ST, DAYTON, OH, 45440 (Jul 1999 - Apr 2012)

DO NOT TRACK - HOW TO PROTECT YOUR ONLINE PRIVACY AND STOP THE DATA MINERS

These days whenever you look at a web page, you can be accidentally sharing a lot of personal data. As has been well reported in the media, web pages frequently store little files on your computer – "cookies" – which then report back when you visit the webpage next time around. You can set your browser to delete 1st and 3rd party cookies, but the problem doesn't end there. The internet cannot work without your computer sharing its IP address with the server of the web page – it has to know where to send the page requested. These IP addresses can be and are stored by servers with data about what IP requests were made. Over the last few years, public concern about the privacy implications of this data mining has been growing.

We tend to see the problem as an individual matter. We tell ourselves that so long as we are careful not to reveal too much about ourselves, we won't get caught revealing too much. If only it were that simple. Your internet browser gives out lots of information about the machine you are using with your IP address and location, and over time this information is capable by use of clever data miner algorithms that generate a fingerprint about your web browsing. The commercial industry which profits from this information gathering is called "data mining." Data miners collect both personal information and information about the collective behavior about certain demographic groups. They buy and sell this information. We've all been mined.

In the USA a campaign has begun which aims to frustrate the worst excesses of the data mining industry. It's called <u>Do Not Track</u>. This is what the campaign says about itself. Do Not Track is a technology and policy proposal that enables users to opt out of tracking by websites they do not visit, including analytics services, advertising networks, and social platforms. At present, few of these third parties offer a reliable method for opting to track out, and tools for blocking the data-gathering are neither user-friendly nor comprehensive. Much like the popular Do Not Call registry, Do Not Track provides users with a single, simple, persistent choice to opt out of third-party web tracking. You can enable the Do Not Track technology for the three browsers: Firefox, Safari and Internet Explorer. There's a lot more information at <u>Do Not Track</u>'s website.

CREDIT REPORT BUREAUS

There are three main credit report bureaus that keep *consumer credit information files:*

- *Equifax*
- Experian
- TransUnion

The Fair Credit Reporting Act (FCRA) is a federal law that regulates credit-reporting bureaus and prohibits inaccurate or obsolete information from being reported in credit files.

<u>Free Annual Credit Report</u>
Under federal law, you can get a free copy of your credit report from each of the three bureaus, every year. Order your report online at www.annualcreditreport.com. When ordering your credit report, you'll need to supply the credit bureaus with some information to identify you including:

- Full Name
- Current address
- Social Security number
- Date of birth

<u>How long does information stays on your credit report</u>?
The law governs how long information stays on your credit report. Information about accounts you have paid off will remain on your credit report even after you have finished paying them. The good news is that well-managed accounts stay on for <u>10 years</u> after they are paid off or closed, showing potential lenders that you handled your finances responsibly. Negative information, however (such as child support non-payment, late credit card payments or abandoned accounts) will stay on your credit report on for up to <u>7 years</u>. If you declare bankruptcy, it will stay on your credit report for up to <u>10 years</u>.

CREDIT REPORT SAMPLE

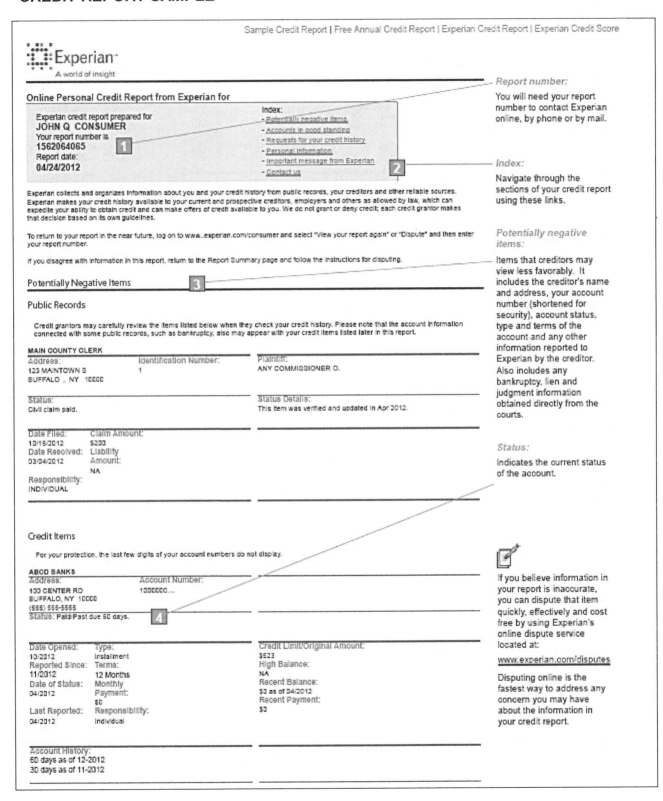

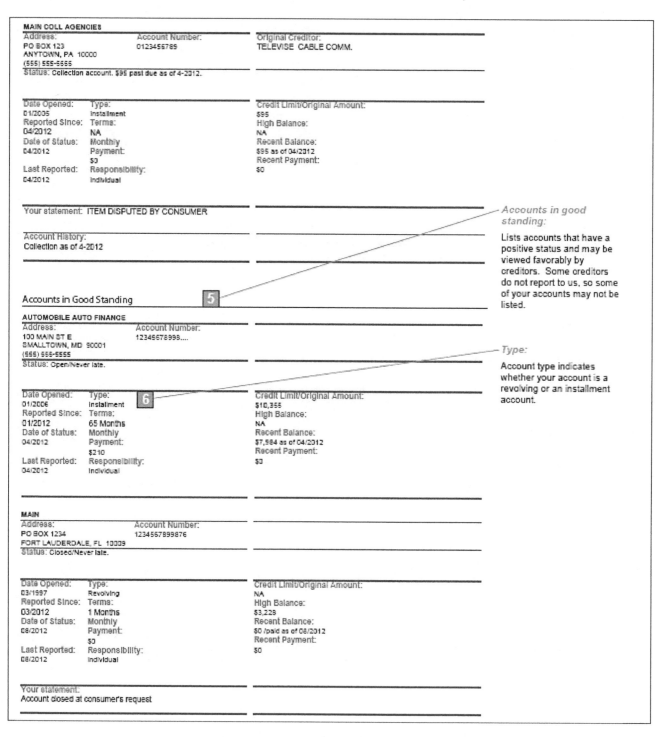

MAIN COLL AGENCIES

Address:	Account Number:	Original Creditor:
PO BOX 123	0123456789	TELEVISE CABLE COMM.
ANYTOWN, PA 10000		
(555) 555-5555		

Status: Collection account. $95 past due as of 4-2012.

Date Opened:	Type:	Credit Limit/Original Amount:
01/2005	Installment	$95
Reported Since:	Terms:	High Balance:
04/2012	NA	NA
Date of Status:	Monthly	Recent Balance:
04/2012	Payment:	$95 as of 04/2012
	$0	Recent Payment:
Last Reported:	Responsibility:	$0
04/2012	Individual	

Your statement: ITEM DISPUTED BY CONSUMER

Account History:
Collection as of 4-2012

Accounts in Good Standing   5

Accounts in good standing:

Lists accounts that have a positive status and may be viewed favorably by creditors. Some creditors do not report to us, so some of your accounts may not be listed.

AUTOMOBILE AUTO FINANCE

Address:	Account Number:	
100 MAIN ST E	12345678999....	
SMALLTOWN, MD 90001		
(555) 555-5555		

Status: Open/Never late.

Date Opened:	Type:	Credit Limit/Original Amount:
01/2006	Installment 6	$10,355
Reported Since:	Terms:	High Balance:
01/2012	65 Months	NA
Date of Status:	Monthly	Recent Balance:
04/2012	Payment:	$7,984 as of 04/2012
	$210	Recent Payment:
Last Reported:	Responsibility:	$0
04/2012	Individual	

Type:

Account type indicates whether your account is a revolving or an installment account.

MAIN

Address:	Account Number:	
PO BOX 1234	1234567899876	
FORT LAUDERDALE, FL 10009		

Status: Closed/Never late.

Date Opened:	Type:	Credit Limit/Original Amount:
03/1997	Revolving	NA
Reported Since:	Terms:	High Balance:
03/2012	1 Months	$3,228
Date of Status:	Monthly	Recent Balance:
08/2012	Payment:	$0 /paid as of 08/2012
	$0	Recent Payment:
Last Reported:	Responsibility:	$0
08/2012	Individual	

Your statement:
Account closed at consumer's request

Requests for Your Credit History

Requests Viewed By Others

We make your credit history available to your current and prospective creditors and employers as allowed by law. Personal data about you may be made available to companies whose products and services may interest you.

The section below lists all who have requested in the recent past to review your credit history as a result of actions involving you, such as the completion of a credit application or the transfer of an account to a collection agency, application for insurance, mortgage or loan application, etc. Creditors may view these requests when evaluating your creditworthiness.

HOMESALE REALTY CO

Address:	Date of Request:
2000 S MAINROAD BLVD STE	07/16/2012
ANYTOWN CA 11111	
(555) 555-5555	

Comments:
Real estate loan on behalf of 3903 MERCHANTS EXPRESS M. This inquiry is scheduled to continue on record until 9-2014.

M & T BANK

Address:	Date of Request:
PO BOX 100	02/23/2006
BUFFALO NY 10000	
(555) 555-5555	

Comments:
Permissible purpose. This inquiry is scheduled to continue on record until 3-2008.

WESTERN FUNDING INC

Address:	Date of Request:
191 W MAIN AVE STE 100	01/25/2006
INTOWN CA 10000	
(555) 555-5555	

Comments:
Permissible purpose. This inquiry is scheduled to continue on record until 2-2008.

Requests Viewed Only By You

The section below lists all who have a permissible purpose by law and have requested in the recent past to review your information. You may not have initiated these requests, so you may not recognize each source. We offer information about you to those with a permissible purpose, for example, to:

- other creditors who want to offer you preapproved credit;
- an employer who wishes to extend an offer of employment;
- a potential investor in assessing the risk of a current obligation;
- Experian or other credit reporting agencies to process a report for you;
- your existing creditors to monitor your credit activity (date listed may reflect only the most recent request).

We report these requests only to you as a record of activities. We do not provide this information to other creditors who evaluate your creditworthiness.

MAIN BANK USA

Address:	Date of Request:
1 MAIN CTR AA 11	08/10/2012
BUFFALO NY 14203	

MYTOWN BANK

Address:	Date of Request:
PO BOX 825	08/05/2005
MYTOWN DE 10000	
(555) 555-5555	

INTOWN DATA CORPS

Address:	Date of Request:
2000 S MAINTOWN BLVD STE	07/16/2005
INTOWN CO 11111	
(555) 555-5555	

Requests for your credit history:

Also called "inquiries," requests for your credit history are logged on your report whenever anyone reviews your credit information. There are two types of inquiries.

i.
Inquiries resulting from a transaction initiated by you. These include inquiries from your applications for credit, insurance, housing or other loans. They also include transfer of an account to a collection agency. Creditors may view these items when evaluating your creditworthiness.

ii.
Inquiries resulting from transactions you may not have initiated but that are allowed under the FCRA. These include preapproved offers, as well as for employment, investment review, account monitoring by existing creditors, and requests by you for your own report. These items are shown only to you and have no impact on your creditworthiness or risk scores.

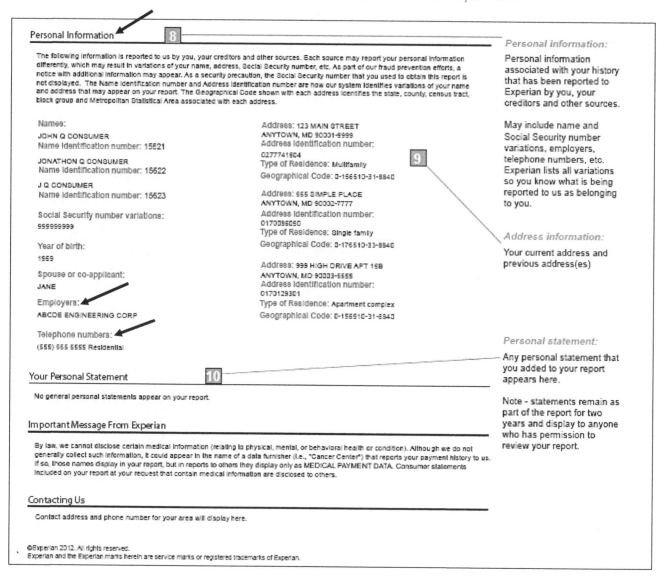

CREDIT HEADER REPORTS AND YOUR PRIVACY

A credit header is abbreviated information in a credit report that gives basic info about the person to whom the credit report applies. A credit header includes identifying information from a credit report such as name, variations of names, current and prior address, phone number, date of birth, sex, and Social Security Number. Note the abbreviated credit header report is modified, so it does not contain your account numbers.

Credit headers are used for target marketing, and are sold in bulk by the credit reporting agencies (CRAs), and can be purchased online. These marketing/data mine companies buy credit header data from the three credit reporting agencies (CRAs - Experian, Equifax, and Trans Union), each of which maintains credit histories on more than 180 million Americans. The credit header data elements include name, aliases, birthdate, Social Security number, current and previous addresses, and phone number (including unlisted numbers that individuals have unwittingly provided to their banks and creditors). Other information is added such as public records data from local, state, and federal agencies - for example, property holdings, motor vehicle records from those states that sell it, voter registration data (again from those states that do not restrict its use), professional license information, UCC filings, and more.

Credit information can be used to access private information, particularly financial information, but the information in a credit header is not generally private in and of itself. The Social Security Number, generally regarded as the most sensitive of the information in a credit header, is used in hundreds of different ways by business and government.

Credit headers came into use after the Federal Trade Commission (FTC) changed its definition of a credit report, in the course of settling a case against TRW (now Experian). At that time the FTC allowed the CRAs to treat headers as "above the line" information and to sell it with no legal protections for the individual. The reasoning was that this information did not relate to credit, and thus should not be considered part of the credit report.

Specifically information in the header or top most portion of the consumer credit report was once not considered to be derived from financial information, because it did not include banking information, credit accounts or financial profiles, per se.

That changed in 2002 when the Court of Appeals for the District of Columbia affirmed rulings in TransUnion v. FTC (2002), the IRSG were unsuccessful in both lawsuits against the FTC that were filed in their efforts to overturn GLBA privacy and in IRSG vs. FTC (2001) when both TransUnion, one of the top three consumer reporting agencies, attempted to have certain data (i.e. credit header information) excluded from the Financial Privacy Rule and the Safeguards Rule.

CAN THEY RUN A CREDIT CHECK OR CREDIT HEADER ON YOU?

For a number of legal and privacy reasons, an individual or a company cannot get a copy of another person's credit report without their permission. The federal Fair Credit Reporting Act (FCRA) specifies under what circumstances a credit report can be obtained and by whom.

Access to credit reports is restricted to businesses with a specific credit debt focused need, and to consumers who request their own report. You may get another person's report if you have power of attorney or are the executor of an estate, or with permission. Limitations on allowing individuals to get the credit reports of other people exist to prevent potential fraud and identity theft risks, along with other uses that would simply be inappropriate. Anyone who obtains a copy of someone else's credit report under false pretenses can be fined substantially and jailed for up to a year.

Only businesses or individuals with a "permissible purpose" can access your credit report. "Permissible purpose" is defined in Section 604 of the Fair Credit Reporting Act (FCRA), and examples of permissible purpose include:
- Accessing a credit report in connection with a credit transaction involving the consumer,
- For a business transaction initiated by a consumer, such as a credit card application.
- For the underwriting of insurance involving the consumer,
- In connection with determining eligibility for a license or government benefit.

Federal law allows potential employers to view a modified version of a potential employee's credit report for employment purposes, which is sometimes referred to as a credit header. The main reason employers may request a modified credit report is to get an indication of a potential employee's personal integrity and honesty. The potential employee's management of financial obligations is considered an indication of integrity and honesty. However, employers must obtain the potential employee's written consent prior to conducting this inquiry. A modified credit report omits account numbers for protection and privacy.

Under the Fair Credit Reporting Act or FCRA, employers must get an employee's written consent before seeking that employee's credit report. Many employers routinely include a request for such consent in their employment applications. If they decide not to hire or promote someone based on information in the credit report, if requested they must give the person a copy of the report and tell them of their right to challenge the report under the FCRA. Some states have more stringent rules limiting the use of credit reports.

CREDIT INQUIRIES – HARD AND SOFT

There are two types of credit inquiries, hard and soft.

A <u>hard</u> inquiry is a credit inquiry pulled for the purpose of obtaining <u>credit</u> for things such as a home, auto or personal loan. Landlord and tenant screening services that utilize credit inquiries are also considered hard inquiries.

A <u>soft</u> inquiry is a credit inquiry requested for <u>informational</u> purposes. If you request your own credit through a legitimate site such as AnnualCreditReport.com, this is considered a soft inquiry and does not deduct points off your score. Additionally, creditors whom you currently do business with can pull a soft inquiry to do an account review and evaluate your current credit worthiness. Offers for pre-approved credit are not counted as hard inquiries. Credit inquiries for insurance and employment also fall into this category, as they are not made for the purpose of granting you credit. When potential lenders check your credit report, they will not see the soft inquiries. Instead, they will see hard inquiries only.

<u>How Many Points Can Be Deducted For A Credit Inquiry</u>?
Each "hard" credit inquiry (meaning the consumer has applied for some form of credit, prompting the creditor to check the credit report or score) that is counted normally subtracts no more than five points from a person's score. Hard inquiries count for 10% of your credit score. While they remain on your credit report for two years, they only impact your credit score for one year.

WHEN OPENING NEW SAVING & CHECKING ACCOUNTS - DO BANKS PLACE HARD OR SOFT INQUIRIES ON YOUR CREDIT REPORT?

Many banks now do <u>hard</u> inquiries against your credit report just to open a checking or savings account. Many other institutions are satisfied with a <u>soft</u> inquiry. Given that soft inquiries get an institution the information they need, why must some institutions damage your credit report with a hard inquiry? It seems unfair that your credit score declines when you are lending your money to the bank.

Banks typically review <u>ChexSystems</u>, an agency that provides info on mishandled checking and savings accounts, and sometimes your credit report data during the process of determining if a customer qualifies to open a new account. This is a separate step from the identity verification. This generally is a soft inquiry but could be recorded as a <u>hard</u> inquiry. Under FCRA regulations, the bank has to have a permissible purpose such as "intending to use the information in connection with a credit transaction involving the consumer" in order to pull a credit report and must obtain the consumer's consent first. A hard inquiry like this could cause a small credit score ding. Some banks check credit reports, and this counts as a <u>hard</u> inquiry; this can show up on your credit report or credit header.

So beware, as your banking institution with your general location could be revealed on your credit report, before garnishment and lien. See the sample on the next page.

ChexSystems Report Sample   (Note your bank address is listed)

ChexSystems^{SM} Report

Receipt Time: 11:22:45   Response Time: 11:22:46
Transaction Tracking Identifier: 02029393499999:38911:TGFUX008_P1:

Consumer
First Consumer Chex Systems^{SM} Response

Closure Information
Paid Closure Quantity: 000   Unpaid Closure Quantity: 001   Consumer Dispute Quantity: 000

Reported Closure
JOHN J CONSUMER
123 ANYSTREET ANYCITY ST 12345
Reported Government Number: 000000000   Closure Reported Date: 08/28/2001

Closure Reasons
Code: A   Text: NON-SUFFICIENT FUNDS(NSF) ACTIVITY
Category Code: 03   Category Text: ACCOUNT ABUSE

Reporting Customer
ACME BANK ,
123456 ANYSTREET ANYCITY ST 12345

SSN Validation
Valid Government Number Text: BECAME AVAILABLE FOR ISSUANCE IN 1983 IN GA SSN:Y
No Previous Inquiries

RENTAL APPLICATIONS - AVOID A CREDIT HARD INQUIRY

Apartment Hunting

You likely will apply at a number of properties when you go apartment hunting, but beware! This apartment hunting can show up on your credit reports. So be very careful in your rental search and about the info you provide. If conducted within a two-week period, credit agencies typically will consider all the credit report requests as one <u>hard</u> inquiry. So it is useful to have your credit report on hand during your apartment search. Leasing agents still may require you to allow them to get their own copy, but if there is anything on your credit that might disqualify you, the leasing agent knows beforehand, and this eliminates their separate inquiry.

Credit Inquiries

The leasing agent will ask for authorization to check your <u>credit report</u> whenever you submit an application for an apartment. When your credit report is checked, a <u>hard</u> inquiry is performed. Hard inquiries have a negative effect, although minimal, on your credit score. Such inquiries occur whenever you put in an application for new credit. Conversely, a <u>soft</u> inquiry has no effect on your credit score and does not show up when your credit report is reviewed. Viewing your own credit score or companies offering you credit without you requesting it, are examples of soft inquiries.

Credit Checks

The landlord or the landlord's agent will probably use your rental application to check your credit history and past landlord-tenant relations. The landlord may obtain your credit report from a credit reporting agency to help them decide whether to rent to you.

Some credit reporting agencies called <u>tenant screening services</u>, collect and sell information on tenants. This information may include whether tenants paid their rent on time, whether they damaged previous rental units, whether they were the subject of an unlawful detainer lawsuit, and whether landlords considered them good or bad tenants. The landlord may use this information to make a final decision on whether to rent to you. A landlord usually doesn't have to give you a reason for refusing to rent to you.

Recommendation

Rent thru a private party (not a big apartment complex) and avoid large complexes that will do a hard check on your credit. Avoid the possibility that an asset searcher with 3rd party access to the credit bureau databases, could find your rental application inquiry and learn your general location.

Sample Rental Tenant Screening Report - *This is nearly equivalent to a Credit Report*

UTILITY SERVICE APPLICATIONS & THEIR BILL NON-PAYMENT REPORTING TO CREDIT BUREAUS

Unless you are moving into a home or apartment where someone else is paying your water, electric or gas bill, (for example, an apartment where utilities are included), you will need to apply for these utility services. The same for some term contract cell phone services. You can apply on the phone, online, or in person, but applying for utility services is applying for credit. Like other creditors, utility companies ask for information like your Social Security number so they can check your credit history, particularly your utility payment history. A good credit history makes it easier for you to get services; a poor credit history can make it more difficult.

Paying a Deposit
If you are a new utility customer or if you have a poor payment history, the utility company may require you to pay a deposit or get a letter from someone who agrees to pay your bill if you don't. This is called a letter of guarantee.

If you don't pay your utility bill, can that go on your credit report?
Yes. Like other creditors, the utility company can send your account to a collection agency. The collection agency then reports you to the credit bureau, and then the unpaid debt becomes part of your credit report. The irony of utility bills and other credit-like payments such as cellular telephone bills, is that if you don't pay the bill the negative information will become part of your credit report. But if you always pay on time, the positive information typically isn't reported, and so it doesn't help your credit history either.

EXERCISE CAUTION WHEN PURCHASING LARGE $$ ITEMS – CREDIT REPORTING

Can car dealers use your driver's license to access your credit report?
Considering all the time we spend fretting about protecting our Social Security numbers, this may come as a shock. Your SSN isn't necessary for a car salesperson to surreptitiously peek at your credit report. They have the technological ability to unlock your file using only the information on your driver's license, and this credit inquiry shows up on your credit report, even when purchasing in all cash with no credit involved. So be wary of these proceedings.

An auto dealership checking a consumer's credit through TransUnion is not required to have the individual's social security number (SSN) to submit the request. Does the dealer need your permission to do that? The dealer does not need permission; rather it needs only certify a permissible purpose (such as extension of credit).

Equifax told us the same thing about the ability to get your credit report without your SSN, but stressed that anyone who pulls your file must get your permission to do so. Experian did not respond to the query. TransUnion prefers to get the SSN, because it more reliably helps locate your exact credit file, but it's not absolutely necessary. The credit report access keys on the license are your name, address, and date of birth, all of which are essentially public information. The driver's license number itself is not relevant, since the credit bureaus don't use that as an identifier.

Car dealers commonly ask for and photocopy your driver's license before they'll let you take one of their cars out for a test drive. If you encounter this situation and are worried that your privacy may be compromised, explicitly tell the salesperson that you are not authorizing use of your license to pull your credit report. Under the federal Fair Credit Reporting Act, a car dealer must always get your permission to look at your credit report. They can get that permission in writing - when you sign a release or a loan application - or by implication without your signature, if there is a legitimate business need.

<u>If I take a test drive, does that give the auto dealer a right to get a credit report on you</u>?
A request to test drive a vehicle does not indicate an intent to initiate the purchase or lease of the vehicle. Accordingly if you ask to test drive a vehicle, the dealer must obtain <u>written</u> permission from you before obtaining a credit report.

<u>If you pay for your car with a personal check, does this give the dealer the right to get a credit report on you</u>?
Yes.

<u>If you want to pay for your car with cash, can the dealer request a credit report</u>?
No, there is not a permissible purpose for doing so.

What does that mean? According to the FTC, simply shopping around, checking deals, and even taking test drives does not constitute a legitimate business need by itself. Rather, it's only when you've gone further along into an obvious purchase transaction that your actions qualify as business that possibly involves a need to check your credit. Only in those circumstances where it is clear both to the consumer and to the dealer that the consumer is actually initiating the purchase or lease of a specific vehicle and in addition, the dealer has a legitimate business need for consumer report information, may the dealer obtain a credit report without written permission.

<u>Recommendation</u>
Buy a car thru a private party with no on-line advertising, and avoid the potential for a credit check with a hard inquiry giving up your location.

INVESTIGATIVE CONSUMER REPORTS AND BACKGROUND CHECKS - FOR EMPLOYMENT, INSURANCE AND RENTAL HOUSING

How does an investigative consumer report or background check differ from a credit report? Some credit reporting agencies and investigation companies compile what is known as "investigative consumer reports." Such reports are defined under the Fair Credit Reporting Act (FCRA) as a consumer report or portion thereof in which information on a consumer's character, general reputation, personal characteristics, or mode of living is obtained through personal interviews with neighbors, friends, or associates.

An <u>investigative consumer report</u> is normally used in limited circumstances including employment background checks, insurance, and rental housing decisions. An investigative consumer report does not contain information about your credit record that is obtained directly from a creditor or from you. For example, an investigative consumer report should not contain information about a late payment. This type of report cannot be used to grant credit. Because the information in these reports is so detailed and may be sensitive, FCRA imposes stricter regulations on CRAs that compile investigative reports.

Federal law requires the requester of an investigative consumer report for employment purposes to obtain permission to conduct the report. An exception would be, for example, if an employee were being investigated for possible criminal activity. If the information obtained in the report is used by the employer to make a negative hiring decision, the employer must give the applicant a copy of the report. You have the same rights to correct and dispute inaccurate information in an investigative report as you have in a credit report.

An <u>employment background check</u> often includes a copy of your credit report, as the three major credit reporting agencies (Experian, TransUnion, and Equifax) provide a modified version of the credit report called an "employment report." An employment report includes information about your credit-payment history and other credit habits from which current or potential employers might draw conclusions about you. An employment report provides everything a standard credit report would provide, however it doesn't include your credit score or date of birth. <u>Nor</u> does it place an "inquiry" on your credit file that may be seen by a company looking to issue you credit.

CAN A PRIVATE INVESTIGATOR GET YOUR CREDIT REPORT?

One of the most frequently asked questions that a private investigator typically receives is, "Can you get a credit report?"

The short answer to this inquiry is "maybe yes, some can with special access," as a few investigators can legally obtain a subject's credit profile report. However there are a few important caveats to consider before asking the question:

Caveat #1 – They must have an "Official" signed release from You, the subject
The first requirement is that they must have a signed authorization or waiver from the subject of the inquiry to obtain their credit report. Due to enhanced federal privacy laws, there are <u>no</u> (legal) means to obtain a subject's credit report unless they have a signed release. Regardless of what "loopholes" another rogue investigator may inform you, there is truly no legal way around it.

Caveat #2 – They must have a "Permissible" business purpose
Access to a subject's credit report is governed by the Fair Credit Report Act (FCRA) which was initially enacted in 1970 and has been amended to address heightened privacy laws. Sweeping and substantial amendments to the FCRA were made in the Consumer Credit Reporting Reform Act of 1996 that further limited access to information contained in a consumer credit report through a set of "permissible purposes" that would later be adopted by the Driver's Privacy Protection Act (DPPA) and the Gramm Leach Bliley Act (GLBA). These federal statutes limit the use of a credit report to certain "permissible purposes" such as a person acting in a fiduciary or representative capacity, for employment screening, or a "legitimate" business need on behalf of the consumer. However, beware a court can order or subpoena your report for arrears enforcement purposes.

So how does a private investigator typically obtain a credit report?
Most can't directly. A few private investigators act as <u>third-party source investigators</u> for credit reporting agencies and have a <u>direct</u> link to obtain a subject's credit report. A direct link is also available only to collection agency investigators, and if they become a paid subscriber of Lexis Nexis Accurint, a data miner company. However the report info is available to PI's thru the International Research Bureau (IRB – a data miner and not a consumer reporting agency), who resell the Accurint data. The end result is most investigators have to utilize <u>outside sources</u> to obtain the information through legitimate third parties, and cannot directly obtain your credit report. Another method if there are significant arrears involved, a PI or asset searcher could thru a lawyer get a court to subpoena your credit report.

Does obtaining a person's credit report affect their credit score?
Whenever a potential creditor (bank, lending institution, utility company, etc.) obtains a person's credit report as part of a lending decision, their score is ultimately negatively affected as a "<u>hard</u> inquiry." However when a subject's credit report is requested by a potential employer or landlord, it is considered a "<u>soft</u> inquiry" which does not have a negative effect on the credit score.

BANK CHECK SCANNERS RECORD YOUR NAME AND ADDRESS - LOW OR NO RISK

Banks and financial institutions scan checks through a check scanner, and create a manageable database system that includes your info listed on your checks including your name and address.

So how does a check scanner work? A check scanner utilizes magnetic ink character recognition (MICR) to read the data on a check. Basically, this MICR technology reads the MICR line on the check, which includes such data as the check number, bank number, and routing number. The check scanner also reads non-MICR information such as the person's name and address, phone number, and check number. The scanner then takes this information and saves it to either a file or clipboard. In essence, the scanner has just created a database of information of customers who pay by check.

Fortunately banks regard your privacy at a very high level, and do not share your info with the data miners or credit bureaus.

USPS MAIL ISOLATION CONTROL AND TRACKING (MICT and MLOCR) - SCANNING OF MAILED ADDRESS LABELS – Criminal Only

Mail Isolation Control and Tracking (MICT) is an imaging system employed by the United States Postal Service (USPS) that takes photographs of the exterior of every piece of paper mail that is processed in the United States. The Postmaster General has stated that the system is primarily used for mail sorting, though it also enables the USPS to retroactively track mail correspondence at the request of law enforcement. It was created in the aftermath of the 2001 anthrax attacks that killed five people, including two postal workers. The automated mail tracking program was created so that the Postal Service could more easily track hazardous substances and keep people safe.

In 2013 the Federal Bureau of Investigation (FBI) revealed MICT when discussing the Bureau's investigation of ricin-laced letters sent to U.S. President Barack Obama and New York City mayor Michael Bloomberg. The FBI stated in a criminal complaint that the program was used to narrow its investigation to Shannon Richardson. The U.S. Postmaster General also confirmed the existence of this program in 2013.

In confirming the existence of MICT, the USPS stated they do not maintain a massive centralized database of the letter images. The images are taken at more than 200 mail processing centers around the country, and that each scanning machine at the processing centers only keeps images of the letters it scans. The images are retained for a week to 30 days and then destroyed.

MICT can be compared to the mass surveillance of the National Security Agency (NSA), revealed in 2013 by Edward Snowden. Basically the USPS is doing the same thing as the NSA programs, collecting the information on the outside of your mail, the metadata of names, addresses, return addresses and postmark locations, which gives the government a pretty good map of your contacts, even if they aren't reading the contents.

A former FBI agent said, "It's a treasure trove of information. Looking at just the outside of letters and other mail, I can see who you bank with, who you communicate with — all kinds of useful information that gives investigators leads that they can then follow up on with a subpoena." The program can be easily abused because it's so easy to use, and you don't have to go through a judge to get the information. You just fill out a form. Law Enforcement Officers (LEOs) are required to submit "Mail Cover Request Forms." Since 2005, there have been a whopping <u>75,315</u> Mail Cover Letters, processing notes and responses requested by local law enforcement and federal agencies.

USPS MAIL COVER - LAW ENFORCEMENT SURVEILLANCE REQUEST – *Criminal Only*

<u>Mail Cover</u> is a law enforcement investigative technique in which the United States Postal Service acting at the request of a law enforcement agency, records information from the outside of letters and parcels before they are delivered, and then sends the information to the agency that requested it. The Postal Service grants mail cover surveillance requests for about 30 days and may extend them for up to 120 days. Since 2001, the Postal Service has been effectively conducting mail covers on all American postal mail as part of the Mail Isolation Control and Tracking (MICT) program.

Mail covers can be requested to investigate criminal activity or to protect national security. On average the Postal Service grants 15,000 to 20,000 criminal activity requests each year; It rarely denies a request.

BANK AND MEDICAL RECORDS - PRIVATE OR NOT?

One receives a lot of mailings from your bank and medical insurers about their Notice of Privacy Practices. Read the fine print, and it states they have the right to use and will disclose your information responding to court orders, legal investigations, or to report to credit bureaus (unpaid bills). Later on, it will state they do this "for law enforcement purposes as required by law." So does this include private investigators who could be snooping and trying to find you?

According to the Association of Certified Fraud Examiners manual, the <u>Right to Financial Privacy Act</u> prohibits financial institutions from disclosing bank records or account information about individual customers to governmental agencies without: 1) the customer's consent, 2) a court order, 3) subpoena, 4) search warrant, or 5) other formal demand with limited exceptions.

The Right to Financial Privacy Act of 1978 protects the confidentiality of personal financial records by creating a statutory Fourth Amendment protection for bank records. Generally, the Act requires that federal government agencies provide individuals with a notice and an opportunity to object before a bank or other specified institution can disclose personal financial information to a federal government agency, often for law enforcement purposes.

The Act states that "no Government authority may have access to or obtain copies of, or the information contained in the financial records of any customer from a financial institution, unless the financial records are reasonably described," and the <u>customer authorizes access</u>, and there is;

1. an appropriate administrative subpoena or summons;
2. a qualified search warrant;
3. an appropriate judicial subpoena; or
4. an appropriate written request from an authorized government authority.

The Act requires that the requesting federal government agency provide the customer with advance notice of the requested disclosure from the financial institution, thus giving the customer opportunity to challenge the government's access to the records before the disclosure takes place. The government agency must serve the customer with a copy of its request or order, or mail a copy to the customer on or before the date which it serves the order or delivers or mails the request to the financial institution maintaining the records. The customer then has 10 days from the date of services, or 14 days from the date of mailing, to challenge the requested disclosure.

The Act only governs disclosures to the federal government, its officers, agents, agencies, and departments. It does not govern private businesses or state or local government. Furthermore, the law specifies which financial institutions fall under the statute's requirements.

Even though the statute is limited in scope and only applies to demands specifically by Federal government agencies, most financial institutions will not release information without one of the above listed authorizations. Even with law enforcement agencies, the most effective way to get bank records or account information is with the customer's consent.

There are many private investigators who claim that they have the ability to obtain bank records, account information, account details and other financial information. While they claim this to be true, the fact of the matter remains – obtaining banking or financial details without specific authority is against federal and state statutes.

<u>How can a "rogue" investigator get your bank or medical records</u>?
The two most common ways that investigators obtain your records or account information is through a source in the industry or through pretexting. Although pretexting does have legitimate and legal uses, the use of pretexting to obtain financial information about another person is protected under the <u>Gramm-Leach Bliley Act</u> passed in 1999, which imposed strict penalties for individuals who obtain information about a third party account through pretext or deceit.

<u>Word of Caution</u>
One may think, "if I hire an investigator to get banking records, it's the investigator's problem, not the person that hired them." Consider this though – if you are ever asked to testify as to how the information was obtained, not only will the evidence be thrown out, but there may be legal implications against you and the investigator.

CHAPTER 10

WHO WILL COME AFTER YOU FOR THE $$

FIRST LAWYERS, THEN PRIVATE INVESTIGATORS, SKIP TRACERS, OR PROFESSIONAL SPOUSAL SUPPORT COLLECTION FIRMS

Lawyers

After your arrears start accumulating, an ex-spouse will typically begin by requesting their lawyer to pursue you and your assets. The lawyer will usually follow thru within their arena of court expertise and obtain a new judgment and garnishment order against you, but beyond that, most don't have the inclination or the desire to pursue you and your money further. This may not seem noble, but most lawyers have little or no experience outside their courtroom-based arena. They may initially attempt to purse the assets listed in the divorce proceeding, and might even have a new asset search performed, but when it shows nothing, what do they do? After some more time passage the client will typically find the lawyer doesn't want to perform or get involved in the detailed bloodhound work to track you down. So the ex-spouse defers to the next line of legal beavers to come after you. All of this takes a lot of time, effort and money.

Private Investigators vs. Skip Tracers

Among private investigators, a "skip trace" is the act of finding a missing person, and refers to "tracing" a person who has "skipped" town. The first thing skip tracing brings to mind is bounty hunting, finding someone who has fled bail. In a broader sense, skip tracing is commonly used to find anyone who has defaulted on a debt which could be alimony or child support payments. The client could be a business owed the debt, a collection agency, or the ex-spouse seeking alimony or child-support arrears who has hired a professional collection agency that utilize PI's and skip tracers.

Skip tracing is used by law enforcement to find suspects or witnesses in criminal actions and by attorneys in civil actions to locate persons of interest to the case. Private consumers hire private investigators and skip tracers for reasons such as locating an ex-spouse or a parent defaulting on child support or alimony.

A PI/skip tracer is hired to find people. Will they hire a Private Investigator or a Skip Tracer to find you? PI's have legal authority; Skip Tracers have none. PI's can also do basic skip tracing work, but they are more expensive than hiring a skip tracer.

In some situations, a skip tracer can get the information wanted for much less than what a PI would have to charge. If they need to research your bank account number, a cheating spouse, a bail jumper, or for anything else, they will need to hire a state-licensed PI.

If your ex-spouse hires a judgment enforcer, a repossession company, or a collection agency to locate your assets or income stream to collect a debt such as arrears, they may not need a licensed PI, as they can save money if they hire a lower cost skip tracer.

Skip tracing is legal when it does not involve performing video surveillance and spying on you, or using false pretenses to find your specific banking information. It is perfectly legal to find out information for their own legitimate purposes. As an example, a repossession company is allowed to spy on a debtor for the purpose of repossessing their vehicle without being a licensed PI. However if they need someone to actually spy on an ex-spouse or a company, they need a PI.

A legitimate judgment enforcer, repossession company, or a collection agency can hire a PI/skip tracer to find you or your asset stream, with the <u>exception</u> of your specific banking information.

PI/skip tracers are able to locate you using various methods including the internet and by talking to your relatives/friends, etc. They can also purchase data miner reports on you, and your credit report only if they are involved in the collection activities of that card. Of course much of their information is obtained by careful and limited lying, which for skip tracing purposes is called <u>pretexting</u>. A large amount of skip tracing is done using deceptive pretexts, but this means skip tracers <u>cannot</u> obtain a bank account number legally. If done properly, pretexting is legal, but they can't pretend to be a law enforcement officer either.

Most skip tracers do not work for original judgment creditors, as they only work for judgment enforcers, collection agencies, and repossession companies. Most charge fees upfront, and one must pay even if the skip tracer produces no useful information. There is at least one company that charges judgment enforcers on a contingency basis, as they only charge if the judgment enforcer is able to recover a profitable payment from you, the debtor.

Contingency skip tracers work continuously with a judgment enforcer, gathering research on the debtor or their assets until the judgment enforcer is able to seize assets. They will look for you on the Internet using Data Miner company information, a phone book, and public records readily available from the Department of Motor Vehicles, or courthouses. They also use paid services to find you, such as hiring a private investigator to go door-to-door at your last known neighborhood and place of employment.

The <u>Fair Debt Collections Act</u> governs the limits of skip tracers and collections procedures, with Section 803 of the Act allowing a skip tracer to obtain the debtor's <u>employment</u> and <u>residence</u> information. A skip tracer must stay within legal boundaries when searching for a person. Harassment of a debtor and unfair actions violate the Fair Debt Collections Act, which may lead to legal action against the skip tracer.

In reality if they attempt to call you at a former listed no., your number should be disconnected. They may also write and should get the returned mailing, "Return to sender address unknown." Now it's time for them to send the claim out to a professional collection agency, who will take the job along with <u>30 – 50%</u> of what they collect (ouch). A month goes by, two months and nothing from the collection agency. Most collection agencies will only replicate the skip tracer's actions, hoping that the letters of suit, etc. will frighten you the debtor - it does not.

As no one took the time to determine if the phone number was real or active, the mail drop address or a former address only a front, and the trail for you goes dead.

Professional Spousal Support Judgment Collection Firms
Last resort, professional judgment collection firms for a 30 – 50% collection fee may utilize combinations of lawyers, PI's and skip tracers to come after you for the money.

PRETEXTING - WHY THEY COME AFTER YOU?

There is a 1999 law, the <u>Gramm-Leach-Bliley</u> Act, that supposedly stops individuals from locating assets, and states that an individual cannot pretext a bank or a financial institution. This law put the asset searching community in a frenzy, and some companies have yet to change the ways in how they locate assets.

Some private investigators or skip tracers will still invest $250 and <u>mail a copy of the judgment to 500 banks and</u> <u>brokerage companies or institutions</u> that surround the subject's place of employment or home. It is a bet as to how many are still out there, and the odds are in their favor for a hit. If that does not work, they can have your trash pulled for old statements (only if they know where you live). There are many ways to locate your assets, so you need to learn quickly that protection should be a part of your personal and business planning.

Head to the local bookstore and watch people reading books about offshore banking, hiding assets or how to disappear. It's usually your typical middle-aged guy dreaming about a new life, with their eyes lighting up at the thought of leaving all their troubles behind. They are reading all those great stories about beach-front living, escaping into oblivion, hiding assets, and not paying taxes. However, not one of those books shares the flip-side. These books don't tell you about the skip-tracer, private investigator or judgment collector who sits in their office and is paid to find people who did what you are dreaming of.

They do it because there is an adrenaline rush, as they get to bill their client and make money. If your name comes across their desk and the money is right, you are the hunt. They will spend their day finding your mistakes, be it through the data miner company info combined with the utility company, the cable TV company, the dentist's receptionist, or that call from your sister. Usually they find you because of the little mistakes you make before departing or while basking in the sun.

You may have questions that can range from - how to get a new passport, a birth certificate and a driver's license. It is repeatedly expressed new identities do not work. If you have ever been finger printed or left behind some hint of your existence, you have a hard time escaping it.

Here are the usual mistakes when escaping or starting a new life: The woman from Denver who called her doctor asking for her medical records to be shipped to Tahiti. A gentleman from New Jersey who stole money from his company and hid in Panama, then had Barnes & Noble change his shipping address to his beach-front condo. To skip-tracers it's a game they get paid to play. They can make as many mistakes as they want; remember the one you make may lead the hunter to you.

THE COLLECTORS, LAWYERS, PI, AND SKIP TRACER'S PRIMARY TOOL – DATA MINER INFO

A "Skip" is a debtor that an asset search or a PI/skip tracer cannot locate or contact for collection purposes. You are typically identified as a skip if at least two of the following has occurred:
- Mail returned from last known address
- Unable to contact at any known telephone number
- Period of non-payment and delinquent account

In the old days, the PI/skip tracer's primary tools were the information available on credit applications provided by the debtor and the PI/skip tracer's ability to lie. Let's face it - none of our friends and few of our relatives will answer the question "Where can I find John Jones so I can sue him?" with a factual answer. Many of us will answer the question, "Where can I find John Jones so I can give him this check I have for him?" with John's address and as many phone numbers as we can think of. In the old days this was a large part of skip tracing, simply because that's all we had to work with. There was no Internet and no data mines companies. All I had was the ability to sound like "Dr. Rosenberg at County Hospital" saying "your kid has been hit by a car, and we need a verbal consent to operate or the kid may die."

Before the Internet, collection agencies approached skip tracing very simply — they reviewed any consumer information they already had and then picked up the phone to call the consumer's relatives, friends and employer in an effort to track down that consumer. PI's and skip tracers had to have very personable telephone voices, had to enjoy working with people, and had to love puzzles. And while those skills still play an important role in today's skip tracing environment, there are a number of additional options and challenges.

With many public records on the Internet and the ability of the search engines to store and cross-reference huge amounts of information, you now have the significant emergence of the "Data Mine" companies - a figurative place (usually the combination of several or many internet addresses) where a lot of information about you can be found. The important part is that a skip tracer can now access a lot of information (some of it accurate, some of it not, some of it relevant, some of it not) about you in a short period of time. What used to take weeks to put together about a skip now takes minutes. So today skip tracing is 49% art, 49% science and 2% pure bulldog determination.

The key is locating you the skip. On a comparative basis of the collection difficulty, currently 35% of delinquent credit card debtors move annually, and half of all collections accounts received require some form of skip tracing, resulting in a recovery rate of between 15 - 35%. Credit card collection charge-offs were $58 billion and growing at the rate of 12% per year.

There are two types of *skip*: *Unintentional and Intentional*

- An <u>Unintentional</u> skip is typically a person who moved from residence "a" to residence "b" and with all that had to be done, simply forgot to notify a lender and didn't leave a forwarding address with the post office. Many lenders send their mail with the notation "address correction requested" on the envelope. This is a request to the post office to provide them with a forwarding address the Post Office may have on file in the event their customer moves. If the Post Office has one, they will provide it (for a fee). If the Post Office cannot provide one, they return the letter to the creditor and the creditor has a "<u>skip</u>" on their hands. Unintentional skips tend to come forward relatively quickly and notify their lenders of their new address. Once that happens, the person is no longer a skip.
- The <u>Intentional</u> skip is a whole different person, as this person moves and deliberately fails to notify creditors. Sometimes, rather than leave no trail for the skip tracer to follow, this person will lay down a false trail - sending the bill collector to places the debtor knows are false. The debtor in this instance is attempting to lose the collector and fully intends not to pay the debt. It is for this person the skip tracer spends the most effort, capital, and time.

<u>How Does the PI/Skip Tracer Trace?</u>
The art of skip tracing involves two basic steps - background research to locate a candidate, and pretexting to actually locate the target and gather valuable information. The days of the collector and/or skip tracer parking themselves outside your door to follow the debtor to work are long gone. Skip tracing is now done from the tracer's desk, with the primary tool, the Internet. The primary options to help them find you are the Internet search engines searching hundreds of databases and <u>Data Mine</u> companies.

<u>The Tracer's Primary Tool - The Internet</u>
- <u>Data Miners</u> are large info data collection companies like <u>LexisNexis</u> with the acquisitions of Accurint and ChoicePoint, that have unquestionably become a major player in the asset searcher's resource book. The credit bureaus are another important tool. The fact is the Internet has become a real wealth of information about people - information that is stored in thousands of different places. Data Mine companies take all these resources and gather all the information that can be found about the subject from all available accessible databases (yes, there are some databases that the Data Miners cannot get to) and place it all in one file, which is then sold to the PI/Skip Tracer.
- <u>Non-Payer or Debtor Provided Leads</u>: In many cases, the debtor themselves provide a resourceful PI/skip tracer with the leads needed to find them, with the principal one being the <u>actual credit application</u>. Obviously the more information on the credit application, the more tools the asset searcher has. People tend to be pretty honest on credit applications for two major reasons. First is

the concern that dishonesty will not get them the requested credit, and second is that material false statements on a credit application constitutes sufficient reason for that debt not to be discharged in a bankruptcy.

On the credit card application, the most useful information a debtor provides are their Social Security number and <u>references</u>. These references are seldom if ever checked before issuing credit, and are always gone over by the <u>credit card collector and PI/skip tracer</u> (with 3rd party access to your credit file). Since it is unlikely the reference will give up much information voluntarily when asked, "Where can I find Ted so I can sue him?" The PI/skip tracer will try to obtain this information through a process called "pretexting." In simpler terms, pretexting is lying and illegal. It is telling the subject a lie in order to elicit that person's cooperation in locating the target.

The good news is the credit card application on which you listed your references is only available to the credit card co. and their collectors, and not to the independent on-line asset searcher or PI. So one should minimize any application info for new credit cards, as your address along with the credit card account shows up on your credit report and abbreviated credit header report.

Asset Search Tracing – Change of Address
If they know you recently moved but don't know where-to, the asset searcher will mail an empty envelope with the subject's last known address and their return address. On the envelope will be printed, "DO NOT FORWARD. ADDRESS CORRECTION REQUESTED." After a week, the asset searcher will receive the letter back their return address with a sticker showing the forwarding address you filed with the post office. Note: This only works if you filed a change of address with the post office within the last year. It is recommended when you move, do <u>not</u> file a USPS change of address.

Asset Search Tracing - Utility Co. Phone Calls
They will call the electric company where they suspect the general area you have moved to, and tell them that they are attorney Bob Taylor. Explaining that you the debtor have retained your services to represent them in a bankruptcy, and they are calling the electric company to ensure that all of your Mr. and Mrs. Debtor's accounts are included in the filing. They have your social security number and need a listing of your accounts, current and past due. They shouldn't make that phone call, because it would be illegal to impersonate an attorney. It is also illegal to call the electric company where they suspect you have moved to, and tell them that you are a Debtor.

Asset Search Tracing - Pretext Phone Call - Beware of this Ploy
- PI/Skip Tracer: Telephone (you) the consumer and say, "Hello, this is Bob Wynn with your electric company. I am calling because your account is 2 months past due and your electricity is scheduled for cutoff on Tuesday."
- Consumer: "I shouldn't be past due, as I made a payment last month and another payment this month."
- PI/Skip Tracer: "How did you make these payments? Did you mail in a check or money order, or did you make a payment directly at one of our payment centers?"
- Consumer: "I mailed in a check for both payments."
- PI/Skip Tracer: "I will try to locate these two payments and get them credited to your account right now. What bank were the checks drawn on?
- Consumer: "First National Bank."
- PI/Skip Tracer: "What is the account number?"
- Consumer: "Let me look; Ok, the account number is 3675309."
- PI/Skip Tracer: "I have located your payments and credited them to your account. The two payments were misapplied, and I have corrected the problem. You are not showing as past due at this time. I apologize for the inconvenience and thank you for your time."

Asset Search Tracing - Phone Break Tip #1 for Your Address
Many times a PI/skip tracer will have a phone number for their skip and need the address that phone number rings at. This is called a "Phone Break" or a "Phone Reverse Search." If they dial 00 on their phone they will get a long distance operator, and tell them they want a reverse listing for the phone number they are trying to break. If the phone number is a listed phone number, the operator will give them your name and address for that phone number.

Asset Search Tracing - Phone Break Tip #2 for Your Address
Be advised, it would be illegal for them to call your phone number they are trying to break for your address and tell you that they are a phone company repairman. They will explain that a truck hit a telephone poll and they are repairing the phone lines. They will then ask you if your phone number is xxx-xxx-xxxx, after changing the last 2 digits of your phone number to some other made-up number. You will correct them that they have called your phone number, and you will volunteer your phone number. They will ask what your address is at the number they called, and 9 out of 10 times you will innocently give your address.

Asset Search Tracing - Phone Hold
You would be surprised how much information people reveal when they are on hold, or when they think they are on hold. The caller will tell you they have to check something with their supervisor, and put you on hold for two minutes, as people will often tip their hand and divulge critical information while they think you have them on hold. So when a caller puts you on hold, you need to put your phone on mute. Consequently, be careful of what information you divulge while someone puts you on hold. Hit your mute button (put them on hold) just to be sure no one is listening.

ASSET COLLECTION COURT-ORDERED TOOLS

There are many legal tools that the asset searchers will use to retrieve your assets, requiring some court time once they have been located or identified:
- Writ of Execution or Attachment – This is a common judicial order that directs the enforcement of a judgment. The writ instructs the sheriff or constable to seize your property for sale at auction after which the proceeds are directed to the creditor.
- Turnover Order – Orders a debtor to turn all non-exempt property over to the judgment holder. This remedy permits the holder of a judgment to cast a wide net to draw in all available assets when the debtor's property cannot easily be attached or seized by the ordinary legal process. This remedy is generally applied when there is no other means that can satisfy the judgment. It is not necessary for the holder of a judgment to first exercise all other remedies before seeking such an order.
- Bank Levy – An order that enables the creditor to attach the debtor's or alimony non-payer bank account, but they have to know the bank and possibly the regional location.
- Blanket Levy – Involves the serving of a Writ of Execution and a Bank Levy on every bank in the debtor's home area. This procedure assumes that the debtor's bank of record is located within a few miles of home or work, which is usually the case.
- Debtor's Examination – This is a legal proceeding during which they can demand that you detail where your bank accounts are located. Fortunately you may have some time (30-day notice) to withdraw funds from your account(s) prior to the examination. But an examination of the bank's records may reveal information on the transfer of funds to another account or bank, or safety deposit boxes.

CAN YOUR MONEY AVOID (OR) HIDE FROM AN ASSET(S) SEARCH?

When an individual such as you wishes to avoid being exposed to paying out money for judgments resulting from alimony/ child support or a lawsuit, it is not uncommon for your substantial assets to be hidden in a variety of ways. For the asset searchers to find or locate your assets, they will immediately run an Asset Search. Any type of asset can be hidden including real property, jewelry, stocks, bonds, vehicles, pleasure craft and the most liquid of all assets – money. When an asset is moved or transferred with the intention to hide, defraud, hinder or delay discovery by anyone, it is then considered to be a hidden asset. This includes hiding of funds from ex-spouses attempting to collect on alimony or child support payments.

What Kinds Of Assets Are Hidden
Most hidden assets are of the liquid variety – bank accounts, stocks, bonds and mutual funds. In most instances hidden liquid assets are transferred into the name of a new spouse, relative, friend, or business entity.

Liquid assets can also be hidden by placing them into safety deposit boxes in the names of relatives or friends or an alias. Another method for hiding cash is to convert it into traveler's checks or savings bonds. Brokerage house accounts don't work as they generate interest reportable on your 1040 taxes, and they can be found thru child support enforcement thru the state FPLS/FIDM program. Or another method of ridding oneself of cash but retaining the value, is to use the liquid asset to pay down a mortgage, overpaying the Internal Revenue Service or pay down credit card balances.

Sometimes a liquid asset is converted into personal property such as works of art, collectibles or antiques. Unless those items are hidden, they can be attached as part of an award in a court ordered judgment, but collection of the property can be difficult to accomplish.

Real property, vehicles, boats, planes and other so-called personal toys can be hidden for the same reasons as liquid assets. When facing a lawsuit which could lead to future judgment enforcement, many people attempt to hide these forms of property by transferring ownership and title to the property to another person or entity.

The best move is to hide your assets, a sophisticated move into a business LLC or corp. with anonymous ownership. NM is the best state, with Wyoming a close 2nd.

How Assets Are Hidden
When looking for the various methods for hiding assets, it is important to remember that when they start any asset search, the obvious will not be overlooked. A basic background check may uncover the use of your alias or use of multiple social security numbers. In addition, the names of your relatives and business associates are often revealed through an initial thorough background search.

Hiding Assets Under Someone Else's Name
This is the most commonly used ploy for creating the illusion that assets are not in one's possession. When a transaction takes place between a subject and spouse or in-laws and the date is close to the date of a divorce, loan default or bankruptcy, a red flag of suspicion can be raised. However proving fraudulent intent is still difficult, especially when attempting to obtain a court order to seize property that is no longer in the name of the subject. Remember, placing your property in the name of a new spouse or other family members can often have a negative impact upon your financial security, if they don't return the property to you.

Hiding Assets as Gifts – When assets are given to relatives or friends as gifts, they can be exempt from creditors or court judgments. But the inherent risk is in having relatives or friends later refuse to return the assets.

Hiding Under a LLC or Corporate Umbrella – Corporations and limited partnerships offer essentially the same opportunities for concealing real estate assets as do real estate trusts. But as with trusts, many states require that deeds cross-reference information to partner's names when they are signatory to real estate documents.

Often corporations will list a statutory or resident agent, and this is generally an attorney who has no actual connection with the owners of the corporation. In most states a corporation is required to file an annual report with the commission that regulates corporate activities. Any information one is able to acquire from corporate records that are available may be useful and give some clues as to hidden real property or assets.

Trust Funds – The most sophisticated asset-hiding method is to transfer property into living trusts, and many of these type transfers are legitimate. When transfers to trusts are made to deliberately avoid payment of debtors or litigants, they are referred to as "preferential" or "fraudulent" transfers. If it can be shown that transfers were made in anticipation of or during litigation or bankruptcy, they can be reversed.

Real Estate Trusts – Most real estate trusts are established for legitimate reasons, but some individuals use trusts to hide real estate as a means of concealment. In such trusts, it is not uncommon for the person hiding the assets to serve as trustee or to have family members serve in this position.

One tactic used that makes tracing the property to an individual quite difficult is having a spouse, child or friend serving as the trustee, buy and obtain a mortgage for the property through the real estate trust. In this manner there is no way a records search will be able to trace the property back to the individual in question. However, this type of relationship relies upon the faith in family or friends to funnel the funds back to the individual at the proper time.

In a few states, real estate trusts do provide a safe haven for the hiding of assets. One may hold 100% of the assets in a trust, but not serve as trustee. Therefore there is no way in which the trustee's name will be cross-referenced to the name of the individual owner. But this only holds true in some states, since the majority of states require that the names of any individuals holding beneficial interests in the trust be revealed.

In many states, real estate trusts are a poor medium for hiding of property, as records of deeds, mortgages, declarations of trust and other such documents are maintained in municipal and county recorder's offices. In half of the local jurisdictions these records are cross-referenced between the name of the trust and those individuals serving as trustees. Thus the paper trail is easy to follow, and the hiding of the asset can be exposed.

ASSET SEARCHES – HOW YOUR PROPERTY CAN BE LOCATED

There are multiple database search services (see Chapter 9) that the asset searchers will use to look for your worldly goods, developed to collect information about an individual's real property and assets. The cost is not large, $140 – 500 using the databases compiled by the data miners.

Tangible assets like your homes, land, automobiles, boats, and aircraft can be discovered. Deed transfer records are thoroughly researched. Family members are listed. Assets in the name of a business you own or are connected to will likely be revealed, and a business credit report of your business(es) will be included. Also included are Uniform Commercial Code (UCC) filings searches, where your account information from loan mortgage collateral pledges will often be revealed.

An asset search can be conducted to ascertain what assets and income you have - to make sure the assets will be available should they win a judgment and come after you. They will perform this asset search before attempting to take possession of your assets - such as a house, automobile or a boat. Fortunately bank accounts and investment financial assets are harder to find, as they don't show up in an asset search. The recourse for the searchers, a subpoena could be served on you or the financial institution if they know which one. So hide it well.

ASSET SEARCH - FINDING YOU AND YOUR ASSETS THRU PUBLIC RECORDS

The term public record has always been very misleading. Even though a record is public and available for public scrutiny in the strictest sense, in reality it may not be readily available. The availability of numerous Internet public records has addressed some of the accessibility issues, and in turn has been a tremendous advancement for the professional investigator and skip tracer. Skip tracers used to have to spend numerous hours driving to and from various courthouses looking for public records, often on a wild goose chase. These days pretty much everything needed is available via the internet.

While skip tracing through online county clerk of court records, most often used the civil and criminal indexes (don't forget traffic citations and parking violations), marriage records, property conveyances and UCC filings, Often accessed are property tax/ownership rolls, and "business tax receipts" (business and occupational licenses) through the county tax collector.

What's available varies greatly from state to state, with many states differing greatly on what is and is not considered "public." The US Supreme Court ruled some time ago that driving records are not "public" records, and therefore will only be available on a very limited basis in every state. Certainly legislation is driving what records are available to the public, but so is the speed at which various records holders are adopting the required technology and digitizing their archives. While records in many counties are online, many courts and other sources of public records are not yet online.

Some states have a plethora of free public record information on the web (such as UCC filings, trademark owner names, corporate records and annual reports), and they also provide the actual images of the full public record. Even when information is considered public, agencies still may not provide free web access to the information. In these instances, skip tracers are no better off than 10 years ago and are forced to use a fee-based commercial database, or send "snail mail" directly to the clerk.

The following are online public records most often used by investigators, and beware differences occur between states and counties.

- Civil Index: A list of civil actions filed through the courts which often include lawsuits, judgments, liens, divorces, foreclosures, affidavits, powers of attorney, etc. The index may also include traffic infractions and parking violations in some areas.
- Criminal Index: A record of arrests and case disposition concerning the accusation of crimes, including felonies and misdemeanors, committed by persons within the record keeper's jurisdiction. The criminal index may also include traffic infractions and parking violations in some areas.
- Real Property Records: Include deeds, titles, mortgages, easements, and UCC filings. UCC or Uniform Commercial Code filings allow a creditor to notify other creditors about a debtor's liens or assets used as collateral for a secured transaction by filing a notice or financing statement in the public record.
- Tax Collector or Assessor: Online information concerning sales and use tax registration, property taxes and assessed values, business licenses, etc.
- Recorder's Office: Handles all recorded documents, marriage and birth records, election information, UCC filings, liens, judgments, military discharges, notaries, archives, etc. Marriage records are excellent for the simple fact that you can find dates of birth, states and cities of birth, maiden names, previous married names, new names and previous spouses.
- Secretary of State Records: Filing information for UCC statements, Corporate, LLP and LLC records, fictitious business name filings, trademark registrations, and Federal liens.
- PACER - Public Access to Court Electronic Records: http://pacer.psc.uscourts.gov/ is an electronic public access service that allows users to obtain case and docket information from Federal Appellate, District and Bankruptcy courts, and the U.S. Party/Case Index via the Internet. Links to all Federal courts and their criminal, civil and bankruptcy records. All registered agencies or individuals are charged a user fee.

HOW THEY MAY FIND YOU THRU YOUR CMRA PMB OR POST OFFICE BOX

Sometimes a PI/skip tracer will be asked to locate and identify the physical address of your PO Box or Postal Mail Box (PMB), often called a <u>Post Office Box Break</u> or a <u>Reverse PO box</u>. Rule #1 – they have to know where it is.

This can sometimes be accomplished with a database search if they have legal access to a credit report database that utilizes <u>credit headers</u>. When people have a PO Box they may use that address for their bills or car payments, utility bills, etc., and the PO Box will appear on their credit headers as an alternate address.

If they locate your PMB/ PO Box they may be able to obtain the initial application information by contacting the United States Postal Service using a form available on the USPS web site. This form requires them to disclose the reason they need the information. The USPS will only reveal the information if they are attempting to serve legal service in proper person, like a subpoena requiring a court case number.

Sometimes these methods will still fail. It could be that the box owner has relocated since they opened the box, and no longer live at the address they provided the USPS. It is even possible that the owner of the Post Office Box provided a former or dummy address or used incidental identification (like an international photo diving license) when they opened the account for the box.

The PI/skip tracer can try to pretext the PMB owner by mailing them professional looking material, free offers, maybe even a love letter, anything to trick the owner into revealing their identity thru a return phone call. These mailings may include a trap line phone number with <u>call capture</u>. If the mail box owner calls back, they'll get your information and can trace you that way.

This may sound difficult for a simple PO box break - Setting up trap lines, obtaining abbreviated credit header reports if they legally can, and printing up pretext post cards. Many investigators like to outsource this type of work and purchase the information from another investigator that's already set up to routinely obtain this kind of information.

HOW THEY USED TO PRETEXT TO FIND YOUR IDENTITY AND INFO

Imagine getting a phone call from someone at a reputable sounding research firm asking you to participate in a survey. The questions they ask seem harmless, including the name of your phone company, investment firm, and even your pet's name. In reality, you may have just been a <u>victim of pretexting</u>.

Pretexting is the practice of getting your personal information such as your Social Security number (SSN), telephone records, bank or credit card numbers, or any other information under false pretenses. In other words, a pretexter pretends they are someone else to obtain your personal information. They will use many different tactics to get your personal information. One of the most common forms of pretexting is when someone claims they are from a survey firm, and they ask you a few questions.

Pretexters claim to be representatives from many different types of organizations -- not just survey firms. Pretexters may also claim to represent banks, government agencies, local law enforcement agencies, Internet Service Providers (ISPs), and many others.

The pretexter's goal is to <u>obtain personal information about you</u> such as your SSN, your bank or credit card account numbers, mother's maiden name, information contained in <u>your credit report</u>, or the existence and size of your savings and investment portfolios.

After getting your info, the pretexter may call your financial institution pretending to be you or someone with authorized access to your account. The pretexter may, for example, claim that they have forgotten their checkbook and needs information about their account.

The concept of pretexting has become much more widely known in conjunction with the Hewlett-Packard boardroom scandal. HP admitted they hired independent contractors (private investigators) who got detailed phone records of HP board members while pretending to be a board member. The contractor also used pretexting to get the phone records of nine reporters.

Pretexters often sell the data they've collected to data brokers, who may sell it to private investigators, or to scammers who want to commit identity theft. Once they know which bank or brokerage firm you use along with your SSN, they can access your account if they can figure out your password.

The concept of pretexting is certainly not new. For example, scammers have used pretexting to obtain individual data from the Social Security Administration by calling when the computers were down. Pretexters are using increasingly sophisticated methods including electronic devices that show false phone numbers on caller ID systems, and paying companies to make calls for them to disguise the true origin of the pretexting call. In fact, scammers today use pretexting to get info from call centers at banks, phone companies, and other financial institutions to gain access to personal sensitive info.

You might be wondering, "*Isn't pretexting illegal*?" There is a US law, the 1999 federal <u>Gramm-Leach-Bliley</u> Act, that makes it illegal for anyone to:
- use false, fictitious or fraudulent statements or documents to get customer information from a financial institution or directly from a customer of a financial institution.
- use forged, counterfeit, lost, or stolen documents to get customer information from a financial institution or directly from a customer of a financial institution.
- ask another person to get someone else's customer information using false, fictitious or fraudulent statements or using false, fictitious or fraudulent documents or forged, counterfeit, lost, or stolen documents.

In addition, the Federal Trade Commission Act basically prohibits pretexting for sensitive consumer information. Unfortunately though, the boundaries of these laws are ambiguous. Although the <u>Gramm-Leach-Bliley Act is limited to financial data</u>, it's unclear whether it also applies to pretexters who obtain non-financial data. Further, some pretexters claim that if the info isn't used illegally, then the law does not apply. Although there may be legal questions, there is no dispute about how it may be possible in rare cases to obtain sensitive personal financial and non-financial information.

The <u>Identity Theft and Assumption Deterrence Act</u> makes it a federal crime when someone "knowingly transfers or uses, without lawful authority, a means of identification of another person with the intent to commit, or to aid or abet, any unlawful activity that constitutes a violation of federal law, or that constitutes a felony under any applicable state or local law." Under the Identity Theft Act, a name or SSN is considered a "means of identification." So is a credit card number, cellular telephone electronic serial number or any other piece of information that may be used alone or in conjunction with other information to identify a specific individual.

Pretexting is the practice of getting your personal information under false pretenses. Pretexting is against the law. Pretexters sell your information to people who may use it to get credit in your name, steal your assets, or to investigate or sue you. Keep in mind that some information about you is public record, such as whether you own a home, pay real estate taxes, or have ever filed for bankruptcy. It is not pretexting for another person to collect this kind of information.

THE REALITY OF AFTER PLAN B - THE HUNT FOR YOUR ASSETS AND INCOME

When your Plan B is executed with some pre-planning, what do you confidently think your odds are of finding your assets? This is hard to answer for obvious reasons, as there is no available success rate data from those that bailed on their alimony and child support (CS). But there are pertinent statistics from the professional judgment collection trade themselves that go after assets:

- 80% approx. remain uncollected, with the avg. collection success rate a low 15-20%.

One may question the comparison of alimony support enforcement backed by a court order and judgment, and is it comparable to professional judgment collection with a court-ordered judgment? Yes, because the ex-spouse's lawyer, PI, skip tracer or professional alimony support collection agency will use the <u>same</u> asset search tools (credit headers, asset searches, paid for data miner info, subpoenas, etc.) to come after your money and your income from wages or other sources. After they obtain a judgment and your bench warrant, they will use a writ for bodily attachment and wage garnishment order that will have been generated by your family courts. As there are no other secret tools they have at their disposal, they cannot just push a PC button and there you are, so one should not run in fear.

For <u>alimony</u> payers (as Chapters 11-12 outline in detail), if you have taken some proactive measures to mask your identity and assets before your Plan B implementation (move out of state, private PMB postal mail box, change jobs, LLC implementation with changing banks and financial assets into new business accounts, no forwarding address, and remembering always loose lips can expose you, etc.), one can expect a low probability outcome they will find you. An important point being when you move, it must be outside the divorce decree state to make that state's judgment and civil contempt bench warrant unenforceable without domestication.

Now throw in the factor that for the ex-spouse to domesticate the judgment, they must spend a lot of their front-ended money and time to pursue you out-of-state. Specifically they must know the state and county you reside in, and then hire a lawyer for some court time.

So the low odds of the alimony enforcer are <u>lowered</u> even further with the ex-spouse's inability, lack of desire and follow thru, or money to come after you. Provided you the payer do one thing - leave the divorce decree state, requiring the ex-spouse to have to hire a lawyer and domesticate their claim to your new state. So when you are stopped by a police officer for a simple taillight infraction and they do their standard state-only bench warrant check, they will come up with <u>no</u> local bench warrants. Otherwise, they can take you in for some short term incarceration while you get your catch-up alimony payments in order.

Unfortunately <u>child support</u> enforcement (CSE) is entirely another game with federal/ state laws and CS agency tools designed to track you and your assets to the ends of the earth in the US, if the CS agencies have their act together. You will have to hide really well in this scenario, have no financial assets, or seriously consider leaving the country. For those of you with child support obligations (not alimony), working as an independent contractor with year-end income reporting of the IRS Form 1099 info to the state CSE <u>doesn't work</u> either, as the IRS reports this info back to the child support enforcement agencies for your wage garnishment or lien.

One needs to assume you can be caught for the simplest mistake, even when your plan is to go invisible. It takes real conviction and dedication to do it. You do not just leave and that is it, because you will be found.

The big picture is a serious hunt for you initially begins with a motion and judgment with a garnishment order for your money, and then possibly a follow-up indirect civil contempt citation with a bench warrant for you missing the court hearing over the arrears. So Plan B can be a viable option for alimony life sentences, and then your life gets to continue on ...

CHAPTER 11

HOW THEY WILL COME AFTER YOU FOR THE $$

Non-payment of alimony or child support is a defiance of the MSA agreement, the judgment, and the courts, and may lead to an indirect civil contempt court order and a bench warrant or worse for you. So here are the incremental steps as to how <u>they</u> (the ex-spouse, lawyers, courts, state child support enforcement agencies, private investigators, skip tracers, alimony collectors, asset search firms, judgment recovery firms or collection agencies) will come after your financial and property assets and you using the following search tools.

There are too many myths and stories out there with many being incorrect; so the following are the documented procedural facts. In preparation for this turning point, you have to have conviction to not turn back, and the will to become invisible from the investigators and asset searchers. This is a critical chapter to read and comprehend to be successful.

ALIMONY ONLY ENFORCEMENT

- **Ex-Attorney Visit and Order to Show Cause (OTSC) Hearing**: After becoming concerned about your arrears, the ex-spouse will usually first go to their lawyer and discuss reopening your case file if closed. They will file the court paperwork awaiting the Notice of Motion or Order to Show Cause (OTSC) hearing date, with perhaps a preliminary Notice of Motion hearing first. Notices will be sent to you about the hearing in 24 days nominal, and it occurs. They will show up at the hearing alone, as you probably do a no-show, particularly if out-of-state. If there is no notification of your new address (since you have moved), the mailing or server-delivery notice goes to your old address and gets returned. If they know you have moved out of the divorce decree state, the judge will then recommend that the ex-spouse retain an attorney in the foreign state they think you live in, and recommend that the case be domesticated there.
- **Rule to Show Cause (RTSC) for Failure to Comply or Appear**: So after you have done your no-show, the court will grant a judgment for the ex-spouse legitimizing the non-payment cause. They may presumably provide a writ order for bodily attachment to come after you along with a civil bench warrant, a misdemeanor charge. The Court may also issue a subpoena and an order for garnishment of your wages and bank records. Sounds easy, but how do they find your wages and money (since those have been moved)?
- **Wage Garnishment or Income Deduction Order (IDO)**: The easiest as the IDO is valid in all states and does not require domestication, but they have to know your current employer and in what state (if you have moved). The wage garnishment is typically mailed by the ex-spouse's lawyer to the employer. So if

you change employers and don't advise the ex-spouse, the only way to find your earnings for serving the new employer the garnishment order, is for them to get a new court order and subpoena for you. Remember the stumbling block is, they have to know your new employer name and location. When you start a new job, only the state and fed gov. get the info about your new employer, because of the W-9 tax with-holding form you filed with your SS #. Your new employment is then reported by your new employer within 20 days thru the National Directory of New Hires (NDNH). Fortunately for alimony only, there is no means for them to access the NDNH data base or the state income tax records that would locate your new employer. The 1999 Gramm Leach Bliley act protects your privacy in an alimony scenario.

- **Judgment, Civil Bench Warrant, and Warrant/Writ of Bodily Attachment for You**: The good news is that when these civil matter items are issued by the state court, the judgments and bench warrants can only be enforced in the divorce decree home state. Alimony non-payment and no-shows are generally misdemeanors at an indirect civil contempt level. So the civil bench warrant is only entered into the statewide law enforcement system, and not into the national Crime Information Center (NCIC) database system reserved for felonies. For enforcement outside the divorce decree state, foreign state domestication is required first.

- **Foreign State Judgment and Domestication Enforcement**: If you have relocated to a foreign state (outside the divorce decree state), the ex-spouse's next step after receiving the divorce decree state's unenforceable judgment, will be to domesticate that judgment for enforcement to within your foreign state. This is not simple. First they have to know which state and county you reside in, then retain a lawyer in that locality with an upfront retainer, and wait for the procedural notice and enforcement procedure to take place. Otherwise the judgment is worthless.

- **Asset Search**: The ex-spouse's lawyer or the private investigator they may hire will probably do this next easy search step, an asset search, for your asset items like car titles, credit cards, etc. Their cost is $200 – 400, so be invisible at this point or your property can go for the hangmen's noose. Asset search and judgment collection firms may also have the same various methods of finding you, such as pulling your credit report or credit header report that may list your employer and references if they are involved in credit card debt or credit collection activities. They can also get the court to issue a subpoena to find the info they need. So do not list your current employer on any credit application or annual credit report update. Here are their other tools to find you:
  - Driver's License and Mailing Address: Your Achilles heel is your SS # associated with your DL, so use a PMB address (not your residence) on your current or next DL, and it is good for 4 – 5 years before renewal. Then move your residential address and go invisible. Or renew your former out-of-state DL by going back to your original state and renewing it at your old marital household address.
  - Vehicle Registration: Transfer ownership to your LLC with your PMB address, to get it off the books and avoid a potential lien. Alternately register and tag the car in another state, but have the registration renewal sent to your PMB.
  - Financial Assets: An important distinction, your bank and financial assets are not disclosed, unless they know the specific financial institutions. A subpoena would have to be served upon you.

- **Subpoena Bank Records and Bank Levy**: Needs a court-issued order and subpoena for your new undisclosed bank(s) or your tax records, and is only effective if you tell them at which bank you have accounts or list them on your income tax returns after they have them subpoenaed from you. There are approx. 7000 FDIC insured banks in the US, and they can't check them all or list them on a subpoena. The 1999 Gramm Leach Bliley act protects your privacy, so list them on your tax return's Form B – Interest and Dividend as Bank #1, Bank #2 … If they know or find your bank, a bank levy will be issued. So be smart, and switch all your bank accounts to undisclosed new banks. Fortunately FIDM (Financial Institution Data Match Program) database reporting of all personal bank accounts is a child support enforcement program, and does not apply to alimony.

Bank accounts can be garnished and when they are, it is almost always a surprise to the debtor. What typically happens is collectors obtain money judgments (usually by default), and then use the judgment to freeze and collect the funds in your bank account. State law and banking rules govern how the bank must handle the garnishment process.

Collectors always notify the bank first and then notify the debtor. This way your funds are frozen before you can take any action such as withdrawing all your funds. Notifying the bank first is perfectly legal, and you typically receive the notice (including your rights) a day or two after your funds have been frozen.

In most states, the garnishment can only freeze funds already in your account at the time of service on the financial institution. During the time the garnishment is in effect, the financial institution cannot honor checks or other orders for the payment of money drawn against your account. This means any outstanding checks will more than likely bounce or be returned for NSF. The exception to this rule is if your account has more on deposit than the amount of the garnishment. In this case, the bank can honor checks up to the amount that will reduce your funds below the amount of the garnishment. When the amount being garnished is paid, the freeze on your account must be terminated.

- **Subpoena Income Tax Records**: Needs a state court-issued subpoena to be served upon you or your former address, so on your future 1040 filings list your banks as Bank #1, Bank #2 ... You also have a 3-year window to file for any IRS refunds, so the longer you wait to file after you break the alimony trail, the less info they will obtain from these unfiled tax records. If they can't find you, the subpoena will probably be issued, so provide preceding caution about your filed tax returns. Fortunately FIDM automated reporting of your banking and financial accounts is only for child support enforcement searches.
- **Postal Mail Box (PMB) Break**: If they ever find your PMB, this will be a dead end as it only replicates the ID info you provided on the USPS Form 1583 when the box was opened. List your LLC business address at this same PMB address, and use your passport as your primary ID which has no address, and some other secondary worthless picture ID. So this effort becomes a dead-end yielding nothing.
- **Writ of Attachment or Execution**: A state court order to attach or seize an asset is issued to a law enforcement officer or sheriff to satisfy a court judgment. A prejudgment writ of attachment may be used to freeze assets of a defendant while a legal action is pending. Common grounds for obtaining a prejudgment writ of attachment are that a defendant has committed fraud or is prepared to hide assets from a court. Important ramification – enforcement cannot cross state lines, as requires domestication to your foreign state first. In fact a separate writ issuance may be required for each county where a writ or levy is to be made.
- **Property Liens**: The court will put a judgment lien on all real property you own if they can find your ownership. Your best asset protection is to transfer all property to the anonymous LLC/ corp. beforehand and then possibly file a friendly lien or charging order to protect your property.
- **Injunctions**: Frequently entered in alimony decree enforcement, an injunction restrains you from transferring, mortgaging, removing or disposing of your property.
- **Judgment Collection Firms**: Ex-spouse's last resort, as the professional collection firms take 30%+ fee of what they recover. After a judgment assignment to collection, these firms for the large money involved may domesticate an out-of-state judgment for recovery and invest the effort to get you. Plan well, and become invisible.
- **Bench Warrants/ Ankle Bracelets/ Jail Incarceration/ Work Release w/Probation and NCIC Criminal Record**: Statewide only and generally not enforceable outside the divorce decree state, unless the ex-spouse domesticates the divorce decree judgment and has a vendetta and connections with the police and legal system. If stopped by the police, they will conduct a statewide check for your warrants including bench warrants. Beware in the divorce decree state, you can be taken in for arrears. Long term incarceration rarely ever done, as work release program (see ankle bracelet) with 90% garnishment of your daily release income, since room and board is taken care of.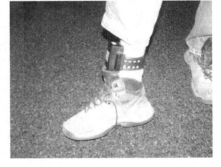
- **Social Security Garnishment**: A state court administrative order is required. First the ex-spouse for your social security for being married 10+ years has to wait until both of <u>you</u> reach eligible retirement age (62 minimum) and <u>start receiving</u> your benefits, at which point they can start collecting the <u>50%</u> matching. If the marriage was less than 10 years, there is no matching SS benefit from you for the ex-spouse. Then under Section 459 of the Social Security Act they can go after your SS benefit, as it can be garnished up to <u>65%</u> for arrears.

CHILD SUPPORT ENFORCEMENT (CSE) - Much Tougher with their Tracking Tools

If there is child support involved, the state's Div. of <u>Child Support Enforcement (CSE)</u> to find you will make your situation far **worse** with their URESA interstate reciprocity, UIFSA enforcements, the federal FPLS and state SPLS parent locater services, and the IRS 1099 program.

Federal Title IV-D regulations allow CSE agency enforcement and collection of <u>alimony</u> spousal support and arrearages, as long as the CSE agency is also collecting child support and arrearages. The state CSE agency must not pursue establishment or enforcement of alimony spousal support only, as <u>no</u> state law authorizes the CSE to establish or enforce an alimony spousal support <u>only</u> order. However, the CSE is responsible for administering alimony spousal support orders, when included in child support orders.

In addition to the alimony search procedures above, your listed residential address can be found, any of your <u>wage earnings</u> and <u>financial institution assets</u> can be traced. Then the following punitive steps will be instituted if they, the state child support agencies, are thorough and aggressive. Some states may throw alimony and CS into the same lot and implement this level of enforcement, so you are in trouble if you reside in one of those states (unless you continue to pay until the child or children are considered emancipated. Don't think you are in the clear because the child has achieved a certain age; some states (like NJ) require a Court Order to have a child declared emancipated. The only real viable option if child support (CS) is involved, disappear and consider leaving the country. They have all the means to find you, if the money makes it worthwhile. You can try to work as an independent contractor with 1099 reporting (although not reported to the NDNH, your form 1099 info divulging your <u>employer and financial income go to the IRS who report it back to the states CSE</u>). Beware your financial assets can still be found if they are diligent, unless hidden well in an invisible LLC with an EIN (Employer Identification Number, and not your SS #). They do not have access to your tax returns, but can seize your tax refunds.

If your unemployment does occur, CS arrears then typically begin, followed by the threat of the Child Support Recovery Act (CSRA) with it's felony conviction potential for over $5000 arrears. Sad but true, the system forces you into a death spiral soon after you lose your job or have a reduction in income. Here is how the trouble starts ...

Rule To Show Cause (RTSC) Hearing
When you do not make your child support payments as ordered by the court or the MSA, the judge will require that you appear before the court and explain why payments are not being made as ordered. If you cannot provide a valid reason for not making the payments, the judge may order one of the enforcement remedies. In addition, the judge has the ability to fine you and/or sentence you to up to a year in jail for failure to pay child support. If you can provide a valid reason for not making the child support payments as ordered, the judge and the CSE staff will advise you of the alternatives available. If you fail to appear for the Rule to Show Cause hearing, the judge will issue a civil <u>bench warrant</u> for your arrest. Then it begins ...

Enforcement Methodology
The Child Support Enforcement (CSE) program is a federal/ state/ local partnership to establish and enforce child support orders, and is sometimes called the <u>IV-D</u> Program, because it was established under Title IV-D of the 1975 Social Security Act. Anyone who has custody of a child who needs child support from a nonresident parent can apply for CSE services. State CSE agencies run the program and can help to locate

a parent to establish paternity or a support order, and they can help to <u>enforce</u> the order. The CSE agency can be in the state's human services agency, attorney general's office, or revenue department.

The <u>Federal Office of Child Support Enforcement (OCSE)</u> provides services to the states, and runs the Federal Parent Locator Service (<u>FPLS</u>) through which states have access to information from the Internal Revenue Service (IRS), Social Security Administration, the <u>National Directory of New Hires (NDNH)</u>, Dept. of Defense and Federal Case Registry (FCR). It also forwards information about past-due child support to the IRS for tax offset and to the US Dept. of State for passport denial blocking future renewals.

<u>Uniform Interstate Family Support Act (UIFSA) Foreign State Domestication</u>: This act provides uniform <u>out-of-state</u> child support enforcement to your <u>foreign</u> state and outlines the interstate hierarchy, but has no means to find your wages for garnishment.

POST HEARING CSE AGENCY ENFORCEMENT: This is how they (the child support agencies and their search tools) will come after you:

- **FPLS – Federal and SPLS - State Parent Locater Service Access**: The FPLS have access to your IRS W-2 and 1099 wage income and bank account interest info, and can search for your residential addresses in the records of the <u>Internal Revenue Service</u>, the <u>Social Security Administration</u>, the Dept. of Defense, the National Personnel Records Center, the Dept. of Veterans Affairs, and <u>State Employment Security Agencies</u>. States also are required to maintain directories of newly hired employees within the state and to report this information to a <u>National Directory of New Hires</u> (<u>NDNH</u>) and the Federal Case Registry within the FPLS, for important data matches to locate noncustodial parents who owe child support. The state's child support enforcement agency will ask the <u>State Parent Locator Service (SPLS)</u> to search for you, the noncustodial parent or CS payer in-arrears. Using your <u>social security number</u>, the SPLS will check the records of State agencies such as motor vehicle registration, unemployment insurance, income tax, and correctional facilities. If the SPLS finds that you have moved to another state, it can ask the other foreign state to search, or send a request to the <u>Federal Parent Locator Service (FPLS)</u>. This is how the state's primary weapon is initiated – wage garnishment, as 96% of CSE child support income is procured this way.

- **FIDM (Financial Institution Data Match Program) Bank Asset Search**: Under the Personal Responsibility and Work Opportunity Reconciliation Act of 1996 (PRWORA), <u>state</u> child support agencies are required to conduct a quarterly <u>Financial Institution Data Match (FIDM)</u> against the records of financial institutions doing business in the <u>state</u> including banks, credit unions, and investing institutions. The purpose of this match is to locate and seize the assets of non-custodial parents who are delinquent in their court-ordered child support payments despite their ability to pay. Also the <u>Federal</u> Office of Child Support Enforcement (OCSE) through the <u>Federal Parent Locator Service (FPLS)</u> assists the <u>states</u> in comparing a state's child support debt records with the account records of multistate Financial Institutions.
The Gramm Leach Bliley Act permits an open search by the state CSE with a court order of your bank financial accounts. If found, the state CSE will issue first a writ of attachment, and your accounts will be frozen during this seizure and collection action.

- **NDNH and SCE Wage Garnishment**: Using the National Directory of New Hires (NDNH), a request will be made by the original state SPLS using the FPLS. Upon the receipt by the State Human Resources Dept. or equal of a Notice of Levy/ Writ of Execution or an Order to Withhold Income for Child Support, the recipient state is legally obligated by federal and state law to withhold money from an employee's paycheck for <u>child support</u>. An employer who receives a letter that expressly requires the company to garnish the wages of one of their employees will include a copy of the court order establishing child support payments. The employer will send a letter to the employee, either with their next paycheck or before to explain the wage garnishment.
Upon service of the legal paperwork, written notification will be sent to the employee documenting when the income withholding will begin and which company has the legal order. The State Human Resources Division only receives notice that money is owed, and the amount that must be deducted from the paycheck. A letter is sent to the employee describing the process and the start date of the Child Support deduction. By the time the employee receives a letter from their payroll office, the employee is already

aware of the monthly support obligation as informed by Child Support Enforcement. Note NDNH new employee reporting includes your home address, so use a PMB.

- **IRS Form 1099 Income Reporting of Wage and Asset and Independent Contractor Earnings (Over $600)**: In 1984 an agreement was signed between the Internal Revenue Service (IRS) and the Office of Child Support Enforcement (OCSE), covering the <u>matching</u> of names and Social Security Numbers received from OCSE with Forms 1099 in the IRS Wage and Information Document Master File. In 1988, IRS agreed to expand the information provided through Project 1099 to include wage and employer information. Information available through Form 1099's includes both earned and unearned income including wages, earnings on stocks and bonds, interest from bank accounts, unemployment compensation, capital gains, royalties and prizes, and employer and financial institution addresses. Note that hired Independent Contractors with Form 1099 reporting only (incomes over $600 per year), the law does not require employers to report them to the NDNH, just the IRS. The IRS gets a listing of people behind on their child support, and then sends the Form 1099 back to the respective state child support agency, for your earnings and assets to be garnished. The information may <u>only</u> be used for the purpose of enforcing child support payments.

- **CSRA - Child Support Recovery Act/ Deadbeat Parents Punishment Act**: The 1998 Child Support Recovery Act, now known as the Deadbeat Parents Punishment Act, makes the willful failure to pay a past due child support obligation while residing in another state a <u>federal</u> offense. It becomes very difficult to obtain employment with a felony conviction. A person convicted of a first violation of the CSRA may be punished by up to <u>six</u> months in a federal prison and a fine. It is important to note that federal Sentencing Guidelines do <u>not</u> apply to a <u>first</u> violation of the CSRA because it is considered a <u>Class "B" misdemeanor</u>. As a Class B misdemeanor which is a petty offense, there is no right to a jury trial. For any subsequent violation of the CSRA, federal Sentencing Guidelines are applicable which effectively increase the presumptive sentence for any subsequent offense to two years imprisonment and/or a fine. A second or subsequent violation is a <u>Class "E" felony</u> which carries with it a <u>maximum sentence of 2 years incarceration</u>. In such a case, there is a right to a jury trial. The Deadbeat Parents Punishment Act (DDPA) of 1998 amended the CSRA of 1992 and established felony violations for traveling in interstate or foreign commerce to evade a child support obligation or for failing to pay a child support obligation which is greater than $10,000 or has remained unpaid for a period longer than two years.

- **FPLS Federal Offset Program (FOP) and CS Arrears Penalties**: The Federal Offset Program (FOP) applies here. If in CS arrears, the state's Child Support Enforcement (CSE) can follow thru with:
  - <u>Credit Bureau(s) Reporting</u>: Report your child support obligation to the 3 credit bureaus as a collection amount, giving you a negative ding for 7 years.
  - <u>Tax Refund(s) Offset Intercept</u>: <u>Automatically</u> submit for tax intercept both your IRS federal and state income tax refunds.
  - <u>Driver's Licensure Suspension</u>: <u>Automatic</u> suspension in many states, but only in the divorce decree state or the state where the enforcement is taking place.
  - <u>Passport Suspension</u>: If you owe $5000 or more in past due child support, the state CSE informs the US Dept. of State who will <u>not</u> issue a new passport or <u>renew</u> your current passport until all past due child support is paid. Note <u>denial or revocation of a passport does not prevent the use of your current valid passport until the 10-year expiration</u>. At this point in time, you will not be able to obtain or renew the passport until arrears are paid.
  - <u>Professional License(s) Suspension</u>: <u>Automatic</u> suspension, but only in the divorce decree state or the state where the enforcement is taking place.
  - <u>Property Liens</u>: The SPLS can issue a lien. So the only protection is to transfer all property to the business LLC, and as an option file a friendly lien or charging order to protect your property. But remember a second outside lien can prevent you from liquidating your property.

- **Bench Warrants/ Ankle Bracelets/ Jail Incarceration/ Work Release w/Probation and NCIC Criminal Record**: Statewide only, and generally not enforceable outside the divorce decree state. If stopped by the police, they will conduct a check for your warrants including bench warrants. Jail incarceration is rarely ever done, as work release program with garnishment of 90% of your daily release income is more efficient, since room and board is taken care of. Ankle bracelet monitoring with work release for CS arrears is being done in N.

Carolina and NJ. So watch out as Florida has jailed 3 defendants, and S. Carolina has up to 1 year policy. Beware the CSRA does have federal crime provisions.

- **QDRO Order by ERISA of Employee Pensions and Profit Sharing**: The federal ERISA law permits assignment of a portion of your employee pension benefits to an ex-spouse as child support or alimony payments. Under ERISA, a Qualified Domestic Relations Order (QDRO) is defined as a judgment, decree, or order (including approval of a property settlement agreement), which is made pursuant to a State Domestic Relations Order that provides child support or alimony payments. A little known aspect of this statute is that it can be used to collect a judgment for alimony or CS arrearage. In cases where there are retirement funds available, a party may request that the court enter a QDRO Order to award the aggrieved party a portion of the retirement funds sufficient to satisfy all or a portion of the arrearage. QDRO orders can be used to access qualified pensions, profit sharing, and stock bonus plans that elect to be covered under the minimum participation rules. ERISA permits the entire accrued benefit to be awarded if the court so orders, in cases where the judgment is equal to or greater than the accrued benefit.

- **Social Security Garnishment**: 1) The ex-spouse for the 10+ years of marriage, may at the point when you reach eligible retirement age and file to start receiving your benefits, they can start collecting the 50% matching of your SS, and 2) then under Section 459 of the Social Security Act (if you are 62+ and start receiving your SS), your SS benefit can be garnished up to 65% for arrears. A state court administrative order is required.

WHY AN ASSET SEARCH HAS LEGAL LIMITATIONS?

<u>Can the asset search find everything</u>?
No, and to do so would be impossible, as not everyone has assets to be found. Further most investigations offered are flat rate, limited scope products designed to capture the most common and most frequently detectable types of assets. With the diversified nature of ownership and registration of assets, it would be cost prohibitive to conduct a guaranteed asset search.

<u>Why can't they openly search for your bank accounts</u>?
The Federal 1999 <u>Gramm, Leach, Bliley Act</u> made it illegal for anyone, lawyers and private investigator's included, to even try to obtain information about a person's financial accounts. This law is very broad and has eliminated all legal viable avenues to getting this information. The investigative methodology used must also comply with all restrictions of the Act, the FTC conditions and the various state and federal privacy acts. There is only one permissible purpose contained as an exemption, and that <u>one</u> exemption is for <u>child support collection</u> in conjunction with a court order. So in effect with your hidden assets, it is difficult to collect on a debt even with a judgment from the court, <u>unless it's for child support (not alimony)</u>.

<u>Can they search for your bank accounts if they already have a court judgment</u>?
No, only if it's for <u>child support</u>, and the judge in your case actually enters an order authorizing such a search. If someone advises the ex-spouse otherwise, ask them how they are able to do this and stay within the strict constraints of the Gramm Leach Bliley Act.

Can they get your Credit Report?
No, credit reports are protected and can only be accessed with your written permission, but with specialized third party access privileges associated with credit debt collection, they may be able to get an abbreviated credit header report.

Can your assets be hidden in someone else's name like a nominee (someone designated to be a hidden owner) or relative?
Yes, but typically the asset search will be limited to the person being investigated. If they need to investigate someone else including an ex-spouse, it means double the work and more money.

Aren't other asset search companies offering to locate bank accounts?
Yes other companies do, but these companies are either breaking the law or taking your money. They then tell you something to this effect, "Based upon the procedures we employed and the results we obtained, no accounts were located." They leave out the fact that the procedures they conducted were to merely look at any court records they found to see if banking information was listed, and that's the end of it. Many companies advertising on the net are also foreign corporations, so the ex-spouse will need to watch their wallet with these outfits.

What makes good Asset Searches different?
A legitimate asset search firm that has licensed private investigators is not an information broker, and does not simply resell old information found in public record archives like the vast majority of competitors do. The search should be conducted by an investigator, not a database search. If there are serious dollars involved, they will come after you.

Why do some firms offer instant results but others don't?
These firms are doing nothing more than running your name through some software that collects information from a number of free public records sources. Their computer then spits out whatever it finds on-line and puts it into a report. They are not investigating anything and most are not licensed private detectives. It takes time, training, expert supervision and a license to uncover information and verify it.

GARNISHMENT OF WAGES AND BANK ACCOUNTS

When facing alimony debt or arrears that can't readily be paid, the best plan of action is to act early, reach some sort of payment arrangement and stick to a repayment plan. Otherwise if alimony goes unpaid and ignored, the courts may intervene by issuing a judgment requiring your employer to garnish or withhold a portion of your wages or bank accounts to pay the alimony. A difficulty for the ex-spouse and the courts may be finding your current employer, assuming your prior employment garnishment stopped to whom the original order was issued. Then finding your new bank accounts can be equally difficult, particularly assuming you have moved your financial assets to new undisclosed locations.

Collection tool of last resort
Garnishment is a legal remedy authorized by a court and should be considered a collection tool of last resort. In most states, the garnishment process can only be initiated by a court order and only if a judgment for monies owed has been entered against you. The paying ex-spouse, you, is often embarrassed when faced with garnishment because their paycheck is involved, which means their employer is aware of their financial situation. Employers are typically required to tell workers about the withheld amount. While it is against the law for an employer to fire an employee whose wages are garnished, that protection goes away after a second and third such judgment, according to the Consumer Credit Protection Act.

Garnished wages
Once an account (or any debt) goes into default, and the ex-spouse finally decides they cannot collect as you are not paying, they may at a last resort sell the debt to a collection company. If the debt collection company is unsuccessful in recovering your debt, then a lawsuit may be filed against you in an attempt to recover its losses. If the ruling in the lawsuit goes against you, a judgment may be issued to garnish your property, bank accounts or wages. Also, if a judgment is rendered in a state where the garnishment law differs from federal law, the law requires the court to adjust the garnishment to the lesser amount.

Garnishment
There are two different forms of garnishment: wage and nonwage. Nonwage garnishment is a procedure where a judgment holder attempts to garnish funds in a bank account. Wage garnishment is used when it is determined the consumer is gainfully employed and has sufficient earnings to attach. If the debtor is not gainfully employed, then the garnishment process begins when a debtor's bank receives a court judgment requesting a debtor's account be frozen to be garnished. Federal law prohibits some money - Social Security, disability or veteran's payments, for example - from debt garnishment, **but not alimony or child support**. The process of separating exempt and nonexempt funds and unfreezing a bank account could take weeks or even months, leaving debtors with no access to bank funds during that time.

As a result of consumer advocates taking issue with the practice of freezing all bank funds and placing the onus on the consumer to prove which funds are exempt, a new rule was passed in 2011 to protect exempted funds from garnishment orders. Electronically deposited exempted funds such as Social Security will now be "tagged" by the federal government, making it easier for financial institutions to separate exempt and nonexempt funds to be garnished. The bank must also provide debtors with the amounts of these protected and unprotected funds once it is served with a garnishment order. Nonexempt funds that are not direct deposited, however, do not qualify as they will not be electronically tagged.

State laws also may add extra rules on bank account garnishment. In NY for example, state law mandates that the first $2,500 in a debtor's account remain untouched if that account received protected (Social Security disability checks, for example) electronic deposits in the 45 days prior to the bank's receipt of the restraining order. Unprotected funds are otherwise protected. It's important to note however that garnishment orders for some specific debt types such as delinquent child support, alimony and federal taxes, can tap into these otherwise exempt funds.

Exempt funds from garnishment
When an employer is notified of a judgment requesting wage garnishment, only a certain percentage of wages can be withheld – based on the total disposable earnings of the employee - allowing the employee some income to live on, according to Title III of Consumer Credit Protection Act. Also protected from garnishment are deductions that are legally required to be paid by the employee, such as federal, state and local taxes, unemployment insurance, state employee retirement system payments and Social Security payments. However, deductions not required by law (health insurance, union dues) are not protected from garnishment.

<u>Garnishing Laws</u>
Policies vary from state-to-state, so it is important to understand your state's laws. State and federal law regulate the amount of money that may be garnished from a consumer's wages or bank account. The states will generally follow the federal regulations.

WHAT IS THE MAX. ALIMONY/ CS WAGE GARNISHMENT LIMIT? - Why Are Debts (25%) vs. Alimony/ CS (50-65%)?

The federal Consumer Credit Protection Act (<u>CCPA</u>) puts limits on your state-imposed wage garnishment 25% percentage amounts for judgment and debt collection, and unfortunately specifies significantly higher percentage limits for alimony or CS. This is because the prescribed CCPA lower debt-only % limits <u>don't</u> apply to <u>child or alimony spousal support</u> garnishments, (as they are treated as an obligation and not a debt).

The federal CCPA specifies the <u>maximum</u> alimony/ child support disposable income paycheck amount that can be garnished as:
*   <u>Up to 50% disposable</u> income if you have another child or spouse to support who are not the subject of the support order; otherwise you could be garnished up to <u>60% disposable</u> income.
*   If you have more than 12 weeks of arrears back payments, you could be garnished an additional 5% for a max. total of **65%** <u>disposable</u> income.
*   For the wage garnishment calculation, your <u>disposable income</u> is your <u>gross</u> income <u>minus</u> any legally required deductions including federal, state and local <u>taxes</u>, unemployment insurance, social security deductions, and state retirement systems. So if you are retired and on Social Security only with no source of taxable income on your IRS 1040, they will typically go after 60 - 65% <u>gross</u>, because Social Security is not an employer, and they have no idea of what your annual income and your lack of deductions are.
*   Note all CCPA prescribed limits utilize <u>disposable</u> income, not <u>gross</u> income. Unfortunately, this terminology confusion is where the misapplication begins by the courts and the lawyers.
*   The confusion continues to amplify during the pre-trial negotiations with the drafts and finalization of the MSA, which can have the percentage exceed the CCPA, because this is a private contracted amount between two parties outside the power of the court. If your garnishment issue went to trial, the judge would have to follow the state and federal CCPA limits. Don't fall for the lawyer threat of percentages that exceed the CCPA Act.

This is an important issue to understand, as during my pretrial MSA final review negotiations I was threatened by the lawyers with <u>50% gross</u> income alimony that would be equivalent to <u>75% disposable</u> income, that ironically is in violation of the federal and state law. I responded at the time questioning the reality of the 75% disposable income alimony, stating that the severity destroyed all incentive for the payer to go out and seek a living. Early retirement with Plan B would be the simple immediate choice.

If you still question (and you will) why your alimony or CS exceeds the federal and your state's garnishment limitations, "*full faith and credit to the original divorce state*" applies, so that your wage garnishment can <u>exceed</u> your current state garnishment guidelines. Your state may have <u>different limits</u> on debt wage garnishment. In cases where the state wage garnishment limits are different from the <u>federal</u> limit (and the state limit may be higher), the one that results in the <u>lower</u> garnishment amount should be used.

So beware, there is a lot of confusion amongst the lawyers, courts, judges, and alimony/CS payers as to what the max. percentage that one can pay (disposable vs. gross), with dollar amounts outlined by the terms of the MSA and explained by the legal teams to their clients when the court renders trial judgments. This concern is justified because some payers are paying <u>more than the legal 60 - 65% disposable income</u> level. Several alimony payers have stated their court-ordered fates of paying higher percentages than allowed by law, so it does happen because of the judge(s) and attorney's confusion in the terminology and the laws. Note the Social Security garnishment utilizes the same 60-65% gross limits.

FEDERAL WAGE GARNISHMENT LAW - CONSUMER CREDIT PROTECTION ACT (CCPA)

Who is Covered
Title III of the Consumer Credit Protection Act (CCPA) is administered by the Wage and Hour Division (WHD). The CCPA protects employees from discharge by their employers because their wages have been garnished for any one debt, and it limits the amount of an employee's earnings that may be garnished in any one week. Title III applies to all employers and individuals who receive earnings for personal services (including wages, salaries, commissions, bonuses, and periodic payments from a pension or retirement program, but ordinarily does not include tips).

Basic Provisions/Requirements
Wage garnishment occurs when an employer is required to withhold the earnings of an individual for the payment of a debt in accordance with a court order or other legal or equitable procedure (e.g., Internal Revenue Service (IRS) or state tax collection). Title III prohibits an employer from discharging an employee because their earnings have been subject to garnishment for any one debt, regardless of the number of levies made or proceedings brought to collect it. Title III does not however, protect an employee from discharge if the employee's earnings have been subject to garnishment for a second or subsequent debt.

Title III also protects employees by limiting the amount of earnings that may be garnished in any workweek or pay period to the lesser of **25%** of disposable earnings or the amount by which disposable earnings are greater than 30 times the federal minimum hourly wage prescribed by Section 6(a) (1) of the Fair Labor Standards Act of 1938. This limit applies regardless of how many garnishment orders an employer receives.

Title III permits a <u>greater amount</u> of an employee's wages to be garnished for <u>alimony/child support</u>, bankruptcy, or federal or state tax payments. Title III allows up to <u>50%</u> of an employee's disposable earnings to be garnished for <u>child support</u> if the employee is supporting a current spouse or child, who is not the subject of the support order, and up to <u>60%</u> if the employee is not doing so. An additional <u>five percent</u> may be garnished for support payments over 12 weeks in arrears.

An employee's "<u>disposable earnings</u>" is the amount of earnings left after legally required deductions (e.g., federal, state and local taxes; Social Security; unemployment insurance; and state employee retirement systems) have been made. Deductions not required by law like (e.g., union dues, health and life insurance, and charitable contributions) are not subtracted from gross earnings when the amount of disposable earnings for garnishment purposes is calculated, so beware.

Title III's restrictions on the wages amount that can be garnished do not apply to certain bankruptcy court orders and debts due for federal and state taxes. Nor do they affect voluntary wage assignments, i.e., situations where workers voluntarily agree that their employers may turn over a specified amount of their earnings to a creditor or creditors.

Relation to State, Local, and Other Federal Laws
If a state wage garnishment law differs from Title III, the employer must observe the law resulting in the <u>smaller</u> garnishment, or prohibiting the discharge of an employee because their earnings have been subject to garnishment for more than one debt.

What is wage garnishment?
A wage garnishment is any legal or equitable procedure through which some portion of a person's earnings is required to be withheld by an employer for the payment of a debt. Most garnishments are made by court order. Other types of legal or equitable procedures include IRS or state tax collection agency levies for unpaid taxes and federal agency administrative garnishments for non-tax debts owed the federal government.

<u>What are the restrictions on wage garnishment</u>?

The amount of pay subject to garnishment is based on an employee's "disposable earnings," which is the amount left after legally required deductions are made. Examples of such deductions include federal, state, and local taxes, the employee's share of State Unemployment Insurance and Social Security, and withholdings for employee retirement systems required by law.

Deductions not required by law - such as those for voluntary wage assignments, union dues, health and life insurance, contributions to charitable causes, purchases of savings bonds, retirement plan contributions (except those required by law) and payments to employers for payroll advances or purchases of merchandise - usually may not be subtracted from gross earnings when calculating disposable earnings under the CCPA.

The law sets the maximum amount that may be garnished in any workweek or pay period, regardless of the number of garnishment orders received by the employer. For ordinary garnishments (i.e., those not for support, bankruptcy, or any state or federal tax), the weekly amount may not exceed the lesser of two figures: <u>25%</u> of the employee's disposable earnings, or the amount by which an employee's disposable earnings are greater than <u>30 times</u> the federal minimum wage.

<u>What about child support and alimony</u>?

Specific <u>higher %</u> restrictions apply to court orders for child support or alimony. The garnishment law allows up to <u>50%</u> of a worker's <u>disposable</u> earnings to be garnished for these purposes if the worker is supporting another spouse or child, or up to <u>60%</u> disposable if the worker is not. An additional 5% may be garnished for support payments more than 12 weeks in arrears.

<u>Are there any exceptions to the law</u>?

The wage garnishment law specifies that the garnishment restrictions do not apply to certain bankruptcy court orders. If a state wage garnishment law differs from the federal CCPA, the law resulting in the <u>smaller garnishment must be observed</u>.

IRS PROJECT 1099 - TO FIND YOUR INCOME AND ASSETS - Child Support Only

One may think that being an independent contractor with IRS Form 1099 income reporting for both wage income and financial assets, escapes the NDNH income reporting which it does. But if child support is involved, the IRS provides income info from your year-end Form 1099 for wage and asset interest income to the child support agencies, and there you are ... You have been found and the garnishment/ lien procedure will begin. An LLC or corporation provides <u>no</u> protection either, unless you utilize your business EIN number for reporting to the IRS. If your social security number is reported, you are a sitting duck, as you are tracked thru your SS number and your address will be revealed.

If alimony is involved, there is no IRS reporting. Case closed.

The IRS Project 1099 allows state child support (CSS) agencies to obtain asset and wage information for noncustodial parents (NCPs). This information is transmitted to the IRS via 1099 forms from financial institutions and state agencies and via W-2 forms that are submitted by employers. ACTS automatically requests 1099 information each October for all NCPs with verified SSNs in active cases that are in the Locate or Delinquency Processing Status.

Since 1984, OCSE has participated in Project 1099 which provides State child support agencies access to all of the earned and unearned income information reported to IRS by employers and financial institutions. Project 1099, named after the IRS form on which both earned and unearned income is reported, is a cooperative effort involving State child support agencies, the OCSE, and the IRS. Examples of reported earned and unearned incomes include: interest paid on savings accounts, stocks and bonds, and distribution of dividends and capital gains; rent or royalty payments; prizes, awards, or winnings; fees paid directors or subcontractors; and unemployment compensation.

The SS number is the key piece of information around which the child support information system is constructed. Federal CSE law requires States to implement procedures requiring that the SSN of any applicant for a professional, driver's, occupational, recreational, or marriage license be recorded on the application (not on the face of the license itself). In addition, the 1996 law requires that the SSN of any individual subject to a divorce decree, support order, or paternity determination or acknowledgment be placed in the records relating to the matter, and that the SSN of any individual who has died be placed in the death records and recorded on the death certificate.

The 1099 project has an extreme level of security. <u>Only responsible caseworkers or supervisors</u> can access 1099 response data, which includes name, address, employer or other source of income, source/amount of assets. To verify income or assets, the 1099 Letter (DSS-4551) must be sent to the entity that provided the information to the IRS. Four types of information can be obtained from the IRS Project 1099:

- The address that the NCP reported to the submitting institution;
- The address of the submitting institution;
- Wage and salary payments made to the NCP; and
- Asset information reported by institutions.

HOW THEY MAY SUBPOENA YOU TO LIST YOUR ASSETS AND BANK ACCOUNTS

A subpoena is a legal instrument that compels some type of action, and can be issued to <u>you</u> only by judges, courts, government prosecutors or parties to a civil suit. As the party to a civil suit, they will not have unlimited power to subpoena whatever and whomever you'd like. Instead, they will have to justify the relevance of the subpoena to the case if it is challenged. A lawyer or an asset searcher might want to subpoena your bank account records include verifying your assets in a claim, but they have to do it first thru you, not thru the financial institution. If you don't respond or cannot be found, they have to know which financial institution. Fortunately, they cannot blanket subpoena every bank in the US.

<u>Procedure:</u>
- A suit will be filed. The power to subpoena is intended to further the progress of a case. In civil matters, a subpoena can only be issued during the discovery period of the suit, which is when both sides exchange information and answer questions. But before this stage is reached, they must file a motion or complaint to be served, and it must not be dismissed. As the defendant, you are supposed to file an answer to avoid default judgment. If you're reading this book, one may presume you will do a no-show.
- A <u>subpoena duces tecum</u> will be served which must be specifically worded to describe the action it seeks to compel and the occasion for compliance. The subpoena duces tecum is the proper instrument for <u>compelling a bank</u> to produce documents and records of accounts. This is simply a document identical to any other subpoena except that it requests the production of documents and includes the words "duces tecum" in the title. The subpoena is not filed in the court; instead it is served directly on the party (or non-party such as your bank accounts) being subpoenaed.
- The court may consider relevance. Personal bank records are generally considered irrelevant and cannot be subpoenaed except for good cause. Examining the party's ability to pay a debt is not good cause (except in cases involving punitive damages). For example, if you're being sued for overdue alimony, your bank records would be relevant.
- You can <u>Oppose Motion To Quash</u> (if necessary), as a subpoena can be contested on a number of grounds with a motion to quash. If such a motion is filed, a memorandum in opposition will have to be filed and argued at a formal hearing. Subpoenas are usually challenged because of some insufficiency of the document, the irrelevance or burden of the request or the party's inability to comply at the date and location specified.
- They can file a <u>Motion To Compel</u> (if necessary). If you refuse to comply and do not file a <u>motion to quash</u>, they can file a motion to compel to get the court involved in your request. A motion to compel

shifts the burden to the other party to prove why the subpoena is improper. If their motion is granted, you can be held in contempt for failing to provide the requested records and documents.

- *This is why it is critical for you and your assets to be "invisible" at this point.*

SUBPOENA YOUR BANK ACCOUNTS (Alimony only, CS has FIDM)

Your bank account(s) are highly liquid, and could be easy assets to attach. So a commonly asked question is, "Does the person have an account at a particular bank?" Fortunately there is no central database that maintains bank account numbers. Prior to 1999 locating bank account information was the most controversial area in an asset search, but new banking privacy regulations have brought about significant changes in data availability. Prior to the banking changes, a variety of techniques such as use of credit reports, information subpoenas and pretext calling were used to uncover bank account information. Under the new law, pretext calls are no longer permitted when attempting to obtain account information. So bank customers and your financial info now have greater protection from searches. However once a bank account has been located and verified with either social security or EIN tax ID numbers, it can be attached for payment of court ordered judgments.

First, there needs to be an actual court proceeding taking place to get a subpoena, and one would like to think they cannot just randomly subpoena something or someone because they want to see it. So assuming there was some kind of civil or divorce court proceeding that has taken place, they would petition the judge with a "Subpoena Duces Tecum" to be delivered to you making a request for your bank records including a description, naming the institution that holds your money, tell them where to deliver them and how long they have to give the info. Once they prepare and file the document with the court, the judge will grant it or deny it. If granted, they serve it on the "statutory agent" of the bank or whoever has the records, and your records may be turned over. The reality is many judges will not scrutinize the subpoena material appropriately and will grant the subpoena without review, if they have personal friendships with the attorneys.

The bottom-line, move all your non tax-deferred financial assets to invisible business account(s) at new financial institutions, and then keep your financial info confidential and hidden. The only item you cannot hide are your IRA/401K accounts that have to be disclosed with your account holder name and social security number, until the point you cash them out.

BANK ACCOUNT SEARCHES - ARE THEY PERMISSIBLE? - Child Support Only With FIDM

Lawyers and other professionals ask whether it is permissible for an asset search company or private investigator to conduct bank, stock, bond or mutual fund account searches on a subject such as you the ex-spouse. The short answer is "no," without a subpoena served upon you.

Conducting a bank, stock, bond, or mutual fund account search is considered to be an invasion of privacy. More important, any company that claims to be capable of conducting bank account searches in this day and age, (and there are a number of them) is doing so by using false pretenses. If that was not enough, the Board of Bar Overseers has also come out and stated that an attorney who has a bank account search conducted on their behalf could be held vicariously liable. Finally, the Attorney General's offices in a large number of states have aggressively sought and obtained injunctions and heavy fines against asset search companies who conduct bank account searches, unless they have authorization through 3rd party searches for credit debt collection activities.

Therefore when the asset searcher has to satisfy their "due diligence" on behalf of their clients when conducting an asset search to find your assets, they will need to contact a reputable company who knows what is permissible and what is not. Most legitimate asset search firms will only use trained asset recovery attorneys to conduct asset searches.

The long answer as to why you are no longer able to conduct a bank account search is the <u>Financial Services Modernization Act of 1999</u> - Privacy Protection For Customer Information Of Financial Institutions. Since then, using false pretenses to obtain bank account information from either banks or bank customers is considered a federal crime. The law applies to all banks and financial institutions, including stock brokerage firms, insurance companies, <u>loan companies</u>, <u>credit card issuers</u>, and <u>credit bureaus</u>. The Act applies to those persons who use false pretenses and any third party requesting the information when it is known, or should be known, that false pretenses will be used.

The good news, there are approximately <u>7000 FDIC-insured US banks</u>, which makes it hard to find the institution and the branch you utilize.

The reality is private investigators must have a <u>court order and a subpoena</u> in hand authorizing the bank investigation. A significant point is that alimony only asset searches by a PI or a lawyer with a subpoena will be unsuccessful if <u>they do not know</u> either: 1) which institution or 2) the state/county jurisdiction to look in.

For delinquent child support arrears, only parties that have legal authority to search for your financial assets using Financial Institution Data Match (FIDM) program include: law enforcement agencies, financial institutions, insurance companies conducting claims related investigations, <u>state child support enforcement agencies</u>, and <u>state-licensed private investigators</u> with a subpoena.

ASSET SEARCHES - WHO CAN GET YOUR BANK ACCOUNT INFO AND WHY?

A quick Internet search for ways to get someone's bank or investment account information returns at least a dozen private investigation companies, that promise to find these records "anywhere in the US and worldwide" for judgment collections, verification of net worth and for "just about any other purpose." But a closer look at these web sites reveals a fine-print disclaimer stating that the information is from public records such as divorce cases and probate filings. And there are a few that do not bother with a disclaimer, providing only an 800 number to call.

Asset searches which may include bank and investment accounts are not illegal; however, certain actions to obtain this information such as pre-texting are illegal. And although there are methods that can be used to obtain financial information covertly, most if not all, are questionable and often futile. There is no clear way for anyone other than the account holder, a designated representative, or a party with a valid court order to get account information without violating the law. Beware there are other options some legal whereupon the asset searcher thru their established CMRA credit bureau connections can come after you, and their methodology may work unless you are invisible.

There is a general misconception that a judgment just by virtue of its issuance, can be used to force a bank or financial institution to disclose account information, but the enforcement of judgments is governed by each state's laws. In California, for example, a <u>writ of execution</u> is necessary. These writs are rendered on a county-by-county basis and direct a levying officer (usually a sheriff) to serve the writ on the named institution. The institution then may be required to freeze the account and in some cases to hand over the account balance. State laws also allow the creditor after a judgment is obtained, to examine and request asset information from the debtor.

The privacy protection laws that govern access to financial information under false pretenses depend on whether the affected customer (you) is a consumer or a business entity. The more significant legislation is directed at protecting consumers, defined generally in the laws and in interpretative decisions as "individuals consuming goods or services for personal or household use." The 1999 Gramm-Leach-Bliley Act (GLBA) prohibits obtaining customer information from a financial institution under false pretenses and imposes an obligation to protect customer information. Under the GLBA, a customer means "an individual consumer," which is essentially the same as the definition of a consumer under the Fair Credit Reporting Act (FCRA). In addition to the GLBA and FCRA, there are other potentially applicable federal privacy laws, as well as a long list of state laws. But even if a specific law may cover only consumers, the financial institution's contract with the business customer would certainly be construed as preventing third-party access.

HOW THEY CAN ONLY SUBPOENA YOUR IRS TAX RETURN FILINGS THRU YOU

They go to court to subpoena your tax return records, as you have hidden all your money in new or undisclosed banks. Can they do this?
Yes, they are going to need to hire an attorney to prepare the subpoena and submit it to the Court. The court then will require the attorney to file a motion, and then go through the discovery process. This will require you to file a financial affidavit as part of a court proceeding. As part of this, their attorney can then also pursue your employment data if you reveal it (vs. being unemployed).

Before the trial, they will go through the discovery process, and their lawyer will most likely serve your lawyer and you with a document called a request for the production of documents. Such requests require you to be served to produce the relevant documents or face sanctions, up to and including losing the case. The discovery request if you comply makes a subpoena unnecessary, but why would you comply?

Will the IRS go for the asset searcher's request of your Tax Returns?
Next step, the ex-spouse, their lawyer, or the asset searcher cannot subpoena anything alone. Instead they must motion the court to subpoena your tax records and show cause why those documents are important discovery to further their case. This will be heard before the judge, with you as the other party being allowed to make an objection to this motion, and then be decided by the court. They will have to limit their request to the data necessary, and should the court grant the motion, the tax return will in all likelihood be submitted to the court and the information that they are seeking provided. So the answer is yes, but they are limited to what they are allowed to read. They can request a subpoena for the records from you, but you have the right to object to the request. If the judge finds the objection reasonable, then in theory the subpoena will not be issued. But don't believe this, as judges rubber stamp many requests for a subpoena, either because of their personal relationships with the lawyers or not really wanting to get involved. This is why you only list your bank interest or capital gain info as Bank #1, Bank #2, and don't identify the financial institutions. If you have gotten this far, you are essentially invisible.

Your Tax Returns: Many people have more than one bank account or brokerage account. Beware your individual tax return can be a good source of information for them with any type of account that pays interest or capital gains, but a court-ordered subpoena or authorization from you is required to retrieve your tax returns. So on your next tax return's Form B – Interest and Dividends, list *Bank #1, Bank #2, Savings #1, Savings #2,* etc. Don't give them a head start.

OBTAINING YOUR TAX RETURNS IS NOT LEGAL WITHOUT YOUR AUTHORIZATION

Although not legal if you by signature did not request copies or transcripts of your filed and processed tax returns, they can help your ex-spouse or asset searchers reconstruct your tax records. Someone (like your ex-spouse) could forge your signature and illegally request a copy of your tax returns, as Form 4506 with a false signature would need to be completed. This is why you should only list your bank interest or capital gain(s) info as Bank #1, Bank #2, and don't identify the financial institutions. Don't give them a head start.

If they suspect that you, the ex-spouse, are hiding income or assets, or if they think you have the potential to do so, they can have you complete and sign a Tax Information Authorization (Form 8821). This form grants them (the ex-spouse) access to your tax related information that has been filed with the IRS. They will have to specify the type of tax (individual, corporate, partnerships, etc.) and the tax years that they are authorized access to. So never sign this form.

What is the difference between the IRS Form 4506 and 4506-T?
- Form 4506 - Request for Copy of Tax Return: A photocopy of your taxpayer-filed tax return, and can take the IRS up to 60 days to complete.
- Form 4506-T - Request for Transcript or Exact Copy of Tax Return: Available generally for current and last six years of returns. IRS Tax Transcripts are obtained thru "Veri-Tax," and usually takes 1 business day to obtain from the IRS. Provides the industry's fastest and most secure method of 4506-T income verification processing directly with the IRS, as they specialize in 4506-T processing and does not offer 4506 services. They are the first company to deliver IRS tax transcripts electronically to lenders nationwide, and the first to provide online ordering of tax documents via its website.

How long is your signature date on the 4506-T good for?
IRS Form 4506-T must be signed and dated by you the taxpayer, with the date good for 120 days. This rule is strictly enforced by Veri-Tax and the IRS. Any 4506-T that appears to have an altered signature or data will be rejected by Veri-Tax and/or the IRS.

The IRS terminology is confusing for:
- A tax return transcript shows most line items from your tax return (Form 1040, 1040A or 1040EZ) as it was originally filed, including any accompanying forms and schedules. It does not reflect any changes you, your representative or the IRS made after the return was filed. In many cases, a return transcript will meet the requirements of lending institutions offering mortgages.
- A tax account transcript shows any later adjustments either you or the IRS made after the tax return was filed. This transcript shows basic data, including marital status, type of return filed, adjusted gross income and taxable income. They are available generally only for the current and the past three years, and the response time is expedited and generally received within 10 business days.

WHY THEY CAN'T SUBPOENA YOUR EMAIL RECORDS

Service Providers Resist
Normally when an internet provider is handed a civil subpoena such as in a divorce, infidelity or child custody investigation, a service provider like Facebook, Hotmail, Yahoo, or Google will resist disclosing the content of a user's communications unless the user consents. A common rationale cited for resistance is that the content is protected under the 1986 Stored Communications Act (SCA) that addresses voluntary and compelled disclosure of stored wire and electronic communications and transactional records held by third-party internet service providers (ISPs).

Compelling You the User to Cooperate
Often the law or the courts will compel you to provide consent to the service provider releasing your records of communications. Some recent cases have been compelling users to turn over to their adversaries, their social media user ID and password.

The Fourth Amendment to the U.S. Constitution protects the people's right "to be secure in their persons, houses, papers, and effects, against unreasonable searches and seizures".. However when applied to information stored online, the Fourth Amendment's protections are potentially far weaker.

Stated simply, under the Stored Communications Act an ISP cannot disclose communications made by subscribers to any person, unless subpoenaed by a grand jury or governmental agency at trial. So an ordinary party to a civil law suit cannot subpoena your email and internet search records from a non-party ISP, regardless of whether the ISP is located out-of-state. If your ex-spouse files a civil law suit and wishes to discover your communications or customer records stored by an ISP, they will need to subpoena them directly from you.

HOW THEY CAN ATTEMPT TO FIND YOUR ID THRU YOUR POST OFFICE/ PMB BOX

This can only be done after discovery of your PMB box's address location, and surprisingly the owner identification process is simple once they find your PO or PMB box address location. You previously filled out USPS Form 1583 (Application for Delivery of Mail thru Agent) info when you opened the box as a customer of a commercial mail receiving agency (CMRA), and may have thought this info would not be made available to the general public or to process servers. However, Form 1583 information will be disclosed only upon written certification of official need such as a subpoena or a court order.

The legal steps are: 1) First they will need a court subpoena. 2) Then they will need to know your PO or PMB box location; and 3) They will then send the subpoena to your PMB with a postage-paid reply envelope requesting the Form 1583 box holder info. Hence make certain there is no useful info on the form 1583 like your real residential address. You will have to provide personal ID info, so use your passport (not your driver's license). The phone number can be your old phone no. Recommend duplicating the PMB address on Form 1583 as your address, as they just scan to see if the blanks are all filled in. The end game, provide no useful info, so it is a dead end for the searchers.

Instead of the above legal approach, it is more likely a private postal box PMB operator would provide your identity info to a PI voluntarily from the Form 1583 if approached in person. Then worst case, a private investigator could expensively stake out your PO box for a couple of weeks waiting for you to come to check your box. So always be on the lookout, and provide no useful info.

CAUTION WHEN OPENING YOUR SOCIAL SECURITY ON-LINE ACCOUNT

Social Security (SS) uses an identity verification service provided by Experian to help verify your identity and protect your privacy when you register with them online. When you make a verification request to establish your account, SS uses Experian who use information from your credit report to help verify your identity. You will be asked for your address, so use an old address or your CMRA PMB address.

From this identity confirmation, you may see an entry called a "soft inquiry" on your Experian credit report. This will show an inquiry by the Social Security Administration with their address and the date of the request. Soft inquiries do not affect your credit score, and you do not incur any charges related to them. Soft inquiries are displayed in the version of the credit profile viewable only to consumers and are not reported to lenders. The soft inquiry will not appear on your credit report from Equifax or TransUnion, and will generally be removed from your Experian credit report after 25 months. Once you have registered for a SS online account, you will not generate additional soft inquiries by logging in to access SS services.

ARREARS BEGIN, THEN JUDGEMENT ENFORCEMENT WITH INTEREST

Is There A Statute Of Limitations On My Arrears Judgment?
Yes. Each state sets a limit on how long a civil judgment is enforceable within the state without domestication, with a judgment typically being valid for 2 - 10 years. After your arrears begin, it is not difficult for an ex-spouse to go pro se before a judge and get an initial judgment and then another. If renewed before the individual state 2 - 10 year expiration, it will be extended for another 2-10 years. Criminal judgments do not require renewal.

Can They Collect Unpaid Arrears + Interest On Your Judgment?
Yes, state statutes provide for of 4-12% interest per annum on the arrears principal money amount remaining of a judgment. Recommend one look at the wage garnishment notice (issued by the court that was given to you at the time of the divorce finalization), and it will show the arrears penalty (20% +/-) plus the state interest penalty (4-12%) also. This 30% +/- penalty can be on top of the 50% net income alimony you already owe – 80% net income total. So don't do your Plan B halfway … Become invisible!

CHILD SUPPORT MIXED WITH ALIMONY - AT CS TERMINATION, THE ALIMONY DOES NOT END ...

There is important to note for those of you who have child support (CS) orders with alimony. The state disbursement units (SDU) units and collection agencies can and do co-mingle CS and alimony, and they do so with absolute awareness of what they are doing. They will label the whole business child support because of the draconian and merciless federally-funded apparatus that exists to punish "deadbeats". Many have waited until their CS was finished to leave the US (the right thing to do), and once they then got the CS order terminated (or so they thought), and then boom unexpectedly the alimony portion magically became a CS issue once they were out of the country for a few months. This is not supposed to happen, but let's be frank - there is no incentive for the courts or the government to do anything to stop this, as the states get extra money for rubber stamping alimony as CS. Fixing your alimony dilemma will require lots of lawyers, court appearances, and oh yeah you'll have to explain to the master why you dared to run away from the plantation without producing your monthly spoil of cotton.

Waiting for the CS to be long dead seems to be a good strategy in retrospect. If you do have a CS + alimony order and you lose your job and go into arrears, magically both will appear on your credit report combined, a big whopping CS order all neat and tidy. If you ever wanted an argument that child support is really just mommy support, now you have it.

CAN YOU STOP YOUR ALIMONY PAYMENTS WHEN COMBINED WITH CHILD SUPPORT?

The simple answer is <u>no</u>!

Bottom-line, one must understand that if you are paying child support, one <u>cannot</u> stop paying alimony. With the state child support enforcement provisions if they are diligent, there are <u>no</u> options for stopping the CS payments of any kind. You must wait until the child support is over, and then get the state court order stating it is. At that time send the court order to the State Disbursement Unit (SDU) so they will make note in your account that the child support has terminated. As a last step, follow up with a phone call to the SDU to ensure they received the court order, and it is duly noted on your account.

As a further demonstration if you really think that you can direct your payments for CS only and not alimony, call the state disbursement office and ask, "Can you stop paying alimony and only just keep sending in CS payments?" The expected response will be, "**No**, as payments are applied proportionally." So if you make a 75% payment intended or annotated for full CS payment only, both alimony and CS will go into arrears proportionally.

Remember your employment wages and employer-listed residential mailing address are tracked thru the NDNH (National Directory of New Hires) and are accessible only by child support enforcement (not alimony). This means for child support cases that if you wanted to continue working in the US, the perceived option of being an independent contractor <u>doesn't</u> work, as your 1099 income and address are reported from the IRS to the child support agencies. Even though independent contractor status has no NDNH reporting, beware the CS agencies still have legal database access to your residential and employer addressees through the IRS Project 1099 info that is sent to them.

Later on if you are dragged back into court for an upward modification of child support, make sure the new order states the CS termination date. This date is for when child support ends, and you can send the order to the SDU eliminating the hassle of having to go back to court for CS termination. Otherwise you are back to court one more time.

Remember, the CS agencies can play all their cards to find you in the US. So for those with CS, the only viable options are:
- <u>The Recommended Option</u> - Continue paying child support till they become adult(s) or emancipated, and then with the final termination of your CS, you can finally deal with the permanent alimony using Plan B as an option, or
- <u>Another Unexplored Option</u> - Leave the country and make private arrangements to continue paying only the child support that cannot be traced easily - (Not utilizing traceable wire transfers, but instead a methodology like a living trust with blind ownership).

<u>Alimony Only</u>
If you have alimony only, one needs to make sure your account is listed as "alimony only" with the state disbursement unit SDU and Child Support Enforcement (CSE) (SDU - where you or your employer send the monthly payments), because the state may try to list it under child support instead for more matching federal incentive dollars provided for CS enforcement. See page 40 regarding the state coupon as to why the comingling occurs. You will have to call the state agency to find this out.

HOW AN ARREARS JUDGMENT IS ENFORCED

This is a summary of how they will come after you, after a state court judgment has been issued against you for arrears. Fortunately with the passage of two Acts, <u>both</u> enhanced your privacy protection: 1) the Gramm Leach Bliley Act (GLBA, 1999) – restricting bank account access and 2) the Fair Credit Reporting Act (FCRA) – restricting credit report and credit header access.

	<u>CAN</u>	<u>CANNOT</u>
Lawyers	<ul><li>Obtain Data Miner reports about your real property ownership such as house, car, boats, etc.</li><li>Prepare subpoenas to obtain information from you about your financial assets and tax returns.</li><li>Obtain a judgment and then garnishment of your wages and financial accounts (if they haven't been moved), and if they know where they are to be found.</li><li>Domesticate a judgment to a foreign state. (But the lawyer has to be licensed in the foreign state).</li><li>Have the court issue a state-only bench warrant for your indirect civil contempt.</li><li>Can get the state court to instruct the SSA to garnish your social security for arrears.</li><li>Get the state court to QDRO your pension and retirement 401K/IRA accounts for arrears.</li></ul>	<ul><li>Pretext.</li><li>Obtain your credit report without your written authorization.</li><li>Obtain your credit header report listing your address and phone number.</li><li>Conduct bank or brokerage account searches.</li><li>Obtain your tax return directly from the IRS without your written authorization. Instead have to subpoena them thru the courts.</li><li>Obtain your email or phone records.</li><li>Find your employment or unemployment insurance, and residential address thru the National Directory of New Hires (NDNH) database, and then initiate wage garnishment.</li></ul>
Private Investigators, Skip Tracers, and Judgment Collection Firms	<ul><li>Obtain data miner reports about your real property ownership such as house, car, boats, etc.</li><li>Thru 3rd party access (if related to debt collection only), can obtain your credit report or credit header report listing your publicly listed address and phone number without your written authorization.</li></ul>	<ul><li>Pretext (not legally).</li><li>Conduct bank or brokerage account searches.</li><li>Obtain your tax return without your written authorization.</li><li>Obtain your email or phone records.</li><li>Find your employment or unemployment insurance, and residential address thru the National Directory of New Hires (NDNH) database, and then initiate wage garnishment.</li></ul>
Child Support Enforcement Agencies	<ul><li>Find your employment or unemployment insurance, and residential address thru the National Directory of New Hires (NDNH) database, and then initiate wage garnishment.</li><li>Find your independent contractor Form 1099 wage and asset income reported to the IRS, as the IRS reports it to the CSE.</li><li>Obtain your listed address from your tax returns.</li><li>Have the IRS seize your state and federal tax refunds for arrears.</li><li>Conduct a Financial Institution Data Match (FIDM) search and find your bank or brokerage accounts.</li><li>Report you to the 3 FCRA credit reporting agencies for CS only arrears, impacting your ability to obtain future credit.</li><li>Report you to the US State Dept. to stop your next passport renewal.</li><li>Report you to the state DMV and get your driver's license and vehicle registration revoked.</li><li>Report you to the state Dept. of Professional Regulation and get your professional license revoked.</li><li>Domesticate a judgment to a foreign state.</li><li>Get the state court to instruct the SSA to garnish your social security.</li></ul>	<ul><li>Pretext.</li><li>Obtain your credit report without your written authorization.</li><li>Obtain your tax return without your written authorization.</li><li>Obtain your email or phone records.</li><li>Enforce alimony only arrears, without having CS arrears also.</li></ul>

CHAPTER 12

HOW THEY REALLY WILL COME AFTER YOU USING THE LAW

These are the aggressive tools provided by the government, the courts, and the state child support enforcement agencies to pursue you for arrears. Note the cards are really stacked against those with child support arrears.

BENCH WARRANTS - ARREST TYPE

Bench warrants are issued in either <u>civil</u> or criminal court proceedings, and often used as tools for fighting <u>contempt of court</u>, a <u>willful</u> disregard of a court order. Bench warrants once issued by a judge, authorize police agencies to pick you up - at home, at work, at school, on the street, any time of the day or night -- and arrest you as they would arrest any other law-breaker. Civil bench warrants are issued when a defendant <u>fails to appear in court</u> as ordered, and can be entered into the <u>statewide law enforcement</u> computer system. In order to file a bench warrant, a judge must generally demonstrate a personal knowledge of the contempt which instigated the warrant, but some jurisdictions will sign anything. Commonly (but not always), the person who is subject to a bench warrant has intentionally avoided a court appearance to escape the perceived consequences of being found guilty of a crime.

A bench warrant is an order issued by a judge or law court for the arrest of a person, charged with contempt of court from alimony or child support non-payment no-show or a criminal offense. Bench warrants are issued for a number of reasons including failure to appear in court, failure to pay a fine, and failure to comply with court orders. A bench warrant is actually a court order given to a sheriff to bring a person into court or to arrest a person. Bench warrants are a variant of arrest warrants, giving police officers the right to arrest you immediately and bring you into court.

Enforcement
When a bench warrant is issued, law enforcement has the authority to pick you up, and bring you to court to address the bench warrant charges. Often if a person is arrested on a bench warrant, the court declares them a flight risk (likely to flee) and orders them held without bail. The authorities may put you in jail and a hearing is held.

For bench warrants, you may post bond in cash or by a licensed bondsman. Typically, judges issue bench warrants for persons deemed to be in contempt of court – possibly as a result of that person's failure to appear at the appointed time and date for a mandated court appearance.

Bench warrants (civil) are only enforceable in the state they were issued, but there is the occasion (1% or less) with child support and large dollar amounts of arrears that become a criminal felony warrant, where the CS agencies and law enforcement will come after you across state lines. This is done by domesticating the judgment to the foreign state and pursuing you to the ends of the earth. Police agencies do not care about out-of-state civil warrants, and most officers do not want to bother with in-state misdemeanor warrants. However, police do have the authority and ability to place you in custody for an outstanding warrant.

There is no standard bench warrant form or uniformity from state to state, but below is one state's form that shows the classic pickup radius PUR territories. Any good information on the enforcement is also hard to find because of the state-to-state and local county variances; just like advice on what to do with permanent alimony. The one uniformity is that a civil bench warrant is typically only good within the state of issuance for a civil misdemeanor, non-criminal case.

Every warrant has what is called a "pick up radius" (PUR 1-5) attached to it, the distance that the issuing county-originating agency is willing to pay to pick someone up for a particular civil or crime offense. There are costs associated with a PUR, so for small offenses the PUR distance is small. Each state and judicial court preferences have slightly different pick-up radius definitions, so there are slight variations to the table below. Generally, a pick up radius (5) warrant is generally county of want only, meaning the county where the warrant was issued is the only place you can be arrested. A pick up radius of <u>one</u> (1) is nationwide, and these are normal reserved for severe criminal felony warrants such as rape or murder. Even if you are in the same state you are fine, as 99% of civil bench warrants fall in the 4-5 category.

Warrants are entered into 2-3 databases: A local database (if there is one), a statewide database, and a FBI <u>National Crime Information Center (NCIC)</u> criminal database. To be entered into criminal NCIC, the pickup radius (PUR) has to be a 1.

<u>Pickup Radius</u>

(PUR)	Description
5	Local County of want pickup only
4	Only adjacent County pickup in the state of want
3	Statewide pickup within 100 miles of county of want
2	Statewide pickup (not NCIC listed)
1	**Nationwide (NCIC listed only for felony criminal charges)**

An alimony non-payment warrant will typically have a misdemeanor charge and a low priority PUR 4 – 5 rating, with entry only into the local state sheriff law enforcement database, providing you did nothing to provoke the indirect civil contempt being converted to direct civil in front of the judge. But beware thru the efforts of the state child support enforcement agencies, large sums of money of child support arrears over $5000 can be converted to felonies and federal status (NCIC listing presumed) by the Child Support Recovery Act of 1992. These are the cases we hear about where the non-payer has been grabbed thru long-arm statutes and domestication.

A bench warrant is also served in the same manner as an arrest warrant. This means that felony bench warrants may be served at any time. However, misdemeanor warrants may only be executed between 6 a.m. and 10 p.m. absent good cause.

STATE OF WISCONSIN, CIRCUIT COURT, _____ COUNTY

| For Official Use |

Case Caption:

**Bench Warrant
Civil**

Case No. _____

Name of Person		Person's Address			
Alias Name(s)			Person's Home Phone Number ( )	Person's Cell Phone Number ( )	
Person's Work Number ( )		Person's Date of Birth	Sex	Race	Driver's License Number
Height	Weight	Eye Color	Hair Color		Other Identifying Characteristics

TO ANY LAW ENFORCEMENT OFFICER:
Arrest and deliver to the sheriff the above named person because this person
- ☐ failed to appear in court as required:
  Date of court appearance: _____
  Type of court appearance: _____
- ☐ failed to _____.

This person may be released upon completion of ☐ any ☐ all of the following conditions:
- ☐ Completing the attached Order for Financial Disclosure and Financial Disclosure Statement, SC-506.
- ☐ Agreeing to appear at a future supplementary examination at a time and place to be determined by the judgment creditor.
- ☐ Paying the amount owed on the judgment $ _____.
- ☐ Paying the statutory sheriff's fees.
- ☐ Paying other costs $ _____.
- ☐ Performing the following conditions as authorized by the court: (All conditions under this section must be specifically authorized by the court.) _____
- ☐ Other: _____

If the person posts the total amount due and is released, the law enforcement agency shall inform the court and district attorney of any new court date.

Geographic restriction:
☐ Statewide   ☐ Within county of ORI
☐ Within adjacent counties of ORI
☐ Other: _____

BY THE COURT:

_____
Circuit Court Judge/Court Commissioner

_____
Name Printed or Typed

_____
Date

Civil Bench Warrant Example (Note statewide or county enforcement restrictions)

If you study the form info above, it is understandable why enforcement is so difficult with the statewide limitation. For an individual that has moved out or state or become invisible, all pertinent info like address, phone numbers are all out-of-date and become unenforceable. Note your social security no. is not listed, but your driver's license no. has the S. S. #. Consequently, only a low percentage of bench warrants are ever served.

The courts do <u>not</u> make an official notification after a warrant has been signed. Beware warrants do not expire, go away or get forgotten by the courts or law enforcement. So if you think you have one with your name on it, you can go on-line and check for them, but only in the state where you think you might have gotten one, because there is <u>no</u> national database for civil bench warrants. If you received one, the smart option is to stay out of that state or the county of want for the remainder of your life.

State extradition laws are set up to deal with criminal cases, not civil cases. If one researches the laws of the state to which you intend to flee, the statutes generally allow for extradition only for criminal fugitives, and that process is dependent upon a prosecutor in the initiating jurisdiction confirming that they want the fugitive to be extradited and that they are going to arrange and pay for the fugitive's return to their jurisdiction. It can be expected that the county prosecutor's office has better things to do with its budget.

CIVIL BENCH WARRANT AND FELONY WARRANT DIFFERENCES

Misconceptions
Understanding the differences between criminal felony (large amounts of child support arrears) and civil misdemeanor bench warrants (alimony) comes down to how they are generated. Failing to appear for court hearings, comply with judgments, or pay fines and costs is considered ample grounds for a civil bench warrant. In that scenario, the judge signs a warrant requesting that the offender be arrested, and brought in for a court hearing. The judge will then address the original charge and may impose further fines and costs, jail time or both, depending on the situation.

Dealing with criminal felony warrants triggers a different set of steps. The process begins with the police department's request for an arrest, based on probable cause to show that person committed the offense detailed in the warrant. Contrary to popular belief, absolute proof is not required for probable cause to stick. The warrant simply states the police department's view of the facts, as the department understands them. Local prosecutors or judges must authorize the felony warrant before police can proceed and attempt to make their arrest.

Distance Considerations
Distance is another critical factor that separates civil bench warrants from criminal felony warrants. Bench warrants usually have a specified radius for the return of defendants caught in other areas - typically from 50 to 100 miles, although some local courts have statewide pickup policies. Felony warrants have no such limitations, and can be served wherever a defendant is found. This triggers another formal process known as extradition, in which the issuing state formally requests the defendant's return to answer the charges. How badly the defendant's home state wants the suspect back depends on the severity of charges, as well as the cost and difficulty of picking them up.

Warning
Treating old warrants as irrelevant is unwise, because as a rule warrants stay in the court system until the defendant is arrested or are recalled, regardless of category. The length of time spent on the run to avoid prosecution does not usually count toward the statute of limitations assigned to a certain charge. Self-surrender is the recommended option for people who find themselves on a warrant pickup list, because it opens the door for a more favorable resolution of the case and resumption of a regular life. Failing to resolve bench or felony warrants can negatively affect many steps that people take for granted, getting a driver's license or passing background checks for a job.

WARRANT/ WRIT OF BODILY ATTACHMENT

If you are first found in contempt for alimony and/or child support particularly after a no-show, a bench warrant combined with an "arrest and deliver" or writ of bodily attachment may be issued. Once the warrant gets into the state system, the Sheriff's Dept. may pick you up if they have your current address, but only within the state of filing. In your divorce decree state, you can be picked up and spend some time in jail for defaulting on alimony (no child support involved). Beware in the state of Florida and a few other states you can spend up to 186 days in jail for the arrears, so this is a serious scenario.

Best advice if a bench warrant and a writ is issued, get out asap of the divorce decree state or the foreign state if they have domesticated the judgment. A simple taillight infraction by that state's police can get you incarcerated and a large financial purge amount initiated.

THE NCIC CRIME RECORD DATABASE - *Child Support Only*

The National Crime Information Center (NCIC) is a branch of the Federal Bureau of Investigation (FBI), providing an online access for authorized individuals about crimes, and in some cases information on criminals. All information that is provided from many criminal justice agencies is designed to be accessible only to authorized users.

NCIC Record File
The NCIC database consists of 18 different files, seven (7) files contain property records, such as boats, guns, license plates and vehicles, and 11 files of records about individuals such as the convicted sexual offender registry, identity theft, immigration violators and missing persons. There is also an Interstate Identification Index which contains automated criminal history record information and is accessible through the network's database.

Record Entry Into The NCIC
This data entry has to be conducted by a criminal justice agency, and this information then becomes accessible to other law enforcement agencies nationwide. For example, an officer from a police department that participates in the NCIC network will key in information on a subject they stop during a traffic stop, to determine if the vehicle is stolen or if the driver has a warrant out for their arrest. However in order for the officer to take action, NCIC policy requires the officer's department to make contact with the other agency that entered the information, to verify the information they have is current and correct. Once the record is confirmed, then the officer can conduct the arrest of the fugitive, or recover the stolen property.

There is a NCIC Record code for alimony arrears, but surprisingly none for child support (which can become criminal for arrears), but don't expect to be entered into the NCIC database as a 3807 for your alimony misdemeanor arrears.
- 3807 Nonpayment of Alimony - Misdemeanor

LONG ARM STATUTES ENFORCEMENT – *Alimony (low priority) and CS*

In US jurisprudence, long arm jurisdiction is a statutory grant of jurisdiction to local courts over foreign (out-of-state) defendants. A state's ability to confer jurisdiction is limited by the Constitution. This jurisdiction permits a court to hear a case against a defendant and enter a binding judgment against a defendant residing outside the state's jurisdiction. That is without a long arm statute, a state court may not have personal jurisdiction over a particular defendant.

Generally, the authority of a court to exercise long arm jurisdiction must be based upon some action of the defendant which subjects him or her to the jurisdiction of the court. In the US, some states long arm statutes refer to specific acts, for example torts or contract cases, which a court may entertain. Some states grant jurisdiction "on any basis not inconsistent with the Constitution of this state or the US."

Unlike URESA (Uniform Reciprocal Enforcement of Support Act), interstate cases established or enforced by long arm statutes use the court system in the State of the custodial parent rather than that of the noncustodial parent. When a person commits certain acts in a State of which he is not a resident, that person may be subjecting himself to the jurisdiction of that State. The long arm of the law of the State where the event occurred may reach out to grab the out-of-State person, so that issues relating to the event may be resolved where it happened. Under the long arm procedure, the State must authorize by statute that the acts allegedly committed by the defendant are those that subject the defendant to the State's jurisdiction. An example is a paternity statute stating that if conception takes place in the State and the child lives in the State, the State may exercise jurisdiction over the alleged father even if he lives in another State. Long arm statute language usually extends the State's jurisdiction over an out-of-State defendant to the maximum extent permitted by the U.S. Constitution under the 14th amendment's due process clause. Long arm statutes may be used to establish paternity, establish support awards, and enforce support orders.

CIVIL CONTEMPT, BUT WITHOUT EXTRADITION ACROSS STATE LINES

The ex-spouse will say you are a "*fugitive from justice*." A bench warrant for your arrest on indirect civil contempt charges may be issued when you fail to show for a court hearing, and the ex-spouse will say, "I want the district attorney to extradite you ... to go to the other state and bring you back."

But the district attorney's office will say that can't happen. They cannot extradite you, because they do not legally have that power. And even if they did, they are not in the business of enforcing civil judgments. The state's priority is to prosecute felonies, not to help someone get their pound of flesh in an alimony civil misdemeanor case.

Even with the county office charged with enforcing alimony support payment orders, the ex-spouse stands little chance of achieving what they believe is justice. There are thousands of ex-spouses in-line ahead of them, chasing ex-spouses in arrears.

The next step for the ex-spouse is to domesticate the judgment to your foreign state, if they know where you are.

DOMESTICATION PROCEDURE FOR A FOREIGN STATE JUDGMENT - UEFJA

When you move out of the divorce decree state, the divorce decree state court will need to issue a judgment that needs to be domesticated to the foreign state you are in. A foreign judgment is a legal order from another state or country. If the ex-spouse would like the support order to be enforced in your foreign state, it must first be domesticated within the foreign state.

For orders regarding alimony, property, debt, or any other non-custody issue, the order needs to be first exemplified in the original state before it can be domesticated. An exemplified copy is also known as a triple certificate, as it must contain three different signatures. First, the clerk of the court where the original judgment was made signs the document. Next, a judge will sign it. Finally, the clerk signs it again, only the clerk's second signature is to ensure that the judge was the one who signed it, and that the judge has the authority to sign it. The next action:
- That the foreign judgment annexed be domesticated and made the judgment of the foreign Court;
- That the defendant be attached for contempt and ordered to comply with the judgment complained of;
- That the defendant be required to pay the Plaintiff's reasonable attorney's fees and expenses of litigation; and

Approximately 47 of the 50 states have adopted the Uniform Enforcement of Foreign Judgments Act (UEFJA), which sets standards for the domestication of judgments from other states. For the remaining three states, the domestication procedure is a little more formal and still can be done thru *full faith & credit*.

Procedure:
1. Obtain an authenticated copy of the divorce decree state judgment by contacting the clerk in the court that rendered the original judgment, and ask for a certified copy. This will comply with evidence rules and prove to the foreign state court that the original judgment is genuine.

2. They will file the authenticated judgment and affidavit with the clerk of foreign state court in a court of competent jurisdiction.
3. Pay filing fees to the foreign state court clerk. The clerk will mail a notification to you, the judgment debtor. After 30 days, the original divorce decree judgment becomes domesticated, and the foreign state collectors can begin using the foreign state law to collect from you, the judgment debtor.

DOMESTICATING OUT-OF-STATE WITH A JUDGMENT RECOVERY FIRM

There is one other option for your ex-spouse to domesticate the divorce decree state judgment to another foreign state, if they don't want to expend the significant personal time and effort required. The ex-spouse will contact a professional Judgment Recovery firm in whatever state you are in and work with them. All the ex-spouse needs to do is <u>assign</u> their judgment over to the recovery firm with a 30-80% collection fee (this makes it legal for them to recover on their behalf). At that point the judgment recovery firm will incur all expenses to domesticate the judgment to your new state, track you and your assets down, seize your assets and then get the ex-spouse paid. It will save the ex-spouse time, but cost them significantly more money. Plus if you move again, they will need to go after you in whatever unknown state you are next in. They will keep the 10 year judgment from going dormant and expiring. So hide well or you may be found.

URESA - UNIFORM RECIPROCAL ENFORCEMENT OF SUPPORT ACT - "Full Faith and Credit" - Alimony and Child Support

The Uniform Reciprocal Enforcement of Support Act concerns <u>interstate</u> cooperation in the collection of spousal and child support. It lays out the procedure for enforcement in cases in which the person owing <u>alimony</u> or <u>child support</u> is in one state and the person to whom the support is owed is in another state (hence the word "reciprocal"). Such acts substantially similar have been passed in all 50 states.

The act includes improved machinery for finding the person owing support; guidelines for the conduct of the trial in the responding state; guidelines for cases where paternity is in question or where there has been interference with visitation rights; and simplified procedures for registering and enforcing out-of-state support orders.

<u>Full Faith And Credit Applicability</u>
Child support is established in proceedings in which the court has personal jurisdiction over both parties, i.e. the mother and father. For post-divorce obligations under the US Constitution Article Four, full faith and credit shall be given in <u>each state</u> to the public acts, records and judicial proceedings of <u>every other state</u>. Therefore courts may use the full-faith-and-credit article to enforce final judgments that have been registered within another state.

When a judgment is not final, there is a problem of registering that judgment in another court, because normally a judgment must be final before it can be registered. A court is free to recognize or enforce a judgment that remains subject to modification under the local law of the state of rendition. Child support orders are considered judgments of this sort.

Under <u>full faith and credit</u>, the state local law of rendition will be applied to determine whether the judgment is modifiable and if so, in what respects. This law will determine whether the judgment is modifiable with respect to past due installments and with respect to future installments. As between states, full faith and credit requires application of the local state law of rendition to determine whether the judgment is modifiable.

UIFSA - UNIFORM INTERSTATE FAMILY SUPPORT ACT - Out-Of-State Or Foreign Enforcement For Child Support Only

The Uniform Interstate Family Support Act (UIFSA) is one of the uniform acts that limits the jurisdiction that can properly establish and modify child support orders and addresses the enforcement of child support obligations within the US. Every US state adopted the UIFSA by 1998, or would have faced loss of federal funding for child support enforcement.

Whenever more than one state is involved in the establishing, enforcing or modifying a child or spousal support order, the Act is implemented to determine the jurisdiction and power of the courts in the different states. The Act also establishes which state's law will be applied in proceedings under the Act, an important factor as support laws vary greatly among the states.

The Act establishes rules requiring every state to defer to child support orders entered by the state courts of the child's home state. The place where the order was originally entered holds continuing exclusive jurisdiction (CEJ), and only the law of that state can be applied to requests to modify the order of child support, unless the original tribunal loses CEJ under the Act.

The Act also provides various direct interstate enforcement mechanisms. For example, it allows a caretaker parent to have an order mailed to the employer of the obligated parent, which will require that employer to withhold pay for the benefit of the child. Furthermore, it allows the caretaker parent to have an order mailed to an out-of-state court to get the other state to enforce the order.

If one spouse moves out of state, the Uniform Interstate Family Support Act (UIFSA) allows the new state to enforce an existing order for child spousal support. However, there are differences in the UIFSA and Uniform Reciprocal Enforcement of Support Act (RURESA) rules involving issues like registering support orders in a new state and asking the new court to modify or change those orders.

In this ever transient society, it is possible that a person seeking enforcement of a support order, whether child support or alimony, may have obtained that order in another state. In an effort to have uniformity among all the States in the US, each State has adopted the Uniform Interstate Family Support Act (UIFSA), which establishes the method to enforce a support order when one or both parties have moved from the State of initial jurisdiction. UIFSA also establishes rules for modifying support orders.

If you have moved to a foreign state from your divorce decree state, and the ex-spouse has either a support order or Judgment of Divorce which encompasses child support and/or alimony, they have to register that order in the foreign State with the Superior Court. Registration can also be done by sending the appropriate documents to a child support enforcement agency (i.e., the Probation Dept.).

Each state which codifies UIFSA, requires that certain documents and information be obtained before registration of the foreign state court order can be proper. Upon receipt of those documents, the order will be filed as a foreign judgment. When that order is registered, the registering tribunal notifies the non-registering party. Notice is to be accompanied by a copy of the registered order, as well as the documents and relevant information that accompanied that order. The non-registering party then has 20 days after the date of mailing or personal service of the notice to request a hearing to contest the validity or enforcement of that registered order. If the non-registering party fails to contest the validity or enforcement of the registered order in a timely manner, the order is confirmed by operation of law.

FPLS - FEDERAL OFFSET PROGRAM (FOP) - Child Support Only

The <u>Federal Parent Locator Service (FPLS)</u> is a collection of systems and programs operated by the <u>Federal Office of Child Support Enforcement (OCSE)</u>, to assist states in locating noncustodial parents, putative fathers, and custodial parties for the establishment of paternity and child support obligations, and enforcement and modification of orders for child support, custody and visitation.

The FPLS assists federal and state agencies in identifying over-payments and fraud, and helps these agencies in calculating the benefits. The FPLS was developed in cooperation with the states, employers, federal agencies, and the judiciary, and was expanded by Welfare Reform to include the:
- <u>National Directory of New Hires (NDNH)</u>: A central repository of employment, unemployment insurance, and wage data from State Directories of New Hires, State Workforce Agencies, and Federal agencies.
- <u>Federal Case Registry (FCR)</u>: A national database that contains information on individuals in child support cases and child support orders.
- <u>Federal Offset Program (FOP)</u>: A program that collects past-due child support payments from the tax refund of parents who have been ordered to pay child support.
- <u>Federal Administrative Offset Program (FAOP)</u>: Intercepts Federal payments in order to collect past-due child support.
- <u>Passport Denial Program (PPD)</u>: A program that works with the Secretary of State in denying passports of any person certified owing child support debt greater than $5000.
- <u>Multistate Financial Institution Data Match (MSFIDM)</u>: A program that allows child support agencies the means of locating financial assets of individuals owing child support.

FEDERAL (FPLS) and STATE PARENT LOCATOR SERVICE (SPLS) - Child Support Only

The Federal Parent Locator Service (FPLS), a national location system operated by the Federal Office of Child Support Enforcement (OCSE) to assist states in locating noncustodial parents, putative fathers, and custodial parties, includes two databases:
- <u>National Directory of New Hires (NDNH)</u>: a central repository of employment, unemployment insurance claimant data, and quarterly wage data from State Directories of New Hires, State workforce agencies, and federal agencies, and
- <u>Federal Case Registry (FCR)</u>: a national database that contains information on individuals in child support cases and child support orders.

The FPLS works in two ways to support state IV-D child support operations in identifying <u>home</u> and <u>work addresses</u> and sources of income and assets:
- First, using a process known as proactive matching, the FPLS compares data from the <u>NDNH</u> to data in the <u>FCR</u>. When there is a match, the FPLS automatically provides new hire, quarterly wage, or unemployment claimant information on custodial and noncustodial parents to any state with a related child support case. The state child support agency uses this information to establish or modify a child support order, or enforce (through income withholding) an existing order.
- Second, at the request of a state child support agency's State Parent Locator Service (SPLS), the FPLS will search external federal agency databases (<u>IRS</u>, the <u>Social Security</u> Administration, Dept. of Veterans Affairs, the Dept. of Defense, and the FBI) in an attempt to locate noncustodial parents and/or their assets, for the purpose of establishing or enforcing a child support order.

<u>What if the noncustodial parent (you) cannot be found locally</u>?
The state's child support enforcement agency will ask the <u>State Parent Locator Service (SPLS)</u> to search for you, the noncustodial parent. Using your <u>social security number</u>, the SPLS will check the records of state agencies such as motor vehicle registration, unemployment insurance, income tax, and correctional facilities.

If the SPLS finds that you have moved to another state, it can ask the other State to search, or send a request to the <u>Federal Parent Locator Service (FPLS)</u>.

<u>What resources does the FPLS have</u>?
The FPLS can search for addresses in the records of the <u>Internal Revenue Service</u>, the <u>Social Security</u> Administration, the Dept. of Defense, the National Personnel Records Center, the Dept. of Veterans Affairs, and State Employment Security Agencies. States also are required to maintain directories of newly hired employees in the state and to report this information to a <u>National Directory of New Hires</u> within the FPLS for important data matches, in order locate noncustodial parents who owe child support.

<u>Can enforcement agencies use the Federal income tax return to find out where the noncustodial parent lives and what he or she earns</u>?
Yes under certain conditions, the IRS may disclose to the government child support enforcement agency information that income earners submit on IRS Form <u>1099</u>. This information is a valuable tool to help find a noncustodial parent and determine their financial assets, and enforcing child support payments, and includes both earned and unearned income, including wages, earnings on stocks and bonds, interest from bank accounts, unemployment compensation, capital gains, royalties and prizes, and employer and financial institution addresses. Any information obtained from the IRS must be verified through a second source, such as an employer or bank, <u>before</u> the government child support enforcement agency can use it.

NDNH - NATIONAL DIRECTORY OF NEW HIRES REPORTING PROGRAM - *Child Support Only*

The Personal Responsibility and Work Opportunity Reconciliation Act (PRWORA) of 1996, requires all employers to report newly hired and re-hired employees to a state directory within 20 days of their start date. All public, private, non-profit, and government employers are required to report their new hires. Failure to report a new employee could result in a fine up to $25 per violation. Good news, state laws do not require <u>independent contractors</u> (1099's) to be reported as new hires, but the IRS reports the Form 1099 income and your address info with your employer into to the CSE agencies for child support enforcement.

<u>What is the New Hire Reporting Program</u>?
New hire reporting is the process by which your employer reports information on newly hired employees to a designated <u>state</u> agency shortly after the date of hire. New hire reports are matched against <u>child support</u> records at the <u>state</u> and <u>national</u> levels to locate parents who owe child support. This is especially helpful for interstate cases (in which one parent lives in a different state from their child), which are often the most difficult cases for states to resolve. With new hire reporting, state child support enforcement agencies have the ability to issue income withholding orders - the most effective means of collecting child support.

The state child support agency does two things with the new hire data. First, the agency compares the information submitted against current state child support files to locate parents. Second, the agency promptly passes the new hire information to the <u>National Directory of New Hires</u>, a component of the Federal Parent Locator Service within the Federal Office of Child Support Enforcement. This service compares the data from the employer's state with child support information from other states and when a match is found, provides the information to the appropriate state agency.

<u>NDNH Data Record Entry</u>: Federal law requires employers to collect and transmit seven data elements to fulfill their new hire reporting responsibilities, as they must submit information on every new hire within <u>20 days</u> of the date of hire. Many employers send W-4 copies as their official new hire report. <u>Beware of this item, and only use your PMB address as your residential address</u>.

Data Element	Definition
Employer Name	Employer Name associated with their Federal Employer Identification Number (FEIN)
Employee Name	Your full name
Employee Address	**Current residential address (USE YOUR PMB ADDRESS)**
Employee SSN	**Nine-digit Social Security number**
Date of hire	**The date services for remuneration were first performed**

<u>Who May Request NDNH Database Info? Authorized Users Only</u>
OCSE receives numerous requests for information in the NDNH or for comparisons of NDNH information with other information for various purposes. Title IV-D of the Social Security Act which governs the NDNH, specifies the entities authorized to request specified NDNH information and the purposes for which the information may be requested. OCSE currently matches NDNH data for <u>8 federal</u> and <u>67 state agencies</u> in addition to the <u>54 child support agencies</u>. The table below summarizes the provisions of the law:

The law allows	But only for this purpose
State Child and Family Service Agencies (IV-B)	to assist states to carry out their responsibilities under programs funded under Part B of the Social Security Act.

FIDM - FINANCIAL INSTITUTION DATA MATCH and WRIT OF ATTACHMENT - Child Support Only

The Financial Institution Data Match (FIDM) program is an enforcement tool used by the <u>Child Support Services Division (CSSD)</u> to collect <u>past-due child support</u>. Using FIDM, CSSD can seize funds from the bank accounts of non-custodial parents (<u>NCPs</u>) who have not paid their child support. Fortunately this does <u>not apply to alimony only payers with no child support.</u>

The FIDM program stems from Federal legislation passed in 1996, where under the Personal Responsibility and Work Opportunity Reconciliation Act of 1996 (PRWORA), state child support agencies are required to conduct a quarterly Financial Institution Data Match (FIDM) against the records of financial institutions doing business in the state, including banks, credit unions, and investing institutions. The purpose of this match is to locate and seize the assets of non-custodial parents who are delinquent in their court-ordered child support payments despite their ability to pay.

The Personal Responsibility and Work Opportunity Reconciliation Act (PRWORA) (also known as Welfare Reform) provided the state child support programs with <u>FIDM</u>, as an additional means for locating the assets of individuals owing child support obligations. State child support programs may issue liens or levies on the accounts of the non-custodial parent to collect past-due child support.

The Federal Office of Child Support Enforcement (<u>OCSE</u>) through the <u>Federal Parent Locator Service (FPLS)</u> assists the states in comparing a state's child support debt records with the account records of multistate financial institutions.

<u>How does FIDM Work</u>?
CSSD compares lists of NCPs who are behind in making child support payments with names of account holders at financial institutions such as <u>banks</u> and <u>credit unions</u>. CSSD then asks the financial institutions to <u>freeze</u> the bank accounts of the delinquent NCPs. When the accounts are frozen, the NCP is unable to access the funds in the accounts. Next, CSSD takes steps to seize the funds in the accounts to use to pay the past-due child support.

<u>When are accounts frozen</u>?
An NCP subject to having their account frozen (a <u>Writ of Attachment</u> is placed on the account) if they owe:

- A monthly current child support and makes no payments during the 30 days after the payment is due.
- A judgment obligation that is 60 days past due.
- Only arrears (and no monthly current support), and the total arrears owed is $500 or more.

When are accounts seized?

The NCP is subject to having the account seized (i.e., having an Order of Condemnation placed on their account) in either of the following situations:

- They are not paying child support directly from their paycheck, and the account contains at least twice the monthly child support amount.
- They are paying child support from their paycheck, owe $5,000 or more in child support arrears, and there is $2,500 in the account.

What Financial Institutions participate in the FIDM data match program?

- Banks, savings and loans
- Federal and State credit unions
- Benefit associations, insurance companies, safe deposit companies, money-market mutual funds, and similar institutions

What account types are subject to the FIDM data match program?

- Checking accounts, savings accounts, money-market mutual fund accounts, and time deposit accounts

How does the Financial Institution Data Match work?

States enter into agreements with financial institutions within their state for the purpose of comparing their child support debt records to the financial institutions' account records, to identify accounts belonging to parents who are delinquent in their child support obligation. When an account is identified, state child support programs may take action to seize the non-custodial parent's assets.

How does Multistate FIDM work?

Currently, state child support programs send OCSE the Federal Offset File (used to intercept federal tax refunds and other federal administrative payments), which includes the names, Social Security Numbers, and child support debt amounts owed by non-custodial parents. The state also indicates whether the non-custodial parent should be submitted for multistate financial institution data matching. OCSE ensures the accuracy of the records, and transmits the file to the multistate financial institutions.

Multistate financial institutions compare the child support data to their open accounts, and transmit to OCSE account information for the delinquent child support obligors. OCSE then transmits the data returned from the multistate financial institutions to the appropriate states.

Based on the information from OCSE, the state child support agency may issue liens or levies to attach and seize the assets belonging to the person who owes child support.

FIDM has a powerful private affiliate website called IDEConsortium (Interstate Data Exchange Consortium), a FIDM management website, that can locate delinquent non-custodial parents' financial assets for child support programs. At this time they are only in 15 states that have fully implemented the IDEConsortium FIDM process, and only have over 4,100 financial institutions actively participating.

CSRA and THE DEADBEAT PARENTS PUNISHMENT ACT (DPPA) - Child Support

The Child Support Recovery Act (CSRA 1992) made it a federal crime to flee one state to avoid paying child support. For the law to apply, the parent who is required to pay child support must owe at least $5,000 or have owed the past due amount for at least one year. The CSRA made it a misdemeanor to violate the provisions of the law and subjected the out-of-state parent to imprisonment of up to six months.

In response to prosecutors who wanted harsher penalties for the most egregious violators, Congress enacted the Deadbeat Parents Punishment Act to make fleeing a state to avoid paying child support a felony in some circumstances. The Deadbeat Parents Punishment Act was passed in 1998 to amend the Child Support Recovery Act by making it a <u>felony</u> for failure to pay child support for a child located in another state.

If a parent who failed to pay child support has owed a minimum of <u>$5,000</u> for a period of at least one year or if the parent owes at least <u>$10,000</u>, the parent may be charged with a felony and if convicted, may be sentenced to imprisonment for a period of up to two years. As a part of the sentence, the court is required to order restitution in the amount of the past due child support. As a condition of probation or parole, the court may also impose a requirement that the parent pay current child support as well as any arrearage still due and owing.

CSRA - CHILD SUPPORT RECOVERY ACT - *Deadbeat Dad Punishment Act (DPPA)*

Federal and state prosecutors have found new ways to use <u>criminal</u> measures to pursue individuals in arrears for child support enforcement. The implementation of the <u>Deadbeat Parents Punishment Act,</u> also known as the Child Support Recovery Act of 1992 allows states to now use using criminal remedies successfully. The intent of the statute was to prevent non-custodial parents from fleeing across state lines to avoid paying their child support obligations and to facilitate recovery of unpaid child support. The Act creates a federal offense for: (1) traveling in interstate or foreign commerce with the intent to <u>evade a child</u>

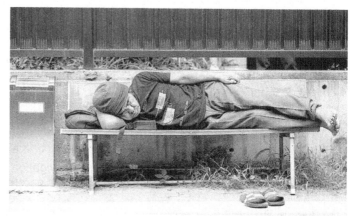

<u>support obligation</u>, if the obligation has remained unpaid for longer than 1 year or is greater than $5,000, and (2) the willful failure to pay a past due child support obligation for a child who resides in a state other than that in which the non-custodial parent resides, if the obligation has remained unpaid for longer than 1 year or is greater than $5,000; the willful failure to pay a past due obligation may qualify as a <u>felony</u> if it has remained unpaid for longer than 2 years or is greater than $10,000.

The Child Support Recovery Act makes it a federal crime to willfully <u>fail</u> to pay a past-due child support obligation for a child living in another State. The past-due child support obligation must be either greater than $5,000 or must have remained <u>unpaid</u> for <u>more than one year</u>. In order to establish willfulness, the US Attorney's Office must prove that the noncustodial parent knew about the obligation, was financially able to meet it at the time it was due, and intentionally did not pay it.

<u>The Penalties</u>

A person convicted of a first violation of the CSRA may be punished by up to <u>six</u> months in a federal prison and a fine. It is important to note that federal Sentencing Guidelines do <u>not</u> apply to a <u>first</u> violation of the CSRA because it is considered a <u>Class "B" misdemeanor</u>. As a Class B misdemeanor which is a petty offense, there is no right to a jury trial. For any subsequent violation of the CSRA, federal Sentencing Guidelines are applicable which effectively increase the presumptive sentence for any subsequent offense to two years imprisonment and/or a fine. A second or subsequent violation is a <u>Class "E" felony</u> which carries with it a <u>maximum sentence of 2 years incarceration</u>. In such a case, there is a right to a jury trial. The Deadbeat Parents Punishment Act (DDPA) of 1998 amended the CSRA of 1992 and established felony violations for traveling in interstate or foreign commerce to evade a child support obligation or for failing to pay a child support obligation which is greater than $10,000 or has remained unpaid for a period longer than two years.

Before a federal prosecutor will accept the case and bring criminal charges against the parent, the prosecutor will require that the parent who is the recipient of child support to first exhaust any civil and criminal state remedies. The federal prosecutor will consider whether there is a pattern of the violator traveling from state to state to avoid paying child support, whether the violator has attempted to conceal his or her identity, whereabouts, or employer to avoid being found; and whether the violator has continued not paying, despite the fact that they had been cited for contempt several times by state courts.

Upon a conviction, the defendant will be placed on probation for a period of years. During that probationary period certain conditions will apply. If any condition is violated, it may result in the defendant serving additional jail time. Common conditions of probation that are imposed for a violation of the DPPA include the following that the Defendant:

- Support his dependents and meet other family responsibilities, and comply with the terms of any court order or order of an administrative process pursuant to the state law requiring payments by the defendant for the support and maintenance of a child or of a child and the parent with whom the child is living.
- Work conscientiously at suitable employment or pursue conscientiously a course of study or vocational training that will equip him for suitable employment.
- Is unemployed, work in community service as directed by the court.
- Appear at all scheduled state/local court child support hearings.

CSRA - CRIMINAL CHILD SUPPORT ENFORCEMENT - DEADBEAT PARENT ACT

Criminal non-support state laws apply when both parents live in the same state and in some interstate cases.

In many states willful failure to pay child support can be a misdemeanor offense (less serious like a parking ticket), or in a few states a felony offense (more serious, like robbery). Often the dollar amount of support not paid determines if the offense is a felony or a misdemeanor. To file criminal charges, non-support must be willful. An investigation will be done to determine whether or not the non-paying parent had the money and the ability to pay the obligation, but chose not to pay or that the non-paying parent voluntarily and intentionally did not have the funds to pay child support.

What is the difference between the State criminal non-support law and Federal criminal non-support law (Deadbeat Parent Act)?
Federal law requires that the case be an interstate case, that $5000 is due or payments have not been received for one year, whichever occurs first. Under this law, a U.S. Attorney files the charges, not the local prosecutor or District Attorney. The case is heard before a federal court not the local county or state court. The U.S. Attorney has the ability to ask the FBI investigate and to ask the U.S. Marshall to travel anywhere in the U.S. to arrest the non-paying parent.

Under state criminal non-support, a local District Attorney can file charges if state law is violated. This varies from state to state. On state criminal interstate cases, the local sheriff has to travel to another state to extradite the non-paying parent back to your state. This is a burdensome process and costs the local county money. In some states it is not available, because there is no state law making non-support a felony offense.

Interstate Cases – They Must Make a Federal Case of It!
If they have a difficult interstate case with a large amount of money in arrearage, they have an option to seek federal prosecution of the law for you, the non-paying parent. Violation of federal law for first offenders is time

served in a federal penitentiary of six months, and a second offense or more is up to 2 years in a federal jail. The non-paying parent must make restitution in the amount of past due support. For your case to qualify:

1. You, the non-paying parent, must live in a different state than the child.
2. It has been determined either under a court order or administrative order that the non-paying parent has a past due support obligation of at least one year or $5000 punishable at six months in jail. $10,000 or 2 year non-support is punishable at up to 2 years in jail.
3. The non-paying parent has willfully failed to pay. Willfulness for these purposes is defined the same as the federal criminal tax law as the knowing and intentional violation of a known legal duty. The government must prove that the non-paying parent had the money and the ability to pay the obligation but chose not to pay.
4. Partial payments do not mean that these charges cannot be filed. However, partial payments may show that the non-paying parent did not have the ability to pay the entire child support obligation. An investigation should be done to determine if partial payments are being made because of the inability to pay or because the non-paying parent chose not to make full payments.
5. Prosecution under this law should take place in the Federal District Court where the children live. Benefits include; the child support agency's records of payments and arrearage are in the children's district; there would not be any transportation costs for the custodial parent and children to serve as witnesses, and if the family is also on welfare, the welfare records are also in the district where the children live.
6. Cases should be referred from the child support agency to the U.S. Attorney's office after all reasonable efforts to enforce the case have been tried and have failed.

CREDIT BUREAU REPORTING OF YOUR ARREARS – Child Support Only

Are child support arrears reported to credit reporting agencies?
Yes, the state Div. of Child Support Enforcement (CSE) is to report all support cases arrears to credit reporting agencies. The credit reports reflect the amount of current child support and the amount of arrearages that are owed. When there is unpaid support on a credit report, it can be more difficult to obtain a loan, acquire a credit card, or make large purchases. If a credit report shows a history of untimely support payments or a large arrears balance, lenders may deny a loan or require that the account balance be paid in full in order for you to obtain a loan.

Are you the non-custodial parent notified that the child support obligation will be reported to the credit reporting agencies?
The parent is notified 30 days prior to the first time that a child support obligation will be reported to the credit reporting agencies. The non-custodial parent will only receive a second notice if the debt had been deleted from credit bureau reporting, and the case subsequently meets the criteria for reporting again.

What happens on a credit report if the arrears balance is paid off, but monthly current support is still owed?
The account will continue to be reported but with a zero balance. If the account was previously past due, it will be reported as current from the time the arrears were paid in full. Credit reporting continues as long as payments are due on an open child support case. CSE follows both the federal legislation for credit reporting and the Fair Credit Reporting Act.

What happens on a credit report if current monthly payments are being paid, but the arrears balance is still due?
If an account has become past due and regular monthly payments have started, the account will show as past due until the arrears balance is paid in full.

What is a child support collection account that is reported to the credit bureaus?
The balance on an account that remains unpaid for 180 days or more will appear on credit reports as a separate collection account. Once a collection account is paid in full, the account will be deleted from the credit report.

TAX REFUND INTERCEPT PROGRAM - *Child Support Only*

What is the Child Support Tax Intercept Program?
It's a method of collecting past due child support and maintenance from tax refunds or credits. A state is authorized to intercept or recover any refund or credit from state or federal taxes, and that amount is applied to past due child support and maintenance. This collection method also is used for other types of debts.

What type of tax refund can be intercepted?
Any federal or state tax refund or credit as determined by the state Dept. of Revenue can be intercepted.

Must the back payments be owed to the state?
No. The child support agency of the state may intercept a tax refund when amounts are owed to the state or to the former spouse.

How does the ex-spouse use the Tax Intercept Program?
A recipient of child support or maintenance payments can apply for the interception of any tax refund from the payer. All they have to do is file a request with the child support agency of the county where the court order for support or maintenance was entered. Any federal or state tax refund then will be certified for interception.

How will you know if your tax refund has been certified to be intercepted?
If you're behind in child support payments and you've been certified for interception of your taxes, your name will be placed on a list of such persons. Before the end of the year, you'll receive a letter notifying you of the certification and the intent to intercept your tax refund.

What if you've declared bankruptcy?
Your child support obligation is exempt from bankruptcy. In other words, any back payments you owe for child support can't be included as a debt and can't be discharged in a bankruptcy proceeding. Therefore, your child support debt will remain unchanged.

When does the tax intercept stop?
Your tax refund can no longer be intercepted when all past due amounts are paid up or, in the case of maintenance, when the order has expired and all payments have been made. If you owe back payments, your refund still can be intercepted after your current obligation to support the child ends (generally when the child is 18 or 19 if the child remains in high school, but subject to state law, and can extend well beyond that. A tax refund also can be intercepted when you've been making regular payments, as long as an outstanding debt remains.

PASSPORT DENIAL AND REVOCATION OVERVIEW - *Child Support Only*

This urban myth stares you in the face until … *passport denial and revocation*. How could the US Secretary of State deny or revoke your passport when you have child support arrears? Once $5000 in child support arrears, they can have your passport revoked (not be renewed). Currently 30 to 40 passports are denied per day. Yes, here's how:

Alimony missed court appearance or civil issues will not affect your citizenship (passport). The State Dept. policy is that passports cannot be revoked for alimony issues, only child support and criminal matters. If you are in contempt of court and a bench warrant was issued, there is no provision in the law to revoke your passport. Further while failure to pay alimony is a civil matter, contempt of court can be criminal.

A federal or state law enforcement agency may request the denial of a passport on several regulatory grounds. The principal reasons for passport denial are a federal warrant of arrest, a federal or state criminal court order, a condition of parole or probation forbidding departure from the United States (or the jurisdiction of the court), or a request for extradition. The <u>Health and Human Services (HHS) child support</u> database and the Marshals Service WIN database are checked automatically for entitlement to a passport. <u>Denial or revocation of a passport does not prevent the use of outstanding valid passports until expiration.</u>

Passport denial is an effective enforcement tool. With this remedy, the US Sec. of State must refuse to issue a new or renewed passport to any person known to owe a child support debt exceeding $5000. Further, the US Sec. of State <u>may</u> take action to <u>revoke</u>, <u>restrict</u>, or <u>limit</u> a passport previously issued to an individual owing such a child support debt, but currently there are <u>no</u> procedures for revocation, restriction, or limitation on a passport.

All cases receiving services through State CSE agencies are eligible for passport denial. Any case that a State submits to the OCSE for the Federal tax refund offset process is also eligible for passport denial if the arrears exceed $5000. OCSE automatically forwards appropriate cases from the tax refund offset file to the State Dept. for passport denial unless the case has been specifically excluded. After a case has been referred to the State Dept., if the noncustodial parent applies for a new or renewed passport, he or she receives notice of the denied application. The notice advises the applicant to contact the listed State IV-D agency for further information. A noncustodial parent then can make arrangements with the State IV-D agency to pay the past-due amount. A State will contact OCSE to remove the case from passport denial status after appropriate payment arrangements are made. So once issued, a passport is <u>valid for 10 years</u>. Proceed with caution in reaching any arrangements to allow the noncustodial parent to pay less than the full amount overdue in order to avoid passport denial. <u>Once a parent obtains a passport, passport denial will not be an enforcement option for another 10 years</u>, even if the noncustodial parent reneges on the agreement.

<u>Passport denial is only available in IV-D child support cases, but here is how revocation occurs.</u>
In many countries, it is not automatic or easy to get permanent residency let alone citizenship, unless you marry (or are already married to) a local. Most places require a citizenship process at least as difficult as the US, which can take several years. During that time, you will occasionally need consular services (for example, in many countries the only place you can get a document notarized by someone in a way that will pass muster for US business/real estate transactions is at the US consulate) and to use international travel, which will be cut off to you if your passport is confiscated or revoked. Beware if you go to the US consulate with large monetary child support arrears that have become criminal, you may be taken into custody and extradited.

<u>Why passports</u>?
As a simple matter, deadbeat parents are difficult to reach outside the country. The State court is more likely to find success if the parents remain in the country within process server and police officer reach. But the same is true if the court just sent these parents to jail, whether or not they had passports. One of those state powers is the power to make and enforce domestic relations orders like child support orders, and another is the power to make and enforce criminal laws, like felony non-support laws. Then what federal interest is there? Money as the Circuit Court of Appeals explained ...

<u>How does the US Secretary of State deny and revoke passports</u>?
Could the US Secretary of State deny or revoke your passport when you have <u>child support arrears</u>? Yes! Congress has provided federal funds under Title IV-D to help the States collect <u>child support</u>, but in exchange, the States must enact federally-prescribed laws to collect support, include the passport laws. These laws must, at a minimum, establish a procedure for the <u>State</u> to certify individual support arrears to the Secretary of Health and Human Services (which administers the Title IV-D program) if the arrears exceed a statutory amount. The amount may be as little as <u>$5000</u>. The laws must also require the State to notify the non-payer of the certification and afford the non-payer an opportunity to contest the certification with the

State. The laws may in addition, allow the non-payer reprieve for personal, proven hardship, a payment plan, or a support modification.

If the Secretary of Health and Human Services receives a State certification, the Secretary must transmit the certification to the Secretary of State for action. If the Sec. of State receives a certification, the Secretary shall refuse to issue a passport to such individual, and may revoke, restrict, or limit a passport previously issued. Additionally, according to the Secretary of State's regulations, the Secretary shall not issue "a passport, except for a passport for direct return to the United States if the applicant has been certified by the Secretary of Health and Human Services as notified by a State agency under 42 USC § 652(k) to be in arrears of child support in an amount exceeding the statutory amount."

Certified arrears individuals appear on a list in the Passport Name Check System. When the arrears are paid or do not exceed the statutory amount, the State sends a subsequent certification through the chain to remove the payer from the list.

Without violating the freedom to travel internationally, the US State Dept. can refuse to let the non-payer have a passport so long as they remain in substantial arrears on the child support obligations. You can be free to work or, but the Constitution does not require that you be given a passport. Considering that enforcement often becomes illusory once the non-payer flees the jurisdiction, the restrictions make sense. Moreover, they are not absolute. The non-payer may pay the arrears, or at least pay them below the statutory amount, may receive a limited passport to return to the US, and may request a waiver for business and family emergencies.

What Can I Do If My Passport Is Denied Or Revoked and the Three Year Support Review?
States receiving federal assistance must have child support review procedures to review orders every three years upon a payer's or a payee's request. In some states, support payers and payees have a "one time pass" every three years to ask the Friend of the Court to review their current child support order. All they need to do is send a letter to the Friend of the Court to request it.

Whatever you do, do not let your arrears build up. The State certifies arrears, and the federal government denies and revokes your passport, no matter what your ex has to say, and no matter how desperately you want a break or how cheaply you can do it. If you wait, you could be out in the cold with no passport, scraping for cash to pay down arrears with penalties.

PASSPORT DENIAL PROCESS, Detailed Federal Rules - Child Support Only

The Passport Denial Program was established by Public Law 104-193, Section 370, to deny passports to individuals who owe child support, and to enforce collection of past-due child support.

The US Dept. of State (DoS) Passport Services issues United States passports. Before a passport can be issued, every passport applicant must establish identity, U.S. citizenship, and eligibility. Every application, no matter what type it is, or where or how it is submitted, is checked against a central database of individuals to determine whether the individual is entitled to be granted a passport. This is called the Consular Lookout and Support System – Enhanced (CLASS-E), and its database includes the names of individuals who have been reported by states to OCSE who owe, or have owed, child support arrearages in excess of the federally-mandated threshold, currently $5000. If a match against CLASS-E occurs, the applicant is denied a passport.

In addition to delinquent child support obligations, individuals can be denied a passport for a number of other reasons, including an outstanding federal warrant for an arrest, or a criminal court order that forbids departure from the U.S. In these circumstances, OCSE has no authority in the case.

If an applicant clears CLASS-E, a passport is issued. When issued, an adult tourist passport is normally valid for a period of ten years; diplomatic, official and regular no-fee (government) passports are valid for five years. DoS began issuing the Passport Card in 2008. The Passport Card is subject to the same adjudication process as the book passport and is valid for ten years. Note that the passport card cannot be used for international travel by air.

Currently, a noncustodial parent's passport can only be denied or revoked (i.e., <u>physically taken</u>) when the passport agency/DoS or US embassy <u>have the passport in hand</u>, such as when they are:

- renewing an existing passport,
- adding pages to an existing passport,
- repairing/reissuing of a damaged passport,
- changing a name or updating a picture, or
- accepting an existing passport as proof of identification.

Here is a caution with large child monetary arrears. When out of the country and if you go into a US embassy for assistance or to get something notarized, there have been instances where your passport was physically taken or revoked and you were placed under arrest for the arrears. Then you might be extradited back to the US. So beware!

Any of the above actions will trigger a search against CLASS–E, enabling the revocation when appropriate. If a passport applicant is identified by CLASS-E as having child support arrearages, federal statute requires that the individual be denied a passport regardless of whether he/she applied for the passport by mail or in person. When the passport is denied, the applicant is instructed in a letter from the DoS to contact the <u>state</u> CSE agency to make appropriate arrangements for satisfaction of the arrearage.

If the passport applicant has never owed back child support, and/or is unsure which state submitted the case, the applicant should contact their state of residence. The contacted state should notify OCSE if it does not have a case for the applicant in its system. OCSE determines if the applicant has a case in another state or if no case exists, and provides that information to the state. If no case exists, the caller must send the DoS passport application denial letter, with their DOB, POB, SSN and a contact phone number, to the Federal Collections and Enforcement Unit. After the identity verification, OCSE informs the DoS of the erroneous denial so the DoS can take the appropriate action.

A passport that has been denied/revoked may not be issued until OCSE under the state's direction, certifies to DoS that the person has made appropriate arrangements for satisfaction of the arrearage. OCSE has no authority to release an individual to obtain a passport unless the state that submitted the case requests it. If more than one state has certified an individual to OCSE, all states must clear the NCP from both TANF and non-TANF certification, if appropriate, before a passport can be issued. The DoS can only receive changes to an NCP's status from OCSE; release documentation should not be sent to the DoS or a passport agent by the state, the NCP, or any representative of the NCP.

Note:
- <u>When a passport is granted, in most instances it will be either five or 10 years before it can be denied again</u>. Only if the arrearages again go over the federally-mandated threshold, the case does not have the passport denial exclusion indicator on it, and the NCP uses a passport service, will there be an opportunity for the passport to be denied/revoked again. Therefore, states are encouraged to carefully review cases and situations before withdrawing NCPs from the passport denial process.
- Although an NCP is automatically removed from passport denial when the arrears balance is reduced to $0, you are not automatically removed when the debt falls below $5000.

Emergency Release from Passport Denial
An emergency release from passport denial applies only to situations of life or death, erroneous submittal, mistaken identity, or <u>NCPs who are out of the country</u>. It may not be used for an NCP who was once legitimately denied a passport based on past-due child support, and has since made payment(s) to bring the arrearage amount down to the state's minimum required criteria for release. The DoS makes the final determination whether to expedite an emergency release from passport denial. NCPs who do not require

emergency travel, or who are not overseas, should be released from the program as described in "Releasing Individuals from Passport Denial."

US Embassy/Consulate/Out of the Country: When an NCP is out of the country and goes to a U.S. Embassy or Consulate to replace his/her passport, add pages, use as an ID, etc., the passport is either denied at the time of application or <u>revoked</u> if the agent has the passport in hand. The NCP is issued a limited validity passport for one way travel back to the U.S. If possible, the individual should provide to the submitting state a copy of the Passport Denial Letter that he/she received from the Embassy or Consulate. After verifying the NCP's identity, the state must then send the denial letter with the completed Emergency Notice of Withdrawal of Passport Denial form (including the specific city and country of the embassy/consulate) to OCSE. OCSE then places the exclusion indicator on the case(s) and sends a release letter to DoS, which releases the passport within 24 hours.

Limited Validity Passports
Limited validity passports may be issued for direct and immediate return only to the United States when a passport is denied or <u>revoked</u> <u>outside</u> of the US. <u>Every US citizen is entitled to return to the US</u>, even if they cannot make satisfactory payment arrangements with the state(s) to repay their past-due support when their passport is denied. The length of time that the limited validity passport is valid can vary from a few days to several months and is determined by the US Embassy or Consulate officer. The new application is subject to the same adjudication as before.

Obtaining a Passport after Clearance of Denial
The DoS does <u>not</u> automatically send a passport to the NCP once he/she has made arrangements to pay off the child support debt and has been cleared in the system. It is the NCP's responsibility to obtain the passport.

QDRO - QUALIFIED DOMESTIC RELATIONS ORDERS - COLLECTING PAST-DUE SUPPORT FROM YOUR RETIREMENT PLANS

A Qualified Domestic Relations Order (QDRO) is a <u>special</u> order that is signed by a judge and submitted to a retirement plan administrator to allow an "alternate payee" (someone other than the non-custodial parent) to receive payments directly from the non-custodial parent's pension or retirement account. QDROs are usually done <u>involuntarily</u> to collect arrears money from a <u>parent who refuses to pay</u>.
- Is your ex-spouse owed alimony or child support?
- Do you the non-custodial parent have a pension or retirement account?
- If so, a Qualified Domestic Relations Order (QDRO) may be the ex-spouse's solution to get your money.

Property held in pensions and retirement accounts <u>cannot</u> be divided until a QDRO has been done, even if it is ordered in a divorce decree. However, many lawyers are unfamiliar with their use, so it is not unusual that an attorney handling a divorce action has not prepared and submitted a QDRO to the plan administrator. If the retirement plan has not been divided in accordance with the divorce decree, the result of a support QDRO would be that the support is paid, in part from funds that should belong to the custodial parent already!

It is also important to determine if the plan is one that is not subject to the Employee Retirement Income Security Act of 1974 (ERISA) – as many retirement plans for government employees fall into this category. These plans <u>cannot</u> be divided using a QDRO at all and may have alternative procedures for dividing the plan proceeds to allow an alternate payee to receive payments.

There are two broad types of retirement plans - defined benefit plans and defined contribution plans. Defined benefit plans are usually funded solely by the non-custodial parent's employer, and will usually pay a pre-determined monthly payment to the non-custodial parent at the time of retirement. Such plans often have the words "pension," "benefit" or "annuity" in the plan name, although the name of any plan cannot be used reliably to determine what type of plan it is. When a QDRO is done for a defined benefit plan, an alternate payee will generally be able receive funds only in monthly installments rather than a lump sum, and usually cannot receive any payments at all until the non-custodial parent retires or reaches retirement age.

Defined contribution plans are usually funded by employee from deposits made directly from a paycheck. Some employers also contribute funds. The name of a defined contribution plan may have the terms "401k," savings, investment or contribution in it. When a QDRO is done for a defined contribution plan, an alternate payee can usually receive the funds prior to the non-custodial parent's retirement and can usually receive them in a lump sum.

The first step in the QDRO collection process is to contact the plan administrator for information about the plan. Don't be surprised if the plan administrator is reluctant to release information - a few will even go out of their way to make the QDRO process difficult and time-consuming. But since fulfillment of the QDRO ultimately depends upon their cooperation, it is worth going out of your way to keep the relationship on good terms. The asset searcher will request a plan summary and a model QDRO, if they have one, and try to determine how long the participant has participated in the plan. This provides a clue as to whether there are sufficient funds to pay arrears, since generally plan administrators will not reveal the amount in the retirement fund.

The next step in the QDRO process is called a "fly letter" - an initial draft of the QDRO is prepared and sent to the plan administrator to see whether the QDRO will "fly," i.e., whether it is qualified under the plan. It is important to get a response from the plan administrator in writing, confirming the QDRO is qualified and will be honored once it is signed by a judge. This helps prevent any last-minute changes of mind on the part of the plan administrator after the QDRO has been signed by the judge.

<u>Domestication</u>: Then the next step is to submit the QDRO to the judge for signature in the jurisdiction of the support order. If you the non-custodial parent are in a different or foreign state, an alternative procedure is to register the support order for enforcement in the non-paying spouse's foreign state and submit it to the judge in that jurisdiction instead. The process of obtaining the judge's signature will usually require a hearing, and you the non-custodial parent must be served with notice of the action.

After the QDRO is signed by the judge, it is submitted to the plan administrator. However, just because the QDRO is signed by a judge does not mean the retirement plan administrator must honor it. The plan administrator reviews the QDRO to make sure it is "qualified" according to the standards of the retirement plan, and a separate board or committee will generally review the QDRO as well. If they determine the QDRO is qualified, the retirement account will be divided according to the amount awarded by the judge.

An important point to remember is that funds taken from a retirement account are always taxable as income to someone, and the taxes will usually be withheld by the plan administrator. Since child support is not taxable as income to the custodial parent, the non-custodial parent should only receive credit for the amount of the payment after taxes have been withheld.

Collecting support with a QDRO is neither a simple nor a fast process, and it could take them more than a year to complete. How complex and difficult the process will be depends upon the rules and policies of the retirement plan, the relationship with the plan administrator, state child support collection laws, the efficiency of the local court system, and the level of knowledge and familiarity with QDROs of the attorneys and judges involved.

SOCIAL SECURITY GARNISHMENT FOR ALIMONY and CS ARREARS

Benefits paid through the Social Security Administration do <u>not</u> escape garnishment in <u>alimony and child support</u> cases, as the state court can get the Social Security Administration to attach your Social Security check for support obligations.

Garnishment Attachment

If the state court that handled your divorce imposes an alimony or child support obligation, it can also issue an administrative order requiring attachment of your Social Security benefits for payment of the required arrears amount. Authorization for garnishment of Social Security benefits can be found in Section 459 of the Social Security Act. Section 466(b)(7) gives domestic support obligations first priority if more than one legal attachment reduces your benefits.

Fortunately there is a limit of up to 65% for child support and/or alimony obligations, that your Social Security benefits and Government pensions can be garnished by the Social Security Administration. The garnishment can also include related expenses such as legal fees, court costs and any interest owed on late support payments.

The Social Security system has to limit the garnishment amount to the lesser of the State maximum or the maximum under the Consumer Credit Protection Act (CCPA) (15 U.S.C. 1673(b)) and is based on the law of the State where the ex-spouse beneficiary resides. The CCPA limit is referred to as the "Federal" limit, and limits garnishment to:

- 50%, if the ex-spouse payer is supporting another spouse and/or child other than the ex-spouse and/or child whose support has been ordered.
- 60%, if the payer is not supporting another spouse and/or child.
- Or another 5% to 55% or **65%** respectively, if your garnishment order is 12 or more weeks in arrears.
- Note this will be % gross income not disposable, because there are no deductions on a social security monthly distribution check.

It is noteworthy SS Supplemental Security Income disability benefits (SSI) cannot be garnished, but Social Security Disability Insurance (SSDI) can be garnished.

WHY THE EX-SPOUSE ALWAYS HAS THEIR HANDS IN YOUR PANT'S POCKETS

Entitlements, when do they stop?

Alimony: First it starts with the permanent alimony, and you are ceremoniously welcomed to the exclusive club of 640,000 US alimony payers. The trouble begins later on if you lose your job, your income decreases, or when you run out of money, you will possibly enter the arena of arrears with penalties and interest. A judgment, civil contempt charge, and a bench warrant could follow if you don't play by the rules. This is just the beginning, as there are three more hefty entitlements going to the ex-spouse after the initial alimony:

1st - Ex-Spouse Can Get 50% Matching Social Security For Being Married For More Than 10 Years: Imagine that years later as you enter your golden years reaching age 62, the ex-spouse can file thru the state courts and get their 50% matching of your SS benefit based upon your work record. This is an additional entitlement, even though you have continued paying the alimony. However, this comes out of the government's pocket, not yours. Your SS benefit is not decreased when your ex-spouse takes this option.

2nd - Ex-Spouse Can Get 65% Garnishment of Your Social Security For Arrears: You will learn firsthand another unfortunate aftermath of the divorce, is that after your retirement when you file for your SS retirement benefit, that the alimony does not stop automatically. Your income will be reduced as you think you have retired, so you begrudgingly play by the rules and go back to the divorce decree state court for a Change in Circumstances, and at best you may get a reduction. Remember there is no guarantee that the alimony is to stop upon your retirement, as only in three states is this automatic by law.

So you continue paying alimony (possibly reduced) and then go into arrears, the ex-spouse can initiate a separate state court-ordered judgment that will get the Social Security Administration to garnish up to 65% of your SS benefit.

This eventuality could happen to you, so do not plan on all of your SS earnings, unless the ex-spouse just gives up. This 2nd entitlement does require the ex-spouse to have some court time either pro se or hiring a lawyer, followed with a judgment and garnishment order issued by the court. The gravy train does not end here.

3rd - Widow Death Benefit for the 10+ Years of Marriage: Now if and when you, the paying ex-spouse die, your ex-spouse is entitled to your Social Security death benefit (Suprisingly only $255), the same as any widow even if your ex-spouse remarried. And if they are married when you (the ex) pass away, they can collect survivor benefits as long as they didn't remarry until age 60 or later. If they are collecting Social Security based on their own work history, they can switch to your survivor's benefits if the payment is larger. Here are the provisions stated more clearly for the surviving divorced spouse to receive benefits:

- You and your ex were married for at least 10 years;
- You, the former spouse, are entitled to Social Security benefits, regardless of the age at which you died;
- The recipient divorced ex-spouse is at least 60 years old, or at least 50 if disabled;
- The recipient ex-spouse is not entitled to a higher Social Security payment on their own record.

CAN YOUR SOCIAL SECURITY DISABILITY BENEFITS BE GARNISHED FOR ALIMONY AND CHILD SUPPORT PAYMENTS?

To answer this question, you must determine what type of Social Security Disability benefits you are currently receiving. The Social Security Administration offers two types of disability benefits: Supplemental Security Income (SSI) or Social Security Disability Insurance (SSDI).

Supplemental Security Income or SSI is a social security disability benefit given to certain qualifying individuals including: the aged, blind and disabled who meet certain income and resource levels. Income and resource levels change each year and can be found on the Social Security Administration's website. Supplemental Security Income is given to these individuals for clothing, housing and food expenses.

The federal government funds Supplemental Security Income through general tax revenues not the Social Security Trust Fund. The federal government treats Supplemental Security Income as a public welfare benefit similar to food stamps and does not consider Supplemental Security Income or SSI to be income for the purposes of child support payments. Therefore, the federal government does **not** allow Supplemental Security Income benefits to be garnished.

In contrast, Social Security Disability Insurance or SSDI was money paid into the Social Security Trust Fund through employment taxes based on a percentage of the employee's earnings. The goal of the Social Security Trust Fund is to allow for the replacement of income for certain employees who become disabled and are unable to work.

According to the federal government, the Social Security Disability Income or SSDI benefit is considered a substitute for lost wages and is **eligible** to be garnished for child support payments. One benefit of Social Security Disability Insurance, however, is children of qualifying disabled workers who receive Social Security Disability Insurance payments may be eligible to receive Social Security Disability Insurance or SSDI benefits until a certain age (18 under most circumstances) and these SSDI payments may be subtracted from the child support amount owed.

THE TRUTH OF INTERNATIONAL CHILD SUPPORT ENFORCEMENT

There are **no** extradition treaties or similar in force between the United States and any other foreign country pertaining to the enforcement of child support or alimony orders or any other court decrees. While some new measures to negotiate reciprocal arrangements with other countries have been pursued, extradition is a big deal involving embassies, consulates, bureaucratic red-tape, law enforcement, etc. A country like Costa Rica or Peru will extradite under the right circumstances for a real crime such as murder or drug trafficking, with sufficient evidence pleaded before their foreign country judiciary.

But for your non-payment of alimony or child support? <u>No</u>, as these are only <u>civil</u> matters in the US and any foreign country. So they are not going to extradite an individual with all the hassle and expense, because some US local county judge issues a bench warrant for contempt for non-payment and no-show. So do not go into an overseas US embassy, or you can get free airfare,

<u>Do Criminal Reciprocal Extradition Arrangements Exist With The Foreign Countries</u>?
The United States has extradition treaties with over 100 countries, of which most are dual <u>criminality</u> treaties with the remaining being list treaties. The list of countries with which the United States has an extradition treaty relationship can be found in the Federal Criminal Code and Rules, following 18 U.S.C. § 3181.

The <u>Extradition of Fugitives Clause</u> in the US Constitution requires States upon demand of another State, to deliver a fugitive from justice who has committed treason, <u>felony or other crime</u> to the State from which the fugitive has fled. 18 U.S.C. § 3182 sets the process by which an executive of a state, district or territory of the United States must arrest and turn over a fugitive from another state, district or territory. In order for a person to be extradited interstate, 18 U.S.C. § 3182 requires:

- An executive authority demand of the jurisdiction to which a person that is a fugitive from justice has fled.
- The requesting executive must produce a copy of an indictment found or an affidavit made before a magistrate of any State or Territory, and
- Such document must charge the fugitive demanded with having committed treason, felony, or other crime, and
- Such document must be certified as authentic by the governor or chief magistrate of the state or territory from whence the person so charged has fled.
- The executive receiving the request must then cause the fugitive to be arrested and secured, and notify the requesting executive authority or agent to receive the fugitive.
- An agent of the executive of the State demanding extradition must appear to receive the prisoner, which must occur within thirty days from time of arrest or the prisoner may be released. (Some states allow longer waiting periods of up to 90 days before release).

In addition to extradition treaties, the US has what is referred to as <u>Mutual Legal Assistance Treaties</u> (<u>MLAT's</u>) with approximately 65 various nations that facilitate foreign countries providing assistance in investigating <u>crimes</u> committed by US persons. A mutual legal assistance treaty is an agreement between two countries for the purpose of gathering and exchanging information in an effort to enforce public laws or criminal laws. This is very important in tax matters, in particular as part of international double taxation agreements wherein the parties agree to deliver information for tax purposes.

This assistance may take the form of examining and identifying people, places and things, custodial transfers, and providing assistance with the immobilization of the instruments of criminal activity. With regards to the latter, MLATs between the United States and Caribbean nations do not cover U.S. tax evasion, and are therefore ineffective when applied to Caribbean countries, which usually act as offshore "tax havens." Assistance may be denied by either country (according to agreement details) for political or security reasons, or if the criminal offence in question is not equally punishable in both countries.

And keep in mind these treaties are for criminal, <u>not civil matters</u>. And even in criminal matters, the country that is being requested to assist generally has to consider the alleged crime a criminal offense under those countries' laws. So for example, if a US citizen were to flee to a country where tax evasion is a civil and not a criminal matter, then the US wouldn't in theory have much success getting any cooperation of the foreign nation in investigating, locating, or extraditing that US person.

The first step in the complicated process of obtaining child support enforcement abroad is for the ex-spouse to contact their state office of child support enforcement. That local state child support enforcement office can provide information about the aggressive techniques now available to pursue enforcement, including garnishment of wages and federal income tax refunds, revocation of licenses, direct contact with foreign employers, criminal enforcement proceedings, etc. If the non-payer owing the child support is employed abroad for a U.S.-based company or for the U.S. government, child support enforcement laws provide a number of steps to obtain enforcement.

In addition, it may be possible to for these state office agencies to initiate formal enforcement proceedings in accordance with local (foreign) law. In many states, the child support office will apply on your behalf. Don't ever say never, because in 1997 the state of Massachusetts working with Interpol, succeeded in having a child support fugitive from its "most wanted" list, who was the subject of an outstanding warrant, deported from the Dominican Republic and arrested on arrival in the United States. The distinction is this warrant became a <u>criminal</u> count, because of the dollar amount magnitude and the fact they left the country.

Initiating Foreign Enforcement Proceedings
If no reciprocal arrangement exists, it may be necessary for them to initiate a child support enforcement action in the courts in the foreign country. This usually will require retaining the services of a foreign country attorney abroad. Note the US Dept. of State and Office of American Citizens Services are not a repository for foreign laws. It may be necessary for the ex-spouse or their attorney to provide foreign authorities with authenticated, translated copies of your non-payer's child support order and any other pertinent documents.

Locating You the Non-Payer Abroad
The ex-spouse will have to contact their local state IV-D child support enforcement agency which will contact all appropriate sources for assistance in locating the non-paying ex-spouse, including the Federal Parent Locator Service (FPLS), Office of Child Support Enforcement, U.S. Dept. of Health and Human Services, Washington, D.C.; That Offices' services involve searching federal databases, including U.S. tax records, that have proven useful in cases involving an absent parent abroad. The U.S. State Dept., Office of American Citizens Services <u>cannot</u> arrange for U.S. embassies or consulates abroad to conduct actual searches for the whereabouts of U.S. citizens abroad who may owe child support. If the person's whereabouts are completely unknown, it may be necessary to retain private detectives through the local foreign counsel or other sources.

CHAPTER 13

YOUR PLANNING STEPS

ARE YOU READY TO BECOME INVISIBLE?

An assessment of the many alimony non-payers or expatriates shows there are three typical escape routes. Unfortunately if not executed well, one could face the eventual loss of all your money with a decline into poverty and possibly some jail time. So plan well, as one of these approaches can become yours:

- **1st Approach**: Liquidate all your assets, put them into a shoe box for safe deposit box placement, and then attempt to lead an invisible life as a fugitive constantly moving, possibly living in an RV. This is the impulsive without thought option, and shows no planning.
- **2nd Approach**: Leave the United States country as an expatriate. This option has a price, as everything you have in the US, you are abandoning. You may not see your family again, including your children. If children are involved, they may well be brainwashed by your ex-spouse who now has total control and access to them (even as adults) and repeatedly hear only their side of the story. Was this the best choice? No!, remember you will still have to file US taxes as an ex-patriot as well as pay the foreign taxes, and you may come back to the US for Medicare after age 65. Also beware IRA/401K accounts have to stay in the US, and cannot be transferred to foreign soil. So for alimony only, it is not worth it! Impulsive, but not the best option either.
- **3rd Approach**: **Stay in the US, work, and live a normal life, but become invisible**. This alternative is viable for you, believe it or not. If you decide neither option above is the suitable route, you have to make the conscious decision to find an alternative. This will allow you to continue leading your normal productive life in the US not as a fugitive, but working, as you probably are not quite ready for retirement. To do this, you have to learn how to become invisible as an individual, and make your employment and financial assets become equally invisible. Bottom-line, you will have to muster the conviction to learn how it could be done, have confidence in your ability without fear, and then do it with six months of preparation. Avoiding bench warrants from an indirect civil contempt citation by moving out of the divorce decree state is a monumental step toward your invisibility.

The expectation and reality for all should be alimony legal reform will not happen in your remaining lifetime ... So how do you make your invisibility Plan B happen for more expediency? Step up to the plate, beat the reform movement, and do it on your own!

THE LONG AND THE SHORT - DO YOU GO FOR IT?

For them to find your money after you become "*invisible*" and stop paying alimony, it will take a concerted effort involving your time, and the ex-spouse's time and money. A majority of ex-spouses, their lawyers and the minimal alimony support services utilizing the state's legal court system and the tools available to them, just don't have the dedication, intelligence, nor desire to spend big bucks and time to find you and your cash. It is not a simple matter for them pushing a PC button and within minutes, the info is simply presented to find you.

Secondly, the government with all their separate databases just isn't that coordinated and smart. There is over $89 billion in unpaid child support, and most states have no financial stake or incentive reward to chase down alimony, as the state does not get rewarded by the federal government for alimony enforcement. For alimony collection, the dollar amount of your monthly alimony may be a factor, as if it is less than $1000/ month there is not a large financial incentive. However those permanent alimony payers above the $1000 - $50,000/mo. threshold with deep pockets are fair game. And remember you can't really wait for the states to retroactively reform their alimony laws for you? So do it on your own.

OPTIONS FOR YOUR FUTURE – CHANGING JOBS and MOVING ON – Alimony Only/ CS?

Ok, so you have been a good ex-spouse, paid your alimony only or maintenance spousal-support, but now due to circumstances beyond your control, you have to change jobs. Perhaps you have just lost your job. Or worse yet, the ex-spouse could be after you for increased payment thru a "Change in Circumstances" court filing. This is a Perfect Storm – lost job, bad economy, and ex-spouse looking for more money. **So consider that a timely opportunity has now been presented to you**.

You have done some pre-planning and are totally invisible with no visible bank accounts (EIN used, and not your SS #), reduced to only one credit card, no ownership of house, cars, etc. except one item - your new employer's wage income will now be based upon a new undisclosed employer at a new location. No one except you, your new employer, and the IRS and the state where you work that will be receiving withholding from your employer, know where you work, but they do know your SS #. You will not divulge your new employer info on any future credit card application or annual credit report request form, or list any usable references on anything. A major decision point for you has come about.

Suggestion if you plan to be on the run or being invisible, get your driver's license and car registered in a state in which you do not live or were divorced, and certainly be in a position to up and leave if the ex finds you and tries to domesticate the judgment.

How do the ex-spouse, lawyer, PI, skip tracer, data miners, asset search programs, and/or the ex-spouse's bounty hunters, how do any of them find you to reinitiate the judgment wage garnishment order at your new place of employment? You have told no one of your new job and to compound matters for the hunters, you have moved out of your divorce decree state to the other 49. Coincident with your new job you have strategically moved, changed your address and now use a private postal mail box that too cannot be found. For these reasons it is not necessary to leave the US and go international. Get the drift, you as an individual in your name, address and phone *no longer exist*.

So at this juncture, why not initiate "*catch me if you can*?" There is not any simple means they can reinitiate your wage garnishment, if they cannot find your new place of employment. Your former $10 - 100,000 a year alimony can now be better spent and saving for your upcoming retirement. If you have no CS, this is a safe bet. So do it!

For alimony there is no legal means or incentive for a state to go after a delinquent alimony payer, because they do not get the Federal reimbursement money like they do for child support, so generally a state will not waste child support resources tracking an alimony-only payer down. Besides alimony arrears is a civil matter, not a criminal matter. Some states do cheat and report alimony payments as child support, to receive child support enforcement incentive compensation from the federal government. Be careful with child support arrears as with the Child Support Recovery Act (CSRA or Deadbeat Dad Parents Act), arrears amounts over $10,000 and 2 years with you living outside the divorce decree state, qualify as a felony if convicted. A second CS arrears conviction gives you a felony – hard to get a job with a record. This is the end for you, and the beginning of your death spiral to bankruptcy.

However what they (the ex-spouse and the asset searchers) can do if on the ball years later but probably not, is first go after your financial assets if they haven't been moved, and then garnish your SS benefit up to 65%. So if you want to run, make sure you are not relying solely upon your SS to support yourself. Also if you have a retirement IRA/401K account, they can later find it and attach it as well, so move it now to another new undisclosed financial institution (utilizing a cashier's check and not a wire transfer). Bottom-line, have all your ducks in a row moved when you get ready to bail.

Big factor if your alimony is a few hundred dollars a month, it just won't be worth the ex's effort to pursue you; but if it is a few thousand dollars a month, the ex may aggressively pursue you and more people will be willing to work for the ex with deferred fees until your assets are taken. So do a good job on becoming *invisible*.

SO HOW LONG DO YOU HAVE AFTER YOU INSTITUTE PLAN B?

How long from practical experience before they come after you?

- <u>Loss of Wage Garnishment Income</u>: It starts usually with the termination of your employment, either voluntary or after being laid off. It does not matter, as this is the moment at which the alimony support withholding income stops.
- 1st Alarm: The first trigger alarm starts with your employment termination, whereupon your former employer sends a required letter notice (originated by the garnishment order) to the ex-spouse that your employment and alimony payments have been stopped. The ex-spouse in a panic recontacts their former attorney, and the timeline for you to get a letter back from their attorney can be as short as a <u>10 day</u> time frame. This notice will state they are aware your former employment stopped, you are to inform them of your new employment, and that the alimony still is to be paid directly to the ex-spouse rather than thru the former state disbursement unit (SDU). Your former attorney may also be copied. Note the SDU will take no action, as they are only a financial depository. This is just a warning letter with no substance.
- <u>Notice of Motion</u>: Next after a delay due to the support checks stopping, the ex-spouse and attorney may decide to go to court to get a scheduled court date in the original divorce decree state and county. You will receive this Notion of Motion occurrence by regular mail, as you have legal rights to present your side of the case, and with a required nominal 30-day period before the court date. Of course, you won't get this, as it goes to your former in-state mailing address.
- <u>Divorce Decree State Judgment and Domestication, Stage #1</u>: The court date in your divorce state occurs, and the ex-spouse may now learn for the 1st time that domestication of the order to your foreign state is required if you have moved out-of-state. The judge may even give the ex-spouse a judgment for the outstanding alimony, except this is only enforceable in the divorce decree state. Meanwhile you may be out-of-state and for any judgment action to be effective, the divorce court venue will now have to be domesticated to your foreign state, for which the ex-spouse will need to hire an out-of-state attorney who practices in the <u>state</u> and <u>county</u> they think you now live in. Note the divorce decree state's judgment has no attached subpoena or bench warrant, so at this juncture there is no investigative power authorized to track you and your assets down.
- <u>Foreign State Domestication, Stage #2</u>: Now the ex-spouse has to decide to hire a foreign state lawyer (assuming they know your new foreign state and county), and the new lawyer will want an upfront retainer to start work. If you are careful, they will have no idea where you have relocated to. They make their best guess and schedule in your foreign court venue a court date to obtain an Order to Show Cause hearing. For this new Order action with a 30 day notice, you will be notified via mail at your old address (assuming you have in this interim moved). They might throw in a subpoena tecus ducem to command you to appear, but it actually will never be served upon you, as you have never received either notice due to moving on with no forwarding address. So don't make yourself visible at your old residential address or work location, move on.
- At the Order to Show Cause hearing in your foreign state, the outcome again will presumably be, you do a <u>no show</u> in court. At this hearing the foreign state court domesticates the divorce decree judgment for the arrears and issues a writ for garnishment. But this works only if they can find your next undisclosed employer that they have no legal authority or available technology to find (alimony only). They may also produce subpoenas with writs to garnish your former financial accounts revealed at the divorce decree, but you have now closed and moved all your money to different undisclosed institutions. The end result for your no-show – the foreign state court may even throw in a bench warrant for indirect civil contempt for you. But it is not worth anything for foreign enforcement unless you get stopped by the police, assuming you are still in this judgment foreign state.
- If this whole procedure is rushed, you can buy yourself some time by continuing to make the alimony payments for a short time, until you are ready for Plan B.
- Then when you are ready to become invisible … Time to move on.

<u>90 - 120 days</u> is probably the absolute minimum for the 1st foreign state court appearance or a garnishment, if they have their act together and only if the ex-spouse comes after you. ***Good Luck From Here and Enjoy Your Life!***

PLAN B CRITICAL STEPS - CHECKLIST

Completed:

☐ Mail Address:
  - o Your CMRA (Commercial Mail Receiving Agency) mail box established with the business LLC or corp. listed as the only addressee.
  - o Your LLC/corp. will be established with the CMRA or PMB private street address. Note a CMRA street address is required (not a PO box) for the business bank and brokerage accounts.
  - o Direct all vital mail (such as the business LLC financial accounts, insurance co. bills, auto registration, etc.) to your new PMB postal mailbox, using only an online address change thru the bank, not a USPS Form 3575 – Change of Address Order. No exceptions, as the Form 3575 enters you into the USPS NCOA – National Change of Address database, that is transmitted to the 3 credit reporting agencies and the mass mailers.
  - o From here on, never provide your current home mail address to anyone including your employer, insurance co., police officers, driver's license, etc. Train yourself to use your private postal mail box (PMB) in all responses only.
  - o If you lose your job, get your postal mail box PMB first to start the transfer.
  - o If you ever start getting uninvited mail at your personal primary (PMB) mailbox, you have been *violated*, and time to move the mailbox to another location <u>immediately</u>.

☐ Identification: From here on for opening business accounts, only use your passport (not driver's license) for ID. Your passport coincidentally has nine digits - the same as a Social Security number. Minimize the use of your driver's license as ID, as it is for driving and tracks you thru your SS #.

☐ Identification – Driver's License: Get a new driver's license using your new <u>PMB</u> address. Do not list your current home address, and request your SS # be hidden if possible.

☐ Business LLC or Corp. Formation: Establish your business LLC/corp. in a state where your ownership invisibility and privacy exists. New Mexico is the best state, and Wyoming a close 2nd.

☐ Business Employment Identification Number (EIN) Number: Now fill out an IRS Form SS-4 on-line to obtain an EIN number from the federal government that you will need for opening your business accounts. This replaces your SS # on the business accounts, with the business accounts reporting to the IRS using your EIN, making your assets invisible.

☐ Open Business Account(s) For Transfer Of Your Financial Assets: Then open a business LLC bank and brokerage accounts with the Commercial Mail Receiving Agency (CMRA) address. A business account application, the LLC Articles of Incorporation, your EIN, and passport will be typically required. This may not prove to be a simple task unless you pick the right bank. Beware opening bank accounts can generate a soft or hard inquiry on your credit report. Find an institution that does a soft inquiry only. You will have to ask during the application process.

☐ Checking Account and Debit Cards: Open a new checking debit card account only with new checks at the new business account bank. Be sure to formally close all former bank savings and checking accounts to avoid damage to your credit report. The monthly service fees will take your account negative, and this unpaid negative balance then gets reported to your credit history. Stop using former accounts except to final pay utility bills etc. before you move.

☐ Transfer of Your Financial Assets To the New Business Accounts: Your financial accounts have all been moved to new establishments and transferred into the LLC name at 2 or more brokerage accounts or banks. Use cashier's checks, no wire transfers. If you don't do this and leave the money at the former known institutions, a court-ordered judgment and garnishment of these accounts may occur within a 3 month period. Beware after a court judgment is issued, your assets can be garnished within a 30-day period.

☐ Checks: Minimum information on your new checks with business name and your PMB postal mail box address. Your name and phone number on the checks is not necessary, so do not include.

☐ Credit Cards: Do not abandon your credit cards, instead cancel <u>all</u> of but <u>one</u> of them. Keep the best one so your credit history is maintained. Don't use them for any future purchases, as they show up on credit reports and asset searches. From here on fill out no credit card applications as the info instantly shows up on your credit header and credit reports. Do update the one card's mailing address to your

PMB only; but be aware this can provide your general location. Recommend this option - an out-of-state PMB can forward your mail to your new state's PMB.

☐ Email: Establish new accounts with new user names and with new passwords. Close out all existing email accounts, by first deleting all messages, and then cancelling the account.

☐ Wage Garnishment Order: A copy should have been given to you in court during the divorce decree finalization. If you did not obtain a copy of your temporary support order or MSA divorce settlement garnishment order, request a copy from your employer. Now watch your bank account(s) to see if a garnishment or a lien occurred from a court-ordered judgment.

☐ Address Diversion: Implement USPS change of address forms (USPS Form 3575) for 1-2 months – utilizing temporary status on a monthly basis, redirecting to multiple locations that are undeliverable. Do not fill out and submit a USPS mail change of address to your new residential or PMB addresses.

☐ Property: Rethink your titled ownership of property – cars, houses, boats, motorcycles. Reassign or change the title to the business LLC, so you have nothing in your name. If the asset searchers do a search and find your property, with the arrears judgment they can file a lien in the county where the property is, restricting your ability to sell it later on. So transfer the title so it cannot be found.

☐ Vehicle Registration: Transfer registration ownership to get it out of your name to the LLC/corp. business you have created, or at the very least switch the mailing address to your PMB mail box as it can be found. Any asset search service will find this asset if left in your name, and if found a lien can be placed on these assets preventing future sale or seizure.

☐ Future Automobile or Large Dollar Purchases: This purchase will generate a hard inquiry on your credit report, and possibly give away your location. Buy from a private party.

☐ Credit Report: Request your report online to see what is known about you, so you can lose the trail. When you check the status of your credit report on-line, use your old residential address.

☐ Cell Phone: Get a new cell phone and phone number, and have it listed using only the business name for your LLC or corp. Do not use your name. Close all old phone accounts, and abandon usage of old phone numbers. Then minimize your contact with your relatives to an absolute minimum. Never get a land line, as your info is reported to the data miners.

☐ Doctors and Dentists: If you have recently paid one of these professionals with your old credit card or check, change your current licensed professionals that you currently use, as your home address could be found by a PI, even though medical records are private. The receptionist could be buffaloed by a PI with a court subpoena/ writ and give up your address. One more reason to use your PMB address.

☐ Insurance: For the same reasons, change your auto and personal insurance company to another company using the PMB, so they cannot be pre-texted for your address.

☐ PC File and Photo Metadata: Metadata is file property basic information about data that contains info such as, author, date created and date modified and file size. Review all computer files you have created or in the future before sending them out or posting on the Internet; confirm that under File – Properties – Summary, your name or employer is not listed as the author. Also beware photos have embedded metadata. Delete the metadata entry, or the internet search engines scan and will pick up this hidden metadata and possibly provide some identity info about you.

☐ Junk Mail Elimination: Label with sticker for 6 months before Plan B. Stop all unnecessary mail. As a good indicator, watching the mail stream to both your PMB mail box and your actual hidden residential mail box is a good indication of how successful you are. There should be no uninvited mail coming to your PMB. None, what so ever or you have been comprised!

☐ Magazine Subscriptions: Allow all to lapse before Plan B is implemented if possible. Do not forward or change of address your subscription.

☐ Utility Accounts and Bills: For any future new utility accounts (gas, water, elec. cable, etc.) applications, start using your middle name along with your last name. Long term, lose your first name. Use your passport with the excuse the driver's license was lost if you can. They will ask for your social security no. to verify your credit worthiness, for reporting to the credit bureaus if your bills go unpaid. So if you can, do not use your residential address; instead use your PMB address, as credit header reports show your utility payment history.

☐ Voting: After moving, do not register to vote. In some states if you are forced to list your voting address with your driver's license renewal, use your PMB address or make up an address.

- Product Warranty Cards and Registrations: Never fill these out, as the info goes into the data miner databases with your address. Same for sweepstakes, festival raffle tickets, as the phone, address and email info could be used to find you.
- Social Networking, Public Message Boards: No Facebook, Twitter, Yelp, Instagram, etc. Put no info out there about yourself. Delete your existing accounts, as best as you can.
- Membership Cards: With membership cards like CVS, Safeway, Costco, public transit passes, etc., be careful and never register your card or list your name with your address or phone no.
- On-line Internet Purchases: For your purchases like Amazon, Paypal, Netflix, Home Depot, etc., use you're your business name and only the PMB address for the shipping address. Do not use your name or your residential address, as it will end up in the data miner files.
- Asset Search: This is an option. After 6 months of cool-down before the big step, now hire your own asset search firm to find and identify your remaining asset exposure (cost $150 - 400), testing your shield of secrecy.
- Secrecy: Tell no one of your Plan B escape plan, either beforehand or afterwards, and never violate this oath to yourself. They will squeal on you if proper authorities or PI's approach them, so tell no one.
- IRA/401K and Pension Beneficiaries: Two critical things to do: 1) Change your beneficiary to be your estate, to make sure your ex-spouse is no longer listed on any existing IRA/401K or pension accounts. 2) To avoid a future Change in Circumstances (CIC) QDRO order when the ex runs out of money, move all your financial holdings to new undisclosed financial institution accounts.
- Change Your Job/ Get New Employment: This is critical to stop the wage garnishment and provide a dead-end for the next employer judgment and wage garnishment enforcement of your earnings. Consider another state different from your divorce decree home base or get a foreign work assignment.
  - Employer Listed Address: Get a neutral PMB address for when your new job employer reports you as a new employee with your home address to NDNH. Use this PMB address on your resume and for your new employer to send your W2's and all employer's mailings.
  - Tell no one your new employer's name, and don't ever enter it into a database, as that employer could be sent a garnishment notice.
  - Employment Background Checks: Be careful here, as your potential employer may want to check your driver's license history and a background check on you. This check generates a soft inquiry hit on your credit report that lists the background searcher's address. So utilize your PMB postal box address on the background check forms, not your residential or driver's license address (this should be your PMB also).
- Move.
- Get an Internet VPN Service: This masks your computer's IP address and obscures your physical address and computer location.

So these are the basics of *How To Disappear* and get off the Data Miner grid. **Take your time, do your research, and then enjoy the freedom.**

Best of Luck, and always be looking behind your back.   ALooking!

INDEX